Investing in the future

United Nations Development Programme

Investing in the Future
Setting Educational Priorities
in the Developing World

Jacques Hallak

Unesco: International Institute for Educational Planning

Pergamon Press

This book has been written and published as part of the *UNDP Inter-regional Project on the Improvement of Basic Educational Services.*

Cover photograph by Dominique Roger, Unesco

English language edition first co-published in 1990 by the
United Nations Educational, Scientific and Cultural Organization,
7 place de Fontenoy, 75700 Paris, France and
Pergamon Press plc, Headington Hill Hall, Oxford, England.
Printed in France by Imprimerie Gauthier-Villars, 75018 Paris

Unesco ISBN 92-803-1138-7 (Limp-bound edition)
Pergamon ISBN 0-08-0407935 (Hard-back edition)
© Unesco 1990

Preface

UNDP and Unesco are convinced that effective educational systems are indispensable to successful development. It is therefore particularly timely that the publication of this monograph coincides with the initiative taken by the United Nations Development Programme, Unicef, Unesco and the World Bank to hold a *World Conference on Education for All* in Bangkok in March, 1990.

The concept for a publication about setting educational priorities in the developing world emerged from discussions between UNDP and the International Institute for Educational Planning. It responds to a shared perception for the need to reappraise the conceptual and practical issues involved in establishing educational priorities to meet the challenges and opportunities of the 1990s and beyond. The economic crisis facing developing countries poses grave short- and long-term problems for education and human resources development. Setting new priorities thus becomes a major concern of all policy-makers in the developing world.

This publication is intended to synthesize fundamental policy issues affecting education today. We also hope it will stimulate discussions on priority setting among governments, multilateral, bilateral and non-governmental agencies, scholars and individuals committed to improving education in the developing world. It should not be interpreted as prescribing a uniform course of action for all societies, but rather as describing a rich mosaic of experiences and approaches from which developing countries may draw in their search for appropriate, relevant and sustainable solutions.

Together with other members of the international community, UNDP and Unesco stand ready at this important juncture to assume a key role in supporting global, regional and national efforts to enhance the performance and relevance of educational systems where they are most needed.

Federico Mayor
Director-General
United Nations Educational,
 Scientific and Cultural
 Organization

William H. Draper
Administrator
United Nations
 Development Programme

Acknowledgements

The United Nations Development Programme, Division for Global and International Programmes, took the initiative for the preparation of this monograph and contributed both financially and substantially to its development. I am particularly grateful to Timothy Rothermel, Frank Hartvelt, John Laurence and Mike Sacks of UNDP for their comments and advice in the preparation of the final draft.

I also drew much benefit from the contributions provided by a number of consultants, in particular André Aujame, Anne Bombenger, Nino Chiappano, Anne-Claire Defossez, Jean Lamoure and Malika Zeghal. Continuous discussion with the staff of the International Institute for Educational Planning constituted a major source of inspiration during the preparation of the monograph.

I should like to express my thanks to all who made critical comments and suggestions on an earlier draft of the text, in particular Malcolm Adiseshiah, Philip H. Coombs, Pablo Latapi, Goran Ohlin, Neville Postlethwaite and Peter Williams.

The preparation of the monograph benefitted from secretarial assistance and typing from Sylvie Munos and Bridget Gargam, also from skilful editing by Eileen Savdié and Kay Brownrigg. Maureen Woodhall played a key role in advising on and contributing to the final draft. Above all, I would like to thank Etienne Brunswic and Gabriele Göttelmann-Duret for their assistance throughout the preparation, writing and revision of the monograph.

Finally, I thank my wife Viviane for her encouragement and for her patience throughout the long hours I spent writing and re-writing this book.

Needless to say, the imperfections and limitations found in the following pages are mine alone.

February 1990

Jacques Hallak,
IIEP, Paris

Contents

Preface   v

Acknowledgements   vii

Introduction   1

Part I. Changing educational priorities: retrospect and prospect   5

1. Two decades of progress: 1960-80   7
2. A decade of crisis: the effect on educational priorities   25
3. Priorities for the 1990s: challenges and constraints for a balanced human resource policy   44

Part II. Memo to policy makers   73

4. Policy choices   76
5. Priorities   97
6. Strategies   132

Part III. Memo to practitioners   157

7. Teachers: priorities for planning teacher supply and demand   159
8. Delivery systems: priorities for selecting educational technologies   180
9. Buildings, equipment, materials: priorities physical planning and utilisation   204
10. Beyond the school systems: priorities in managing non-formal educational programmes   238
11. Managing the system: priorities for management and administration   255

Part IV. Memo to donors   277

12. Priorities for international assistance   277

Investing in the future

Setting educational priorities
in the developing world

Introduction

Investing in the future:
an urgent priority

Broadly defined, human resource development (HRD) relates to the education, training and utilisation of human potentials for social and economic progress. According to UNDP, there are five 'energisers' of HRD: education; health and nutrition; the environment; employment; and political and economic freedom. These energisers are interlinked and interdependent, but education is the basis for all the others, an essential factor in the improvement of health and nutrition, for maintaining a high-quality environment, for expanding and improving labour pools, and for sustaining political and economic responsibility. Little wonder, then, that all countries place major emphasis on educational policy in designing their plans for accelerating development. This book will treat some of the conceptual and practical issues involved in establishing educational priorities.

No standard or uniform solutions can be prescribed to all societies. We will therefore avoid prescriptions and refrain from making specific suggestions. What we hope to offer is the benefit of the experience of others. How have others formulated policy, and how did it work best? How have they set priorities, conceived strategies, attracted financial assistance, implemented programmes, and followed through? Where have they made costly mistakes? In knowing where others have succeeded or failed, may lie the key to our success.

The book is divided into four distinct parts addressed to specific categories of key figures involved in education and development: the policy-makers of the developing countries, in particular ministers of finance, planning, education; the practitioners, responsible for the management and provision of education; and the community of education donors. It is also intended for participants in the various courses and seminars offered by universities and training institutions, including the IIEP. It is hoped that the book will stimulate discussion among scholars, researchers and individuals committed to improving education in the developing world.

While recognising the universality of educational challenge and the complicated interrelations of educational problems and solutions in both developing and industrialised countries, we shall concentrate on those of the former, referring to the latter as and when comparison is pertinent to this overview of the various policy issues and ways in which they might be addressed.

We have allowed ourselves two major qualifications in the preparation of this monograph -- first, we define education in the broadest of senses, and second, we plead for constant appreciation of the element of time.

There are those who perceive education as a human right,[1] and there are those who see it primarily as an investment in economic development.   There are those who favour general/academic education and those who favour specific training and the development of skills.   There are those who argue for basic literacy and numeracy for all, restricting access to post-basic education and training, and those who would give the latter priority for the sake of economic development.   And somewhere between these points of view, policy-makers must judge where to allocate the scarce resources available for education. For reasons explained in the course of the book, these distinctions are neither always useful nor entirely justified. We shall take as our benchmark the general advancement of continuing education, and define our bias, which is towards the ethical imperative of providing universal education.

Priorities in education are dependent on complex and volatile factors, some of which are usually recognised and taken into consideration in planning and decision-making -- at least in the rhetoric -- such as certain societal goals (political, cultural, etc.), on the needs of economic development, and particularly on national capacities for financing manpower training.   The impacts of environment -- family and home backgrounds, and in a more extended way, social and cultural factors -- are sometimes not adequately taken into consideration by donors. Educational policy and strategy must be solidly anchored in local traditions and values, reoriented in promising new directions, on the basis of successful experiments, if disruption and social turmoil are to be avoided. The time factor must not be neglected in any of the introduction, design, or implementation phases of large-scale educational adjustment. Habits are changed over generations; one must not think it will take less time to change teaching and learning mindsets.

To come to the content of the book: Part I is a comparative overview of the past, the present, and what we see as the future conditions under which education must continue to progress in the developing world. It is argued that in spite of the many difficulties and constraints, progress has been more positive than is generally acknowledged. Because of their late start, the developing countries are beset with old problems which persist along with new problems which compound them. All must be addressed by policy-makers in establishing educational priorities. In all societies, industrialised and developing, goals of improving and expanding HRD are amply justified on ethical, cultural, social and economic grounds. The problem lies in choosing.

Part II, addressed to policy-makers, is the core component of the book. It seeks to discuss and review the various concepts, issues, factors, and methods which must be taken into consideration in setting objectives, priorities, and strategies for educational adaptation and expansion. It is argued that present methods of arriving at priorities leave much to be desired, and suggestions are offered which might lead to more informed policy decisions, more pragmatic and effective ways of adopting priorities, and more feasible strategies for reconciling resource constraints with pressing needs and legitimate ideals.

Part III is for the particular use of planners and local administrators and managers, and deals with the implementation of educational policy, planning, programmes and projects. A discussion of implementation issues such as the proper management of resources -- human and material -- and new possibilities for educational delivery offered by technology and the media is followed by an outline of the special needs of the marginal groups which are un- or insufficiently served, and a review of general suggestions for the institutional or organisational improvement and strengthening of administrative machinery. Questions of finance, procuring and dissemination of information, training and incentives are considered.

Finally, in Part IV, which is addressed to donor agencies, the implications for international co-operation are examined. Observers of the educational scene in developing countries tend to be negative in assessing past performance, and unrealistic in proposing future change. By taking into consideration more of the infinite ways in which information and skills can be transferred from those in possession of them to those who are not, and by advocating more suitable assessment of both past and future from the point of view of time, we hope to encourage the formulation of policies which might lead to less discouragement and a better ambience in which to carry them out.

---

1. The adoption on 20 November, 1989, by the UN of the International Convention on the Rights of the Child is a particularly significant event in this respect.

Part I

Changing educational priorities: retrospect and prospect

Over the last three decades, the developing countries have made tremendous efforts in education aiming to concretise a basic human right and to promote, at the same time, economic and social development. In view of the present signs of stagnation or even deterioration of educational coverage and quality and the by no means direct linkage between HRD and economic progress in practice, there is an urgent need for setting priorities in education and implementing programmes for improvement.

The first part of this book will attempt to give an overview of what has really been achieved during this period, and of the inconsistencies and difficulties affecting educational development especially since the recession in the late seventies.

Moreover, it will give some insight into the legitimate grounds for policies aiming to successfully link human resource development with global development processes, and at the same time look at the constraints and complexity of such policies. Today, this challenge is greater than ever before for many developing countries, especially those confronted with dwindling resources. A tentative mapping of educational priorities, which policy-makers might set in the light of past achievements and economic, demographic and technological prospects characterising their respective countries, closes the first part of this book.

Although the close interconnection between socio-demographic development, health, education and training, in the overall process of HRD are dealt with here, as well as in other parts of this book, the main focus is on education. Within the vast educational field, we have mainly concentrated on formal education; because of lack of adequate data only some references are made to non-formal and informal education and their successful linkages with school education.

At this stage, it is useful to state that the concepts of 'formal', 'informal' and 'non-formal' education used throughout are inspired by the following definitions:

•   *Formal education:* the 'educational system' with its hierarchic structures and chronological succession of grades, from primary school to university, which in addition to general academic studies comprises a variety of specialised programmes and full-time technical and vocational training institutions.

•   *Informal education:* the lifelong process par excellence, whereby each individual acquires attitudes, values, skills and knowledge through everyday experience, through the educational influences and resources of his or her environment, namely family, neighbours, workplace and leisure, in the market, the library and through the mass communication media.

•   *Non-formal education:* all those educational activities that are organized outside the established formal system -- whether functioning separately or as an important part of a broader activity -- and designed to serve identifiable clientèles and educational objectives. According to this taxonomy, the term 'out-of-school education' refers to informal and non-formal education, while 'in-school education' may also possess informal and non-formal functions or structures.[1]

---

1. This taxonomy was proposed by P.H. Coombs, R.C. Prosser and M. Ahmed, In: *New paths to learning for rural children and youth,* New York, International Council for Educational Development, 1973.

Chapter 1

Two decades of progress: 1960-1980

Developing countries made impressive efforts and progress in education in the 1960s and 1970s. Quantitative indicators, including both the number of educated people -- the stock of human capital -- and enrolment rates -- the additions to that stock -- show that considerable progress was made between 1960 and 1980. Both governments and individuals gave high priority to education and the development of human resources during this period. This expansion in the stock of human capital took place against a backdrop of considerable political change, as many countries achieved political independence, and took responsibility for determining their own educational policies and choices. Governments gave high priority to education in allocating their resources, reflecting both a strong political will to generalise access to education, in the conviction that it would help foster national unity and satisfy social justice and respect for an essential human right, and at the same time an urgent need to develop their human resources in order to contribute to the economic and social growth of their societies. Parents and children shared the view that education would improve their living conditions, and pressed hard for access to schooling -- so much so that, when governments did not respond rapidly to their expectations, they opened their own schools (this happened for example in the Ivory Coast and in Kenya in the mid-1960s). It is the convergence of strong government commitment, together with strong social demand for education that explains the fantastic explosion of school enrolment over this period. But this is not to suggest that the trend occurred without problems -- far from it, as we shall see in the following chapters of this book.

The huge investment in education that took place during this period was not confined to formal schooling. People learn and acquire skills and knowledge in a wide variety of ways, and this book is concerned not only with the formal education system, with schools, colleges and universities, but with non-formal education, including literacy classes for adults or children who have dropped out of primary schools, agricultural extension services for farmers, which aim to develop their knowledge and technical skills, and on-the-job training provided by employers in the workplace. Equally important is the vast network of informal learning opportunities, through which both adults and children acquire information, knowledge and skills. Informal education is provided through a huge variety of channels, including the family, the local community, religious organisations and the media, including broadcasting as well as books or newspapers. The last three decades have seen a tremendous growth in radio and television ownership and in book and newspaper production in the developing world. This represents a formidable increase in the opportunities for informal education, and the implications of this for literacy and for promoting links between formal, non-formal and informal education are discussed later in this chapter.

Despite the importance of non-formal and informal education, there is a lack of accurate information and statistics, and therefore any attempt to measure the educational progress achieved in developing countries in past decades will tend to concentrate mainly on formal schooling, about which there is a wealth of statistical data available through Unesco and national bureaux of statistics, which provide a fairly detailed quantitative picture of the enrolment of young people in pre-primary, primary, secondary and tertiary institutions in virtually every country from 1960 to 1986. Unesco statistics also give graphic indications of such elements as enrolment by sex, primary retention rates, public spending, and costs per student, which can serve to highlight some qualitative as well as quantitative aspects of educational development. Partial information is available on adult and non-formal educational efforts, but there are less data in Unesco and national statistics about non-formal or informal education than formal schooling.

It is these Unesco statistics that are the starting point in this and the following chapter for a brief summary and review of the changing priorities in education and human resource development in developing countries in the past two decades. This chapter gives a picture of the impressive educational efforts and achievements of developing countries since 1960. These achievements have been accompanied by growing problems however, and the next chapter examines the difficulties and the economic and educational crises that many countries have faced.

Changes and trends in education are long-term phenomena which must be considered in their historical context. Educational progress cannot be completely separated from that of other social and political institutions, and both the progress and the problems of education in developing countries need to be viewed in a long-term perspective. It is difficult, of course, to generalise about experiences which occur in different social contexts at different times in history, but the histories of educational development in Europe and North America in the nineteenth century are interesting, and of some relevance in interpreting and assessing trends of enrolment in developing countries over the past three decades. With much higher levels of industrialisation and more propitious socio-economic conditions, it took the USA and European countries such as France, Germany, and the United Kingdom from sixty to one hundred years to achieve universal primary education, and their rate of expansion of secondary and higher education was much slower than in today's developing world.

This serves as a reminder that the progress made since 1960, in educational expansion and human resource development in developing countries, is a truly impressive performance, despite the problems and set-backs that have undoubtedly occurred.

We start, then, with a summary of this progress, based on statistics on enrolment of both children and adults and the growth in expenditure and in teachers, buildings and equipment that made this expansion possible.

1. School and higher education enrolment

From 1960 to 1980, the total world enrolment of children in all levels of formal education nearly doubled, and most of this increase took place in the developing world. There are wide differences from country to country, which reflect many factors, including both political and economic forces. Some countries with low levels of income per capita have nevertheless achieved faster growth in enrolments than some middle-income countries, which started from a higher base in 1960.

In fact many countries that faced extremely unfavourable socio-cultural, administrative and financial conditions have given very high priority to achieving rapid expansion of formal education.

The result is that between 1960 and 1980:

- Primary school enrolment increased by 106 per cent. Demographic growth of the school-aged population partly explains the increase, and part of it may be explained by high rates of repetition. But on average the proportion of children of primary school age who are enrolled in school was 20 to 30 per cent higher in the 1980s than in the 1960s, and a number of countries, among them China, Sri Lanka, Indonesia, the Philippines, Jamaica, Tunisia, Syria, and Singapore, have almost achieved universal primary education, despite the fact that in 1960 there were many children unable to go to school. In some countries pre-primary education also rose rapidly during this period.

- Enrolment increased by 280 per cent at the secondary level, and 346 per cent at the tertiary level. These high rates of growth are partly the result of the combined effect of (i) much lower rates of enrolment than the primary in 1960 ("smaller grows faster than larger") and (ii) the interdependency of growth of the various components of the system. When a wave of growth in primary enrolment reaches the secondary level, its effect is amplified and the effect will in turn be felt at the tertiary level, but this is not the whole explanation. Many developing countries gave the highest priority to developing skilled human resources, through rapid expansion of secondary and higher education.

2. Out-of-school enrolments

Not only has there been a great expansion of children in schools and young people in colleges, universities and other formal higher education; at the same time there have been growing numbers of adults engaged in non-formal education and programmes have been set up for young people who drop out of the school system.

The diverse nature of such activities makes it difficult to assess the target population, content, duration, and effects of the various programmes, and to collect and interpret statistics, but a study carried out for Unesco in 1985 of 84 industrialised and developing countries[1] drew the following conclusions:

- The total number of adults served by non-formal programmes in developing countries is estimated to be about 23 million (13 million in Asia, 5 million in Africa and the same in Latin America). This figure is still small in relation to the total needs, as measured by the number of illiterate adults.

- There seems to be a correlation between size of adult population served and income level of the country; the developed countries have higher percentages of educated adults, and probably more regular programmes for adults, than low-income countries.

- Developing countries, where basic learning needs are less widely met or which suffer from wider illiteracy, tend to have weaker adult education programmes, with the exception of a few centrally planned economies that give high priority to adult education.

- While the experience of individual countries varies considerably, there was a general trend toward increased adult enrolment from 1960 to 1980, which peaked in 1979.

- Adult education tends to supplement or extend formal schooling opportunities in many countries, rather than be a substitute for them. For example, a recent study in Kenya[2] found that adults were more likely to participate and remain in adult education if they had had some previous experience of formal schooling.

3. Expenditure trends

Such rapid expansion of enrolments required a considerable increase in expenditure. Unesco figures show that total public expenditures for education increased in the developing countries from US$8 billion in 1965 to about US$40 billion in the mid-1970s, and to more than US$93 billion by 1980. Much of this apparent increase was the effect of inflation, but if expenditure is measured in terms of constant prices it still shows a marked increase between 1960 and 1980.

Table 1.1 shows that public educational expenditure, expressed as a percentage of GNP, increased on average in the developing world from 3.3 per cent in 1970 to 3.6 per cent in 1975 and 3.9 per cent in 1980, after peaking at 4.3 per cent in 1977. The figures show variations between regions, but the general trend is clear: developing countries devoted an increasing share of GNP to education until the late 1970s, when a decline began in several regions.

Table 1.1 Public expenditure on education as a percentage of GNP, 1970-1980

Region	1970	1975	1976	1977	1978	1979	1980
Developed countries	5.6	6.0	6.0	6.0	5.9	5.9	6.0
Developing countries	3.3	3.6	4.1	4.3	4.1	4.0	3.9
- Africa (excluding Arab States)	3.4	3.9	4.3	4.4	4.1	4.0	5.2
- Asia (excluding Arab States)	3.5	4.2	4.7	4.8	5.0	5.0	4.6
- Arab States	4.7	5.9	5.9	6.2	5.6	4.9	4.5
North America	6.6	6.4	6.2	6.5	6.6	6.5	6.9
Latin America and the Caribbean	3.3	3.5	3.6	3.9	4.0	4.0	3.9

Source: Unesco, *Statistical yearbook, 1978, 1980, 1981, 1982, 1984*, Paris, Unesco.

Part of this increase was due to the rapid rate of demographic growth in developing countries, which resulted in a rapid growth of the school-age population, while GNP per capita rose more slowly.

Nevertheless, the fact that developing countries devoted an increasing share of their total national income to education is a measure of the high priority given to education and human resource development in the 1960s and 1970s. Unesco figures also suggest that the gap between industrialised and developing countries in terms of educational expenditure per capita has narrowed. In 1970, the ratio of expenditure per capita in developed and developing countries was 28:1, but in 1982 this had fallen to 15:1, reflecting a substantial financial effort on the part of developing countries.[3]

These figures are based only on public expenditure. Data on private educational expenditure are difficult to obtain and often unreliable, but in many countries parents contribute substantial sums in the form of fees or expenditure on books or materials, and Unesco figures suggest that there was an increase in private school enrolments in many developing countries in the 1970s. The total national resources devoted to education therefore rose even faster than Table 1.1 suggests.

4. Teachers

An enormous effort has been made to recruit and train teaching staff at all levels, to meet the challenge of enrolment growth between 1960 and 1980. *Table 1.2* shows the increase in enrolment, compared with the increase in the numbers of teachers at primary, secondary and tertiary levels.

Table 1.2 Growth index of enrolment and teachers, 1960-1980 (1960=100)

	Primary		Secondary		Tertiary	
	Enrolment	Teachers	Enrolment	Teachers	Enrolment	Teachers
Africa	390	372	1 010	844	1 124	846
Asia	206	224	310	352	513	435
Arab States	285	365	652	574	874	812
LAC[1]	228	252	577	421	843	585
Developing Countries	240	255	447	453	684	558

[1] LAC = Latin America and the Caribbean

Source: Unesco Statistical Yearbooks, 1976 and 1988.

The rapid growth in primary school enrolment was matched by an equivalent increase in primary level teachers, but at the secondary level the number of pupils rose faster than teachers in Africa and Latin America, and student enrolment grew faster than teacher numbers in all geographic regions at the tertiary level. This means that student-teacher ratios increased at the secondary and higher education levels as enrolment expanded, but in primary schools many countries saw a decline in pupil-teacher ratios. In 1960, 41 out of 156 developing countries had average primary pupil-teacher ratios over 40, but only 34 countries had such high ratios in 1980, showing a significant improvement in average staffing ratios during a decade of fast-growing enrolment. There are still a number of countries, however, where ratios remain high.

5. School buildings, equipment and books

The substantial increase in the number of children in school has meant a huge investment in new school buildings. Between 1950 and

1985, more than 1.3 million new primary schools were built, representing an increase of 280 per cent. Of course, many of these buildings are poorly equipped, but the sheer scale of new school building in many developing countries was enormous in the 1960s and 1970s, and a number of countries, for example Kenya and Indonesia, developed significant 'self-help' programmes involving community participation in school building.

Many countries produced no local textbooks in 1960 and there are many examples of countries that have had to overcome considerable obstacles before implementing successful local school book production programmes. Given the complexity of management of such programmes, and the lack of institutional capacity, it is not surprising. But there have been a number of success stories in school book production, both with and without foreign financing, for example in India, Thailand, and the Philippines.[4] In some cases this has meant that countries that were formerly completely dependent on imported textbooks from abroad (for example the Philippines and Ethiopia) have succeeded in reducing their dependency on foreign textbooks, and improved the quality of their education by producing books more suited to their own educational needs and cultural setting, sometimes at lower cost.[5] One recent study showed that in 13 developing countries the number of school textbook titles produced locally doubled between 1970 and 1986.

6. Innovation and the use of technology

Significant efforts have been made in many developing countries to experiment with new methods of teaching/learning and to introduce new delivery systems, based on radio or television, although traditional teaching still dominates at most levels of formal education.

There have been many studies and evaluations of new educational technology. Results have been very positive regarding the use of radio in developing countries, but the high costs of television and computers have limited their use for teaching purposes in the formal education system.[6]

A survey of the use of radio in schools and in non-formal education[7] suggests that:

(i) Radio is a cost-effective delivery system, with a wide variety of potential uses and advantages, including:
- the enrichment of learning experiences through occasional specialised lessons that the classroom teacher would find it difficult to provide;
- direct instruction; that is, carrying the major burden of instruction in one or more subjects;
- extension of in-school education, by means of radio instruction which can lead to a qualified teacher being replaced by a monitor;
- distance learning, in which radio programmes combined with textbooks and occasional personal interaction entirely replaces the teacher and classroom.

(ii) The most successful examples of the use of radio -- in Nicaragua, Mexico, Tanzania, Kenya, Sri Lanka, Colombia, Indonesia, the Dominican Republic -- resulted in:
- improving access to schooling through distance learning;
- improving the quality of education through direct support to teachers;
- reducing costs by reaching large active audiences;
- adding to teachers' skills through in-service training and distance learning.[8]

(iii) In the non-formal sector, radio can be used for:
- promoting of strategies of rural development, for example improvements in health and nutrition;
- promotion of literacy campaigns;
- broadcasting radio forums and other interactive programmes, for example for agricultural extension services.

(iv) Access to higher education can be expanded through 'open' university systems, made possible through the combined use of traditional and new technology. Unesco statistics show enrolment in open universities in developing countries ranging from 1 per cent (in Jamaica) to 55.5 per cent (in Thailand) of the total university enrolment.[9] In China, radio and television distance education involves several million students at the secondary and higher levels.

Between 1960 and 1980 developing countries introduced, tested, and adopted a number of reforms and innovations in structure, content and methods. A very popular example, with obvious possibilities, is the 'Escuela Nueva', which is spreading throughout rural Colombia and moving the country towards a more open, participatory model of classroom learning. This is only one example of a wide rage of innovations. Many more examples are given throughout the book.

7. Increased reliance on non-formal and informal education

The overall picture shows a considerable expansion of knowledge, experience, and know-how in developing countries, sometimes at great expense. The sharing of experiences and information has greatly enriched the backgrounds on which decision-makers can draw. But innovation seems to be less frequent in the formal areas of learning than in the informal, where innovations in communications technology and the media mean that there has been a marked increase in the opportunities for both adults and children to learn informally -- in their homes, villages or towns -- rather than only in schools. *Figures 1.1 - 1.4* show a considerable rise in the number of book titles produced per million inhabitants, in the circulation of newspapers and in the availability of radio and television. This represents a huge increase in the opportunities for reading or watching or listening to informative broadcasts, news programmes, entertainment, films -- and these extensions in the informal learning environment often help strengthen other, more formal, educational activities. In Africa, for example, the number of televisions went up from 2 per 1,000 inhabitants in 1965 to 25 in 1986, and in Asia the increase was from 18 to 48. The increase in radios was even greater (from 33 to 170 per 1,000 inhabitants in Africa).

On the other hand, a conflict of social values between the new media or other informal channels, and traditional channels of communication and instruction may limit the effectiveness of new media in some traditional societies, or may elicit outright rejection. But the new media can also be instrumental in opening minds and encouraging acceptance of change, thereby helping to promote modernisation.

Figure 1.1 Book titles per million inhabitants

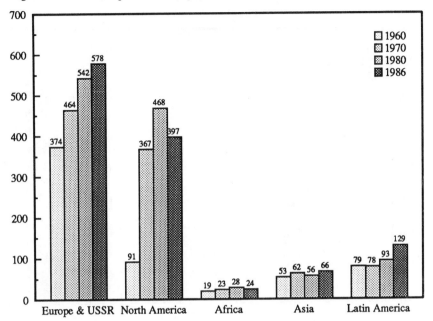

Figure 1.2 Circulation of daily newspapers per thousand inhabitants

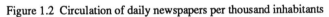
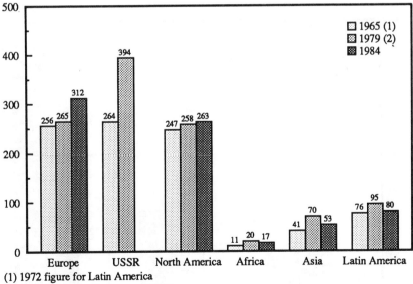

(1) 1972 figure for Latin America
(2) 1977 figures for Europe and USSR

Figure 1.3 Radio receivers per thousand inhabitants

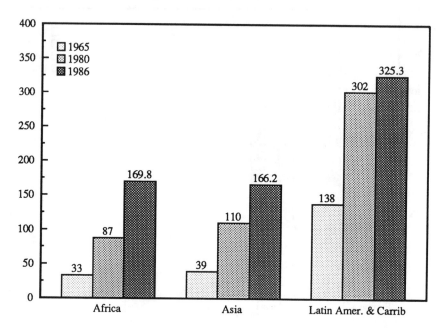

Figure 1.4 Television receivers per thousand inhabitants

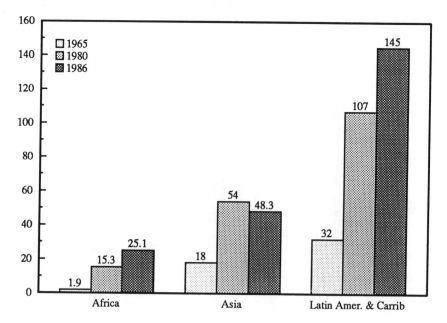

One striking trend in some countries is the increased efforts to promote non-formal education in rural areas through the development of community schools and new media.[10] Through these initiatives, educational services can be delivered to all ages, and members of the community can be drawn into decision-making processes. Rapid population growth has led to a strong demand for education in rural areas in many countries, but there are still wide disparities between urban and rural areas in terms of both access and quality.

Other important innovations have been achieved in adapting formal education to the needs of non-traditional learners: for example, women have been enrolled in literacy and adult-education activities, working children have been integrated, and marginalised ethnic groups have been attracted by the use of their own languages. A project called 'Street school for street children' in the Philippines,[11] is an interesting example of attempts to extend non-formal education to meet the needs of those who are not served by the formal school system.

While the formal school remains in general the dominant -- or at least the largest -- component of most educational systems, a wide range of other educational possibilities have proliferated beyond its borders, and played important roles in relating education to the various sets of social, cultural and economic conditions in developing countries. However, experience shows that the links between formal education and non-formal and informal teaching and learning are very complex and imperfectly understood, and later sections of this book explore in greater detail the possible uses of non-formal education.

8. The effects of educational expansion on indicators of human resource development

To assess the development of the human capital of a country, we need an accurate idea of the size and composition of its population and changes over time. A categorisation by educational level might include some who are totally illiterate, some who are barely literate and numerate, those who have reached basic or more advanced levels of knowledge and understanding of the world and the environment in which they live, those who could apply that knowledge and contribute to the development of their society. If trends in the distribution of the population among these groups could be measured, it would be possible to assess changes in human resource development over time with some precision.

Unfortunately, there are rarely enough accurate data even to indicate levels of formal schooling in many developing countries. We know very little, even in developed countries, about the extent to which rote memorisation remains the backbone of the educational process, or whether problem-solving or creativity are encouraged. It is even difficult to ensure consistent definitions of literacy and numeracy, and the effort to assess the achievements of developing countries in human resource development must inevitably resort to imperfect and proxy indicators, such as:

(a) percentage of the total population that has had no schooling at all;

(b) number and percentage of literate adult population;

(c) numbers of students enrolled in secondary, technical and tertiary institutions.

a. Proportion of population with no schooling

Census figures from 32 countries show that the proportion of the population with no schooling at all has declined significantly since the 1960s. For example, Unesco statistics for 1984 show that 39 per cent of adults aged 25 to 34 in Tunisia had had no schooling, compared with 84 per cent of those aged 45 to 54, which means that in spite of population growth, the proportion of the adult population that has benefited from some kind of schooling has increased considerably. As *Figure 1.5* shows, in the developing countries generally, 28 per cent of 6- to 11-year-olds had never been to school in 1980, compared with 43 per cent in 1960.

b. Literacy

Perhaps the most striking educational achievement is the overall expansion of literacy in the developing countries since the 1950s. The number of people who have at least passed through primary school, and the number who have actually become literate, has vastly increased as the opportunity to attend school has widened. As these young people grew into adulthood they often became fervent supporters of education for their children, which helped to foster a

Figure 1.5. Percentage of 6- to 11-year-olds with no schooling, by region

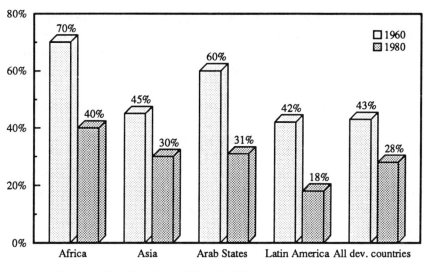

Source: Unesco, *Statistical Yearbook, 1988,* Paris, 1988.

strong social demand for schooling. For the late 1960s, Unesco statistics showed rates of illiteracy falling below 50 per cent, which implied that the number of literates actually outstripped the number of illiterates, perhaps for the first time in the history of mankind. By the mid-1980s, the proportion of the adult populations of developing countries classified as illiterate had fallen to 38 per cent, and overall and numerically the total literate adult population of the world grew from about 900 million in 1950 to 2,300 million in 1985. The figures are all the more impressive when seen in the context of rapid population growth, resulting from progress in health and life expectancy.

However, population growth also meant that the absolute number of illiterates was growing; from 700 million in 1950, they reached 880 million in 1985. In absolute numbers, the largest pockets of illiteracy are concentrated in a few countries in Southern and Western Asia, a few in Latin America, and more in Africa. Nevertheless, in relative terms, the percentage of illiterates in most developing countries diminished between 1950 and 1985, and from a historical perspective, the performance of the developing countries is extraordinary, when compared with the much longer time taken by industrialised countries to eliminate illiteracy in the nineteenth century.

Of course, better conditions of health, nutrition, and shelter contribute to the elimination of illiteracy, and improvements in education in turn contributed to raising standards of health, nutrition and life expectancy. A well-nourished child will obviously profit better from educational opportunities than an undernourished one, while educated parents tend to have healthier children than illiterates.

c. Participation in secondary and higher education

Not only have an increasing number of children attended primary school and achieved literacy and numeracy, the numbers and the proportion of the relevant age-group attending secondary and higher education grew substantially between 1960 and 1980, as *Table 1.3* shows.

Table 1.3 Secondary and higher education enrolment in developing countries (in 000s)

	1960	1970	1980	1986
Secondary[1]	33.696 (14.9%)	83.889 (15.8%)	157.930 (19.5%)	191.796 (23.1%)
Higher	4.015 (1.5%)	7.320 (1.8%)	18.096 (2.2%)	26.800 (2.8%)

[1] Includes general, teacher training and vocational
Source: Unesco, *Unesco statistical yearbook, 1989*, Paris, Unesco, 1989.

Trends vary considerably from one country to another. Middle-income countries such as Uruguay doubled their secondary enrolments during the period 1960-86, while Mexico's increased twelvefold. On average, low-income countries multiplied their tertiary enrolments by four and lower middle-income countries by ten. However, relative priorities varied between countries: in some developing countries eradicating illiteracy, and expanding primary education had the highest priority, while others emphasised higher education and some produced many more university graduates than their countries could immediately absorb. This high priority for university graduates reflected the desire of many newly-independent countries to replace foreign nationals with locally recruited manpower. In the mid-sixties, developing countries had to rely heavily on specialists from abroad, especially in teaching and the civil service; by the 1980s, many developing countries had replaced the majority of foreigners by their own nationals. This is not to say that all of these people are adequately trained, or that educational and training systems are adequate to the countries' needs for highly specialised engineering or technical manpower, but considerable progress has been achieved.

9. Summary: trends in human resource development

To summarise, developing countries have been able to reduce or overcome many of the effects of unfavourable cultural, social, institutional and financial conditions, and to make significant and sustained educational progress in the 1960s and 1970s, because of the convergence of the political will of governments with social demand for education. Even though it is difficult to compare different societies at different times, it can be said that enrolment and literacy grew at much faster rates in the developing countries in the three decades between 1950 and 1980 than in industrialised economies at similar stages of development.

However, this rapid expansion brought problems of increasing costs and low quality that assumed crisis proportions in many countries in the 1980s, and it is to this decade of educational and economic crisis that we turn in the next chapter.

---

1. Roy Carr-Hill, John Lintott, *Comparative analysis of statistical data on adult education for 84 countries,* Paris, Unesco Office of Statistics, 1985.

2. See G. Carron, K. Mwiria, G. Righa, *The functioning and effects of the Kenyan literacy programme,* Paris, Unesco:IIEP, 1989, (IIEP Research Report No. 76).

3. K. Lewin, *Education in austerity: options for planners,* Paris, Unesco:IIEP, 1987, (Fundamentals of Educational Planning, No. 36).

4. D. Pearce, *Textbook production in developing countries: some problems of preparation, production, and distribution,* Paris, Unesco, 1982.

5. D. Pearce, *A guide to planning and administering government school textbook projects, with special emphasis on cost reduction factors,* Paris, Unesco, 1988.

6. Unesco, *The economics of new educational media,* (In three volumes), Paris, 1980.

7. D. Jamison, E.G. McAnany, *Radio education and development*, London, Sage, 1975.

8. L. Mählck, E.B. Temu, *Distance versus college-trained primary school teachers: a case study from Tanzania*, Paris, Unesco:IIEP, 1989, (IIEP Research Report No. 75). See also A.W. Dock, W.A. Duncan, E.M. Kotalawala, *Teaching teachers through distance methods*, Stockholm, Swedish International Development Authority, 1986, (Education Division Documents No. 40).

9. Unesco/IBE, *A review of education in the world: a statistical analysis*, Paris, Unesco, 1988, (ED/BIE/CONFINTED 41/REF 1).

10. The experiences of about forty countries are referred to in Keith Watson, 'Forty years of education and development: from optimism to uncertainty', In *Educational Review*, Vol. 40, No. 2, 1988, p. 152.

11. See Assefa Bequele, In: 'The emergent response to child labour', *Conditions of Work Digest*, Vol. 7, No. 1, 1989, p. 188

Chapter 2

A decade of crisis:
the effect on educational priorities

A radical change in any social trend can be a source of tension, imbalance, and possibly crisis, requiring painstaking adjustment from the old to the new set of circumstances. We have seen in Chapter 1 that, since 1960, a radical change has taken place in education in many countries. By the late 1960s, there were signs of an emerging 'world educational crisis'.[1]

The signs of an emerging or potential crisis included escalation of costs and expenditure, declining quality, doubts about the relevance of the curriculum for emerging social and economic needs, imbalances between supply and demand for educated manpower, leading to further imbalances between educational aspirations and employment opportunities, a growing problem of educated unemployment in many countries and continuing or widening gaps between standards and participation in rural and urban areas. It required time and social stability to solve these problems, and in many developing countries it was impossible to find time or to achieve social stability. The problems were thus not overcome, but continued throughout the decade of the 1970s into the 1980s.

The early 1980s saw a new crisis developing. The major recession which began in the industrialised countries after the oil price shock in the mid-1970s spread throughout most developing countries in the late seventies and early eighties, and led to balance of payments and budget deficits which severely affected the capacities of governments to finance education. This added a new dimension to the problems and imbalances that were already rooted in the educational systems. So new problems developed, as consequences of the recession and of political and economic responses to it; yet others have resulted from changes in educational policies that were introduced in an attempt to get on with educational development or to overcome previous difficulties. Successive waves of economic and educational crisis affected the efforts of governments and social demand for education, so that both the general tensions in the development of education and the imbalances that had emerged in the previous two decades were aggravated.

1. Tensions in educational development in the 1980s

This section examines several indicators of the tensions and problems facing education in this decade.

a. Public spending on education

Trends in educational expenditure summarised in *Table 2.1, Table 2.2* and *Figure 2.1* show:
 • With few exceptions, the 1980s have been a period of worldwide declining growth in real public spending on education. In many developing countries, especially in Africa and Latin America, the growth rate has been lower than that of national incomes. Unesco estimates that between 1980 and 1986, real public educational expenditure per inhabitant has decreased on average in developing countries from US$29 to $27. There was a decline in overall public budgets in real terms in the wake of two world recessions compounded by marked fluctuations in oil prices, aggravating debt crises throughout Latin America and Africa and in some countries of Asia and the Middle East, and high rates of inflation.

Table 2.1 Public expenditure on education as a percentage of GNP, 1980-1986

Region	1980	1982	1983	1984	1985	1986
Developed countries	6.0	6.2	6.1	6.1	6.2	5.8
Developing countries	3.9	4.3	4.0	4.0	4.1	4.0
- Africa (excluding Arab States)	5.2	4.4	4.8	4.9	4.7	4.4
- Asia (excluding Arab States)	4.6	5.1	4.7	4.5	4.7	4.4
- Arab States	4.5	5.3	4.7	5.5	6.4	6.7
North America	6.9	6.9	6.9	6.8	6.4	6.5
Latin America and the Caribbean	3.9	4.2	4.0	4.4	4.0	3.5

Source: Unesco, *Statisical yearbook, 1982, 1984, 1985, 1986, 1987, 1988,* Paris, Unesco.

Table 2.2 Increases (+) and decreases (-) in the proportions of central government expenditure on (i) defence, (ii) education, (iii) health, (iv) social security, welfare, housing and community amenities, (v) economic services and (vi) government expenditure as a percentage of GNP, 1972-1986. Figures relate to number of countries (for which data are available).

	Defence		Education		Health		Social Security, etc.		Economic services		Other		Total Gvt. expenditure as % of GNP	
	+	-	+	-	+	-	+	-	+	-	+	-	+	-
Low-income economies	7	4	3	8	5	6	5	6	6	5	5	6	8	3
Middle-income economies	6	9	4	11	5	10	9	6	6	9	10	5	10	5
Upper middle-income economies	4	5	4	5	5	4	5	4	1	8	6	3	6	3
Sub-total	17	18	11	24	15	20	19	16	13	22	21	14	24	11
Industrial market economies	0	14	1	13	8	6	8	6	1	13	11	3	14	0
Total	17	32	12	37	23	26	27	22	14	35	32	17	38	11

Source: Compiled from the World Bank, *World Development Report 1988*, Washington, D.C., 1988.

Figure 2.1 Public expenditure on education per inhabitant (in U.S.$ at current prices)

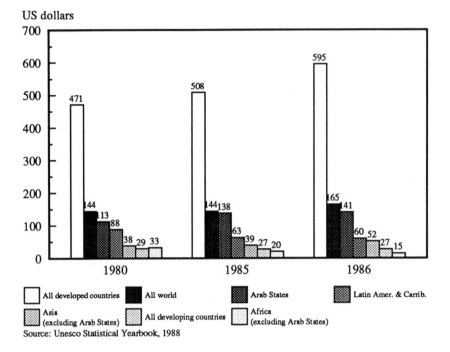

US dollars

Source: Unesco Statistical Yearbook, 1988

- Economic recession and austerity and political pressures have caused some governments to shift priorities away from education towards health, or other social services, or towards defence. In other words, when objectives conflicted, the vulnerability of the education sector was clearly revealed in some countries, although in others, governments chose to protect the education sector.

- In a context of scarcity of resources, secondary and higher education have been cut in some cases, but primary education has borne the brunt of the cuts in many countries where the political influence, prestige and autonomy of higher institutions, and the social demand for access to them, have resulted in a high government priority for higher and secondary levels, to the detriment of the primary sector.

- The way in which governments have responded to financial austerity has varied considerably. In some cases salaries have been protected by cuts in expenditure on maintenance and upkeep of schools, or by shifting the burden of financing books or materials to families; construction and equipment orders may be simply cancelled, or postponed. But such measures are not usually enough, by themselves, and in many countries the real salaries of teachers have declined, and in some cases the number of teachers has also fallen.

b. Enrolment

Since 1980, average annual growth rates in enrolment have declined, in comparison with 1960-80, in most educational levels and in geographical regions (see *Figures 2.2, 2.3* and *2.4*). At the primary level, rates of growth dropped dramatically in Africa and in Latin America, more moderately in other regions. But there were wide differences within regions. Some countries suffered a decrease in enrolment -- note that this is not a decrease in the rate of growth, but a decrease, albeit small, in actual enrolment -- while others managed to increase enrolment rates in the 1980s, indicating radical differences in government attitudes, in pressures from families, and in the strength of expansion in primary enrolment rates between 1960

Figure 2.2 Average annual growth rates of enrolment (Primary education level)

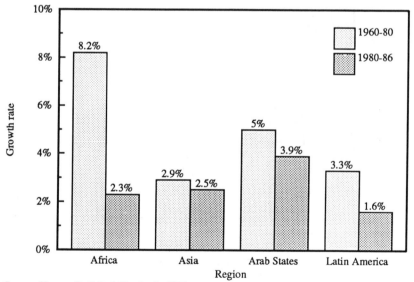

Source: Unesco Statistical Yearbook, 1988

29

Figure 2.3 Average annual growth rates of enrolment (Secondary education level)

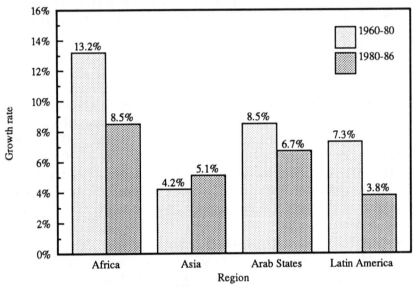

Source: Unesco Statistical Yearbook, 1988

Figure 2.4 Average annual growth rates of enrolment (Higher education level)

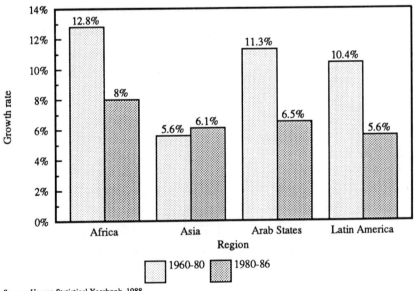

Source: Unesco Statistical Yearbook, 1988

and 1980. Little in the way of general conclusions can be drawn, apart from the obvious one that many poor countries are still a long way from universal primary education, and some are even slipping backwards.

There was a decline in the average rate of enrolment growth at the secondary and tertiary levels in all developing regions except Asia, where a sharp increase in enrolment at the upper levels in the 1980s can be explained by differing government policies, less stringent budget situations due to sustained economic growth, already high income levels and previous growth in enrolment. By 1980, China and India had already reached high enrolment ratios at the primary and secondary levels compared with many developing countries, and this resulted in a faster expansion of higher education in the 1980s.

Despite the difficulties involved in completing primary and secondary schooling in many countries, and growing problems of unemployment among secondary school leavers or graduates, there is still strong social demand for secondary and higher education. Rightly or wrongly, the students and their families are convinced that it is worth the effort, and that the private return on investment in secondary and higher education justifies any sacrifice.

As noted in Chapter 1, adult education programmes in several countries declined around 1979. Many governments appear to have found it easiest to drain funds from adult and non-formal education and literacy programmes, which were the first to suffer budget cuts in many cases and proved to be more vulnerable than the formal system. The beneficiaries of these programmes are never the most powerful lobbyists, and by 1980 many governments had not yet seen the value of sustained action, and were financing programmes piecemeal. Literacy campaigns especially require determination on the part of governments, which must initiate, implement, and follow up with post-literacy activities, to ensure success. Target groups must be mobilised and illiterate environments must be transformed into literate environments. Some countries have gone in this direction, but many have not, and without post-literacy projects, newly literate adults feel only frustration. Countries must find ways and means, and sustain their efforts tenaciously, and the international community, Unesco in particular, must participate, if the simple benefit of being able to read a newspaper is to be made available to all.

c. Unit expenditures

The combined data on enrolment trends and expenditure confirm that countries at different levels of development are facing very different education problems. The policies they have followed since the recession are also very different, which has led to marked differences in trends in expenditure per student. The figures since 1980 show that:

• in low-income countries, primary education expenditure per pupil, which was already very low (about US$40) in 1980, declined to less than US$30 by 1986. At the secondary level, where low- and lower middle-income countries spend about the same per student, troubled governments moved quickly to make cuts;

• at the secondary and tertiary levels cost per student is higher, as a percentage of per capita GNP, in poorer countries than in higher income countries.

To summarise, low-income countries are devoting a heavy share of their resources to education. It might even be argued that spending the 'right' amount per student, especially secondary and tertiary students, is among the most critical goals of today's developing countries. Quality formal education is expensive. It requires textbooks, equipment, and teaching materials, and teachers must be trained and paid. Some non-salary cost elements are determined by markets -- worse, international markets -- and have to be imported and paid for in hard currencies. Paper, for example, represents 60 per cent of the production of a textbook in a developing country. Below a certain minimum funding, education cannot be provided at all. Yet low income may make it impossible for a developing country to provide formal education of adequate quality for very many of its citizens. Under these circumstances it is hardly helpful to compare its efforts with those of an industrialised country. It might be more appropriate to focus on non-formal education or alternative approaches that might be within the reach of a country too harassed to dream of 'traditional' schoolrooms and playgrounds for all.

Intersectoral competition for scarce financing seems to have exerted greater pressure on some governments, which shifted priorities towards health or defence, than others, which tried to protect education (See Table 2.2). But the dominant trend remained downward, that is to say counter to two other decisive trends: rapid growth in the school-age populations of the world's poorest countries, and an increase in average expenditure per pupil enrolled as cohorts of pupils passed from low-cost primary to higher-cost secondary and university. Most African countries, and particularly Latin American countries, have tried to deal with this dilemma by reducing real spending per pupil at all levels. Others have simply not kept up with population growth, with the unfortunate consequences of large numbers of children not in school, and increasing imbalance between urban and rural areas.

2. The effect on quality

Increases in enrolment between 1960 and 1980 were not always accompanied by commensurate expansion in the capacities of the schools. Even where growth rates fell or stagnated, it has been difficult for some countries to provide enough teachers, enough school places, enough in the way of materials to maintain quality. A word of caution: it is not suggested that all developing countries suffer from all of the problems discussed here. Certain Asian countries fare better than other developing countries, while others, particularly in sub-Saharan Africa, face gigantic difficulties. Every country is unique, but all face financial constraints that affect quality.

a. Buildings and equipment

Despite the huge increase in school buildings between 1960 and 1980, continued population growth means that many more buildings are needed, especially in urban areas, where the annual growth rate is often around 6 per cent. Obviously, a 6 per cent increase in the number of schools, just to keep pace, is already beyond the finances of most developing countries, and existing buildings, new or old, have to be used intensively and are often very overcrowded and inadequate.

At the primary, and often at the secondary level, in many African and Latin American cities, the multiple-shift system is typical. While dual use of a building makes sense in a poor country, some buildings are the daily scene of three entire schools. Maintenance and cleaning are slapdash if not non-existent, the classrooms are increasingly drab and impersonal, and both teachers and students become more and more demoralised as time goes by.

If a building is to support double shifts, it must have safe storage facilities, but these are rarely available. Equipment is confined to what teachers and students can carry away each day. Teachers are unable to set up projects, charts, continuing experiments or displays of pupils' work, which play such an important part in good primary teaching. They cannot even get into their classrooms to write on the blackboard before class. They cannot linger with eager students to follow up an activity that has interested them. Schooldays are progressively truncated, and there begin to be wide differences from one week to the next.

Pupils in grades 1 and 2 suffer most in very overcrowded schools, particularly in poor districts in urban areas; sometimes they can attend only a couple of hours a day. But often pupils in higher grades can also be accommodated for only a few hours a day.

A 1985 study[2] of classroom conditions in urban schools in 12 African States showed that nearly half were inadequate. Classrooms designed for 40 are accommodating 70. Only half have sanitary facilities. Furniture is either non-existent or in poor condition, and often at least two students share each desk. Budget cuts are usually applied first to maintenance. In a country like Guinea for example, many primary school buildings are in serious disrepair, probably hazardous to health, and the urban playgrounds are miserable if not worse. In Yemen, expenditure for maintenance and repair has not increased at all over the past ten years, despite an enormous increase in the number of buildings.

These conditions are not due exclusively to the financial squeeze. In many countries, the education ministries' building departments are funded for investment, but rarely for maintenance. Sometimes repairs are left to local communities, and while studies in Guatemala and Honduras, for example, suggest that the more closely involved the local communities are in the life of the school, the better the condition of the buildings, in other cases school maintenance is beyond the resources of the local community.

Expenditure on instructional materials (see *Table 2.3*) can also serve as a parameter for assessing educational quality, and while it may not be surprising that industrialized countries can afford to spend ten times as much as Latin America, on average the situation in some countries can only be described as alarming, given the importance of books for the quality of a school.

Table 2.3 Expenditures of 66 countries on instructional materials per pupil at the primary level, 1980 (in US$)

Area	Number of countries	Yearly expenditure
Low-income countries	34	1.69
Middle-income countries	32	6.14
Industrialized countries	16	92.32
Sub-Saharan Africa	16	2.49
Middle East and North Africa	4	3.28
East Asia and the Pacific	6	2.06
South Asia	4	1.26
Latin America	15	8.99

Source: B. Fuller, "Primary school quality in the third world", In: *Comparative Education Review,* Vol. 30, No. 4, Nov. 1986.

Table 2.4 Percentage of students without textbooks in selected countries

Burkina Faso	33
Comoros	67
Guatemala	75-100
Haiti	75
Pakistan	50
Rwanda	87
Sierra Leone	25-65
Uganda	40
Nigeria	98
Paraguay	67
Peru	67

Source: World Bank (1989), op. cit.

The lack of materials or equipment can be especially serious in primary schools, where children from illiterate or bookless homes are being introduced to written figures and words -- strange symbols to which very simple material could give concrete meaning. Generally speaking, as *Table 2.4* shows, it is especially in low-income countries that the availability of textbooks is critically low.

Even the teachers are sometimes without textbooks, and often without manuals. In Malawi, fewer than 15 per cent of teachers surveyed in 1983 by the World Bank had received a teacher's manual for any subject other than English, and only 44 per cent of the teachers in rural Brazil had received manuals.

b. Staffing

(i) Teachers

In many developing countries the increase in the supply of teachers has not kept pace with enrolments. Unesco statistics show that in Africa, 18 countries have average pupil:teacher ratios higher than 40, and 8 out of 29 low-income countries have average ratios over 50. While class-size is not a reliable indicator of quality of education, particularly at secondary and tertiary levels, overburdened teachers and overloaded facilities do mean that quality suffers. In Bangladesh, the recommended maximum is 40 primary pupils per classroom, but the average in urban areas is 52. It is in the dense urban areas that the situation is most stressful for both teachers and students.

At the secondary level, the teacher shortage often results from imbalances in supply and demand between disciplines. Sri Lanka in 1984 graduated 400 too few science and mathematics teachers for its needs, and 14,400 too many teachers in the humanities.[3] Shortages of teachers generally are most acute at the senior high-school level, and in science and technology at both secondary and tertiary levels. Of course, shortages of science teachers are not uncommon, even in industrialised countries, but research shows that appropriate subject qualifications are an important determinant of quality of instruction (see *Table 2.5*).

Table 2.5 Percentages of underqualified teachers, in selected countries, 1980

	Primary	Secondary	Primary and Secondary
Bangladesh			46
Barbados	15		
Cameroon	48		
Chile			20
Cuba			40
Ecuador	3	1	
Guyana			30
India	37	20	
Jamaica			23
Mauritius			3
Nicaragua			70
Peru			22
Tunisia	1		
Venezuela	22	27	

Source: ILO/Unesco, *Report of joint ILO/Unesco committee of experts on the application of the recommendation concerning the status of teachers,* Geneva, ILO, 1983, p. 126.

During rapid expansion in the 1970s, unqualified teachers were recruited at both primary and secondary levels in many countries and this fact too reflects on the quality of education. An ILO/Unesco survey[4] in 1980 showed that in Bangladesh, Cameroon, Nicaragua and Venezuela nearly half of primary and secondary school teachers were underqualified. The proportion of qualified teachers normally drops in periods of rapid expansion, and in some cases remains at critical levels for some time. In 10 out of the 33 sub-Saharan African countries for which data are available, the majority of primary teachers have not even completed secondary education.[5]

Compounding the fact that there are not enough teachers in low-income countries, cuts in the real level of teacher salaries means that morale is low and it may be impossible to keep trained teachers in the profession. Studies in several African countries show that teachers earn less than stenographer/typists[6] and that their salaries fell on average by 17 per cent in real terms between 1980 and 1985. In many countries the decline in teacher salaries was even faster. In Congo and Togo, primary and secondary school teachers earned 30 per cent less, in real terms, in 1985 than in 1980.

(ii) Administrative and supervisory staff

School principals or department heads frequently lack the training or resources to be effective supervisors, administrators or managers, and it is not uncommon to find secondary schools, both general and technical, without any department heads at all. Principals are thus tied to supervisory duties that they have neither the time nor the technical knowledge to carry out effectively, especially in large schools, and it is difficult to see how even a concerted campaign can succeed in raising standards of teaching under such circumstances.

At the primary level, supervisors often have no transportation, and a trifling and irregular allowance for public transport. Some supervisors in rural areas are virtually cut off from their more distant schools, unless, as sometimes happens, parents' associations raise the money to finance a visit. In most districts, routine administrative duties such as collecting statistics and inspecting buildings take up most of their time, and very rarely do they actually see a teacher in the classroom. The number of teachers per supervisor is often too high, and the area under his or her supervision too large, to be adequately served. Of course, motorcycles and other forms of transport will not necessarily turn a supervisor into an effective agent of the education system, but without them, supervisors can be as isolated as the teachers they are supposed to assist and guide.

c. Student flows

Poverty, disparities between urban and rural areas, boys and girls and different religious or ethnic groups all help to determine the rates of educational participation and drop-out in developing countries.

(i) Access and attendance

Studies in a variety of countries show the extent of regional and other disparities:
• in India and Nepal enrolment rates among the children of the richest families are 50 to 100 per cent higher than among those from the poorest[7];
• in the Côte d'Ivoire 30 per cent of rural children of school age have no opportunity to attend school[8];
• in Guatemala 56 per cent of urban 7-years-olds are in school, compared with 25 per cent of rural children[9] ;
• in Afghanistan, Nepal and Pakistan, the gap between male and female enrolment has widened;
• on average, in all developing countries, 25 per cent of all school-aged children are not in school, but the percentage for girls is 40 per cent.

(ii) Drop-out and repetition

Once they are enrolled, keeping children in school is a major problem in many developing countries, where high rates of repetition and drop-out lead to inefficiency and a waste of scarce resources. A major factor leading to drop-out is poverty. For example, in North-Eastern Brazil, the repetition/drop-out rate in primary schools is 66 per cent -- much higher than the national average -- and poverty is most frequently cited by parents as the reason their children leave school.[10] A study in Dharmapuri, in India, showed that financial difficulties and the need to help parents in their jobs were the reasons given by 80 per cent of the drop-outs in the city. Nearly 75 per cent of the drop-outs belonged to scheduled castes or tribes, and 71 per cent came from families with an average monthly income below US$ 6.00[11]

At the primary level, temporary dropping out at harvest time may generate discouragement and lead to permanent drop-out. One solution may be to adapt the organisation of the school year to better fit with the work constraints of the parents and children.

Even if children do not drop out of school, they may be obliged to repeat a year or more, thus pushing up costs. In several African and Latin American countries, 20 to 30 per cent of all pupils enrolled in secondary schools are repeaters and at the primary level it is closer to 50 per cent in some countries. And the average repetition rate has increased in low income countries since 1980. The problem is often linked with absenteeism. In many developing countries, teachers' salaries are low, and they are obliged to take second jobs and be absent from school. Parents are poor, and children must try to earn money or help in the fields or at home, and so miss school. The school year may already be short and absenteeism makes it even shorter. In Haiti, the official school year is 180 days, but in fact a typical school year is around half of that. If the time spent in school helps to determine how much pupils learn, then this has a powerful influence on the quality of education. In addressing the issue of high repetition rates which affect many countries, the question of absenteeism should not be overlooked.

3.   The outcomes of schooling

Comparative studies of student achievement indicate predictably that, on average, children from industrialised countries achieve higher scores than those from developing countries.[12] Mean reading levels of low-income countries' primary graduates are typically 1 standard deviation below those of industrialised countries. But more recent assessment studies suggest that the situation is more complex than this. The latest 'science study' of the International Evaluation Association[13] tested children in a range of science subjects in 26 countries, of which 10 are in the developing world. Lower secondary pupils in Japan and Hungary scored consistently well in all aspects of science, while those from China, Korea, Papua New Guinea and Thailand scored well in specific aspects of science. In upper secondary schools, Hong Kong and Singapore scored highly, while Ghana, Nigeria, the Philippines and Zimbabwe scored consistently poorly in comparison with other countries. To sum up, the study suggests that there is great variation among developing countries in levels of science achievement, with children from some developing countries scoring better than those from more developed economies. On the other hand, in some developing countries children need twice as long (in terms of years at school, even though the length of the school year differs) to reach the same level of achievement as children from developed countries.

Whatever the level of instruction attained, students do not necessarily acquire the skills to meet their needs or the social and economic needs of their countries. The problem of educated unemployment is a symptom of the mismatch that may occur between the world of work and the world of education, although in some cases it may be more a result of a fall in the number of jobs available -- perhaps because of recession -- than the fault of the graduates or their preparation. According to ILO statistics, the number of unemployed persons who have had employment experience in 'professional, technical, and related' fields or in 'administrative, executive, and managerial' functions, has increased in 39 of the 47 countries for which statistics are available.[14]

In Ecuador, for example, the number of productive jobs increased between 1970 and 1982 at an annual rate of 1.5 per cent, while over the same period, the student population increased annually by 25 per cent, resulting in a surplus of graduates. In Argentina, economic growth has hit a low of 0.3 per cent, while the enrolment ratio at the university level is about 39 per cent -- higher than the average in Europe.[15] Imbalance between supply and demand for skilled manpower is also illustrated by the case of Mali, where only 30 per cent of the 1986 university graduates got jobs, and in Guinea, where the unemployment of graduates resulted in a 40 per cent reduction in the number of university enrolments.[16]

A mismatch between supply and demand can result in educated unemployment, but an irrelevant curriculum may also contribute. The content of the secondary and tertiary curriculum in many countries is far removed from the world of work, and there are many instances of well-equipped vocational institutions with sophisticated apparatus that are under-utilised and a curriculum unsuited to the requirements of the local labour market.[17] A summary of African case studies[18] shows that few workers use the vocational skills they have acquired in school. The useful ones are learned on the job. That is, many developing countries are dominated by an unorganised agrarian sector, and do not have the necessary industrial base to absorb the products of a western-oriented vocational course of study. General secondary and tertiary curricula are too rigidly organised, and the distribution of enrolments usually too heavily weighted against the scientific fields, to adjust to specific labour demand.[19] However, attempts to increase the proportion of science students at the university level frequently fail because of a shortage of suitably qualified school leavers.

4. Summary: The effects of a decade of crisis

The economic recession that began in the late 1970s and continued into the 1980s had wide and grave repercussions for education and human resource development in developing countries. There are certainly considerable differences between countries, but certain problems and trends have emerged -- throughout Africa, Asia, and Latin America -- and become all too familiar. Growing demand for school places is accompanied by heavy drop-out rates; sluggish flow and repetition, by fierce competition for admission; over-concentration on the academic aspects at the secondary level; neglect of technical and vocational courses, especially the terminal ones; wide disparities of highly vulnerable non-formal programmes; literacy campaigns that cannot be finished, not to say followed up; converging pressures of the financial squeeze and of sheer numbers threatening timid advances in the quality of education; and the growing threat of unemployment at the end of it all.

There are certainly exceptions to this gloomy picture, but in all too many countries there is a growing frustration as education tries to respond to ever changing needs with dwindling resources.

In the period 1960-80 the challenge was how to cope with the consequences of rapid growth. Today, it is the dangers of stagnation and decline that face policy-makers and practitioners in many developing countries. How to set priorities in the face of this challenge is the subject of this book.

1. See P.H. Coombs, *The world educational crisis: a systems analysis*, New York, Oxford University Press, 1968; and *The world crisis in education: the view from the eighties.* New York, Oxford University Press, 1985.

2. J. De Bosch Kemper, M. Hugh, *Les installations scolaires en Afrique francophone*, Dakar, Unesco, 1985, (BREDA/PUB/PMF/86/02).

3. L. Dove, *Teachers and teacher education in developing countries: issues and planning, management and training*, London, Croom Helm, 1986.

4. ILO/Unesco, *Report of Joint ILO/Unesco Committee of Experts on the application of the recommendations concerning the status of teachers*, Geneva, ILO. 1983, p.126.

5. A. Zymelman, J. DeStefano, *Teachers' salaries in sub-Saharan Africa*, Washington, D.C., World Bank, Population and Human Resources Division, 1988.

6. A. Edwards, *Teachers' salaries in developing countries,.* Washington D.C., World Bank, Education and Training Department, 1985.

7. D. Evans, 'The educational policy dilemma for rural areas', In: *Comparative Education Review*, Vol. 25, No. 2, 1981, p. 232-243.

8. P. Glewwe, *The distribution of welfare in Ivory Coast in 1985*, Washington D.C., World Bank, 1988, (LSMS Working Paper no. 29).

9. S. Lourié, *Inequalities in education in rural Guatemala*, Paris, IIEP, 1982, (Paper presented at IIEP seminar on inequalities in educational development).

10. Robert E. Verhine; Anna Maria Pita de Melo, 'Causes of school failure: the case of the state of Bahia in Brazil', In: *Prospects.* Vol. 18, No. 4, 1988.

11. K. Venkatasubramanian, *Education for integrated rural development: the problem of wastage at the primary level of education in Tamil Nadu State, India*, Bangkok, Unesco/ROEAP, 1982, (Education and the rural community, 1).

12. S. Heyneman; W. Loxley, 'The effect of primary school quality on academic achievement across 29 high- and low-income countries', In: *American Journal of Sociology*, Vol. 88, No. 6, 1983.

13. T.N. Postlethwaite; D.E. Wealey, (eds). *Science achievement in 23 countries: a comparative study*, Oxford, Pergamon Press, 1990.

14. Bikas C. Sanyal, *Higher education and the labour market*, In: 'International Encyclopaedia of Comparative Higher Education', New York, Garland Publishing Inc., (forthcoming).

15. E. Parker, 'L'éducation peut causer des catastrophes', In: *Futuribles*. No. 131, 1989.

16. Miala Diambomba, *Les universités en Afrique francophone*. Paris, Unesco:IIEP, 1988.

17. J.P. Lachaud, *Le désengagement de l'Etat et les ajustements sur le marché du travail en Afrique francophone*, Geneva, International Institute of Social Studies, 1989, (IIES DP 14).

18. Visvanathan, Selvaratnam, 'Limits to vocationally-oriented education in the Third World, In: *International Journal of Educational Development*, Vol. 8, No. 2, 1988.

19. Unesco, *A review of education in the world: a statistical analysis. A contribution to the International Conference on Education*, Paris, 1989, (ED/BIE/CONF 41/Rev.1).

Chapter 3

Priorities for the 1990s: challenges and constraints for a balanced human resource policy

After having discussed and reviewed in Chapters 1 and 2, past trends, achievements and issues, the main purpose of this chapter is to argue for an expanded and sustained mobilisation of national resources for human resource development (HRD). Section 1 will develop the case for HRD on both ethical, economic, social, cultural and ecological grounds. Section 2 will make a case for an integrated approach to HRD. Countries' experiences show that a policy of HRD becomes a successful driving force for economic and social development only when it is integrated within an overall development policy and when both policies are implemented in a favourable national and international setting. Section 3 describes those trends that are likely to have determinant effects on the future development of education systems in the developing world. Finally, Section 4 attempts to map out the main priority areas for the consideration of educational policy-makers operating in different regions and groups of countries in the developing world, with different economic constraints and educational achievements.

1. The case for education and HRD

On both empirical and theoretical grounds, many arguments suggest that education and the development of human resources should receive special attention from governments aiming at promoting economic growth and human development. But perhaps, above all, it is for the sake of individuals and societies themselves that efforts should be made to expand and improve the education of youth and adults.

a. The ethical dimension

Experienced political leaders know that they must go beyond the economistic and psychometric views of education and deal with its fundamental ethical and human dimension. Above all, education is a human right and as such should receive priority in the allocating of national resources. It is a very shortsighted view to keep education bound and gagged in the role of manufacturing skilled manpower, or to judge one's success by the number of children and adults who have efficiently consumed a learning package.

If education is considered to be a human right, it is because it leads to individual creativity, improved participation in the economic, social and cultural roles in society, and hence a more effective contribution to human development.

As Mayor put it: "Education is a prerequisite not only for the full exercise of the individual's rights, but also for understanding and respecting the rights of others".[1] In this way, education can become a powerful factor in promoting social cohesion and material understanding. Unfortunately, however, there are societies in which access to education is determined on principles of power, and the human right principle remains problematic.

b. Improvement of health and nutrition

Education contributes to improving the health and nutrition of children and parents; hence it can help to reduce mortality and increase life expectancy. Malnutrition causes deterioration in the old as well as the young, but in children it is particularly devastating in its effects on resistance to disease and physical and mental development. Inadequate systems of distribution of food, and discrimination of distribution, even on a family level, can contribute to the painful injustice of hunger. Education helps remedy these serious problems, not only by increasing the income of a parent, but also because of its influence on the parents. The more educated the parents, the better the nutrition conditions of the children. Moreover, studies show that it is more important to the nutrition of a child that the mother be educated than the father. There is also fair evidence that education in health and nutrition can be more effective and less costly if it is simultaneously part of general education and tied to community organisations or other influential channels of communication.[2]

More generally, despite improvements throughout the developing world over the past three decades, the health care situation is still alarming, especially in the poorest countries. In some, it became impossible even to monitor certain indicators at the time of the recession.[3] In addition to its function in improving access to health care, education can contribute to preventive information which will reduce illnesses as well as infant and maternal mortality, regrettably still rampant in many countries. World Bank studies in 29 developing countries have shown that infant and child mortality is in inverse correlation with the education of mothers: each year of schooling means, on the average, 9 per 1,000 fewer infant and child deaths. Countrywide longitudinal studies also confirm the effect of literacy on life expectancy.[4]

c. Economic development

Despite some remaining controversial issues, there is virtually general agreement[5] on the close connection between HRD and economic growth.

Primary education unquestionably exerts a decisive impact on economic productivity. The impact of different levels of educational achievement on the output of farmers in subsistence agriculture is more easily measured than that of other sectors, and comparative studies have observed that four years of primary education increased their productivity by 8.7 per cent across countries.[6] But the effect of education is not the same from one country to the next, and its contribution to rural development can be any of several: (i) a direct increase in productivity or interaction with other factors in production; (ii) improvement in the marketability of products through the application of effective agricultural techniques; (iii) the association of education with the decision of a farmer to try modern practices. Surveys of rural areas in Bolivia, the Dominican Republic, Guatemala, and Paraguay have led to the conclusion that education has a positive and significant correlation with rural productivity in two of the four countries, and that a strong link exists between education and the modernisation of an environment.[7]

When no direct measure of productivity is available, earnings serve as proxy; research in developing countries has found returns to primary schooling averaging around 27 per cent, returns to secondary around 15-17 per cent.[8] Literacy and numeracy alone have been observed to explain differences in the wages of secondary school completers.[9]

It is more difficult to demonstrate a relationship between education and economic growth. However, there is historical evidence to support the opinion that none of the presently rich industrialised countries was able to achieve significant economic growth before attaining universal primary education.[10] Furthermore, the most successful of the newly industrialised countries -- Korea, Singapore, Hong Kong -- and those with the fastest-growing GNPs in the 1960s and 1970s -- Thailand, Portugal, Greece, and others -- had usually achieved UPE and near-universal literacy just before their economy began its ascent.[11] Yet, cross-country analyses suggest that high performance in literacy and schooling are not automatically followed by sound and sustained economic development; and the outstanding performances of Japan and Korea were apparently not founded solely on mass literacy and numeracy but on socio-economic regulation, land reform, and modern economic management. Education should probably be looked upon as a necessary, but not sufficient, condition for economic development.

d. Technological development

In the modern-day context of accelerated technological change, education has a crucial role to play.

A developing country's capability of participating in the benefits of technological progress, and of contributing actively to technological innovation, depends on a number of educational prerequisites. High-level researchers, engineers, and technicians must be trained and used effectively. It is not because developing countries must look to others to provide technology that they need not produce their own professionals, managers, technicians and skilled workers. Without them, they cannot assess the possible choices, select appropriately, or apply what they choose to their own contexts. Without them, there is no choice but to fall behind forever.

A country's engagement in the development and use of new technologies has serious implications in terms of employment and skill requirements.[12] With the introduction of new technologies, especially informatics, fields of employment in which repetitive unskilled and skilled jobs have so far prevailed, tend to shrink ; others, building essentially upon high- and middle-level professional personnel with creative skills, able to improve the quality and management of their work, seem to be expanding without making unskilled labour obsolete. Similarly, getting involved in the application, let alone the development, of biotechnologies, electronics, information processing and other complex technologies will require that the traditional disciplinary limits in both research and training be changed. Manual and specific skills will increasingly have to be complemented with broad views of systems in which technologies are applied. For advanced studies, sound basic literacy and numeracy skills, middle-level technical and organisational skills, and to an increasing degree, high-level cognitive skills -- abstract reasoning and problem-solving -- will be the cornerstones of the mastery of technological advance.

e. Socio-cultural change

According to some researchers,[13] schooling promotes 'modern' attitudes, and 'rationality,' but we must be cautious in the use of normative terms for subjective phenomena. In taking measurements of individual modernity, defined as consisting of rationality and empirical opinions, it was found that these increased with the number of years of schooling. Secondary school instruction in arts and sciences proved to be most 'effective' in producing attitudes considered to be modern. Some evidence, but little documentation, indicates that the number of years of schooling correlates with 'rational' savings and consumer choices.

There is evidence to support the observation that education has an impact on fertility. Formal education of girls has a significant influence on age of marriage and family planning practices.[14] Since nearly 50 per cent of women in Africa, 40 per cent in Asia, and 30 per cent in Latin America and the Caribbean are married by the age of 20, and childbearing is common among adolescents in developing countries, reduction in fertility rates is no small contribution to development.[15] A survey of 14 countries shows that women without education have more children than those who have had some, and the number decreases with level of education.[16] The education of women is the key to population control, family health and hygiene, nutrition, and the educational motivation of children. Indeed it must be said that their role is central to economic life, and because education changes attitudes individual by individual, it can promote or jeopardise national unity.

Imported concepts and values disseminated in schools can contribute to disaggregation of a cultural centre of gravity, aggravate social cleavages, and reinforce the marginalisation of local languages in schools and literacy programmes. The overwhelming evidence of the importance of mother-tongue schooling and of literacy as a prerequisite to educational development dramatically points out the necessity for building educational transmission channels at the grassroots level.

Education is also determinant in narrowing or widening the cultural gap that is frequently observed in developing countries between their highly educated élites, who have access to varied facilities and an international system of communication, and their excluded majorities.

f. Inequalities and HRD

Education is a major social institution which can contribute to democracy and equality. Through education, a culture is transmitted and transformed, social functions and status reproduced and created. Culture acts upon and is acted upon by education, and the problem of inequality of educational opportunity, be it geographical, sexual, and/or socio-economic, is closely linked to inequality of distribution of income, cultural goods, and political power. It is widely agreed that in the developed countries a student's performance correlates with the socio-economic position of his or her parents, but this does not necessarily apply in the developing countries.[17] The comparatively young educational systems of developing countries may thus have some chance of reducing social inequalities, or at least encouraging a certain degree of upward mobility. Some countries began immediately after independence to work toward classless societies. Whatever the social context, the function of transformation of education is undeniable, and as it reaches economically and socially deprived groups, the transformation will be egalitarian.

Presuming a favourable social structure, and an economic context which permits upward mobility, education will produce a richer, more varied human capital, and will reduce the social disparities that plague communities across the spectrum of development.

g. Ecological development

Education has a vital role to play in improving the relationships between man and the environment.

The time is over when GNP used to be widely accepted as the only valid indicator of development and progress in a society. Since the early 1970s, there has been growing awareness of the fact that development aimed at a better quality of life is seriously affected by imbalances in the human environment, which are often caused or reinforced by human behaviour itself. In industrialised countries, one can no longer ignore that pollution and its physical and biological effects are the unwanted consequences of uncareful industrialisation and unlimited striving for growth. In developing countries, inadequate water supplies, floods and famines caused by over-exploitation of land and soil, malnutrition among the young and the vulnerable, very fast urbanisation, and a host of others, are environmental problems symptomatic of under-development or 'ill-development'.[18]

Education in a broad sense can make major contributions to a better understanding and to the addressing of these environmental problems. The initiatives which have been taken in various countries with this end in view are already encouraging indeed[19]:

The mass media, but also associations organising mobile exhibitions, excursions, etc., have already proved to play an important part in creating public awareness of environmental problems. But genuine environmental education is needed to change people's outlook and enable them to acquire new knowledge and to act in a different manner. National initiatives essentially placed major emphasis on the training or retraining of experts and technicians so as to extend the specialised personnel needed. However, at both national and international levels, it became evident that no viable solutions to environmental problems could come into effect unless changes were made in all sectors and at all levels of general education.

Education for environmental literacy via out-of-school activities, aimed at making people able to draw from their own resources to satisfy their basic needs, has proved to be a most powerful tool for changing human behaviour towards the environment. At the school level, increasing attempts have already been made in some developing and several industrialised countries to incorporate environmental education across the curriculum into various subject matters. Experiences suggest that by introducing environmental dimensions into science education -- e.g., in the light of a country's or a local community's specific living conditions and problems -- one can enhance children's understanding of environmental issues and also improve their access to scientific knowledge.[20] Increased efforts will have to be made and innovative actions developed to make environmental education a lifelong, forward-looking education that keeps abreast with the changing environmental problems and their possible solutions.

2. The need for an integrated approach to HRD

Experience suggests that education and human resource development policy become driving forces of development only if synchronized with and reinforced by general development policy and if both are supported by a favourable national and international environment. The likelihood of successful HRD consequently varies with the prevailing specific conditions from one country to another and within a country from one phase of development to another. In practice, the task is far from being simple. It requires sustained efforts and permanent control and correction of imbalances, mismatches and gaps within the educational system, as well as between the human resources 'trained' in the latter and the human resources needed for development.

From several decades of development experience one can draw the lesson that it takes a long time to consolidate HRD, and that accomplishments of one period are strongly influenced by what has been gained years and even decades earlier. A cross-country comparison of trends in literacy shows that most countries with literacy rates of between 90 and 100 per cent had already figured among the achievers (with literacy rates of 65 per cent and over) of 1950. No developing country can allow the deterioration of today's instruction and literacy effort and expect to succeed in developing human resources in the near future.

Sustained effort is necessary to increase enrolment in basic education in a number of developing countries so as to achieve universal primary education, and this will require the mobilisation of vast resources -- a difficult task given the low national income and the economic recession from which many of these countries suffer. Poverty is obviously not a favourable factor, but it is not sufficient excuse to halt progress in human resource development either. A low-income country, Burundi, had remarkable success in increasing access to primary and secondary instruction between 1979 and 1985 because of a strong and expressed intention on the part of the government, as well as the parents and local communities that participated actively in financing the programmes.

Parallel efforts to maximise the quality of primary schooling are also necessary. Primary education of poor quality impedes human resource development at all levels; it discourages demand for schools, lowers efficiency, and contributes to wastage of resources. Last but not least, the job opportunities of school leavers and graduates correlate closely with the quality of their instruction.

In many countries a serious difficulty is that social pressures for secondary and higher education often exceed public financing capacities and public school quality is perforce lowered. Heterogeneous private educational services at these levels lead to overproduction of graduates in fields that labour markets cannot absorb. At the same time, economic development is hampered in agriculture, industry, the informal sector and the public services by the lack of manpower with adequate literacy and numeracy skills and of middle- and high-level technicians.

When looking for country cases in which not only basic education but also the development of education at various levels and its articulation with economic progress seem to have been successful, one is impressed by the success of the newly industrialised East Asian countries; this success can at least partly be attributed to heavy investment in secondary and tertiary education, particularly in engineering and other applied areas. Higher education in many Latin American and African countries, by contrast, has laid emphasis on law, the humanities, and the social sciences. It is not suggested here that these disciplines are unimportant; the plea is for more balanced distribution. The experience of the newly industrialised countries also shows that basic scientific education with strong emphasis on technology and engineering must be fairly strong before a country can expect to diffuse or adapt new technologies to local conditions on the shopfloor. Recent evaluations of educational outcomes[21] show that secondary scores vary with quality of science education at primary level, a fact which does not obviate the need for improvement of secondary science teaching.

Visible success will not be achieved overnight. A 'critical mass' of engineers, scientists, technicians must be trained, and the level of literacy of a population raised to a point where it can foster and promote economic and social development.

Moreover, trained specialists can make their full contribution only if they work in correctly oriented institutions, and it takes time, and sometimes special government and private action (such as that of industry associations), to orient an institution correctly. Investment in HRD is a continuous process: even when economic development appears to be on a safe footing, investment must be sustained. Otherwise the rapidity of obsolescence of knowledge will cause the country to fall back.

Finally, cultural traditions are key determinants of future trends. When they are ignored by policy-makers, they may assert themselves in unexpected ways. They are capable of affecting the future of educational systems, if not destroying them, and too rapid change in an educational 'model' without paying due attention to cultural factors can have serious consequences. It takes time to cajole the opinion of a society and the amount of time, as well as the chances of being able to make the change at all, vary widely from one country to another.

The following 'country parables' (all of which draw on authentic national experiences) may illustrate the importance, the difficulties and some of the possible ways of deploying comprehensive, coherent and sustained efforts of HRD within global development processes.

a. The rocky road to balanced HRD

Our first country is in Africa. Shortly after independence the government decided to give top investment priority to education, to eradicate widespread illiteracy, and to provide the educated human resources needed for national development. Massive investment in industry (most of it foreign) promised the country's imminent economic takeoff. A large part of government resources were devoted to education, and within the education budget to: (i) speeding up universal primary education with the aid of modern educational technologies; (ii) expansion of agricultural extension schemes; and (iii) developing quality vocational and technical training. Adult literacy programmes were neglected in the educational budget. However, the public had high hopes that its children would be educated, and could look forward to increasing well-being. Primary schooling was rapidly extended, putting pressure on the secondary and higher levels. Government efforts to control access to upper levels, particularly secondary, failed, and there was a rush for white-collar jobs. But after a decade and a half of apparent growth, the world economic recession tarnished the picture: instead, the situation was one of investment withdrawn, industry at stalemate, negative growth in agricultural production, bitter disillusionment.

Among other pressing questions, government officials ask themselves whether pumping all that money into education has been such a good idea: They have educated a lot of young people. Those schooled in rural settings have massively migrated to urban areas but the pace of industrialisation and economic growth is now too sluggish to accommodate them. The country is still predominantly rural, and the rural areas are crying out for skilled labour, whereas they suffer from low quality primary schooling and high (although decreasing) illiteracy. The migration of rural schoolleavers have split the rural populations into modern/traditional camps, and the division exacerbates the critical social and economic consequences of not always successful rural development policies.

* * *

What is the lesson from this 'parable'? Obviously, it takes more than money to develop education. In a context of high illiteracy on the one hand, and beginning but rapid industrialisation on the other, planners and policy-makers must control and ensure parallel progress across the school spectrum, and combine adult literacy with basic education and sustained rural development policies.

b. The difficult 'quality-quantity' equation

The second experience is that of a Latin American country. Building upon slow but sustained economic growth over years, and high (albeit not quite universal) literacy, the government started accelerating expansion of secondary and higher education in the late 1960s. Universal primary education was a fait accompli, except in a few rural areas, and pressure was increasing on the upper levels of the educational system. A broad base of middle- and high-level skilled manpower -- especially in technical fields and engineering -- needed to be developed in order to respond to the requirements of national economic development: expansion of the service sector, industrial development aimed at import substitution with local production, and sustained competitiveness of agriculture and related production sectors.

Until the outset of the 1980s, the government's steady increase of resource allocations for the expansion of secondary and tertiary enrolment met with reasonable success. The private sector also made a significant contribution. But insufficient attention to the quality of general and vocational education and to steady enrolment growth in those fields of higher education and training which were most needed for development cost it dearly. In a context of economic stagnation and indebtedness, the low quality of preparation of the country's workers and technicians was widely criticised. The lack of engineers in the productive sector became part of a vicious circle of growing debts and dwindling investment (and production), partly due to lack of confidence in the country's economic capacities, and its inadequate labour supply.

* * *

The lesson here is that deficiencies in the control and monitoring of educational quality and student flows can obviously cause serious HRD gaps, and contribute to the erosion of a country's economic competitiveness.

c. A smooth take-off toward development

A third example is an Asian country in which, at the start of its industrialisation, the vast majority of the population were living off the land, and in rural areas. The economy was essentially self-oriented, foreign trade almost non-existent. In its efforts to accelerate and strengthen national production and to widen the range of industrial and service sectors, the country worked on its literacy score. With a view to underpinning productivity in small-business industries such as textiles and clothing, food and agriculture, tourism and transportation, the country focused on universal primary education, improving the quality of primary education, and increasing enrolment at the secondary and tertiary levels. The economic environment was fairly favourable, the country having access to markets with high purchasing capacities, and it found diversification not too problematic in any of the sectors: primary, secondary or tertiary.

* * *

In this case, priority allocation of public educational resources to primary education followed by a slight shift towards secondary education and substantial contributions by the private sector to higher education helped to achieve the set educational goals. The country has coped with human resource needs via an educational policy paying particular attention to social studies and humanities at secondary level and accepting limited enrolment in vocational education and in sciences and engineering at the tertiary level. This was not in contradiction with the country's sustained economic development which had hitherto been based on sectors requiring lower and middle level skilled manpower. Economic and technological development in the future, however, could raise questions about the policy so far adopted.

But the country's smooth and lasting take-off has obviously been promoted and consolidated to a significant degree by a HRD policy rooted in quality general education and synchronised with the national economy's needs.

d. Making the dragon strong for sustained development

Finally, we take the case of a country in South-east Asia, which around 1970 found itself at a crossroads. A decreasing but still substantial proportion (over half) of the labour force was deployed in agriculture, while industry -- food and textiles primarily -- was rapidly expanding. A clear option was taken to accelerate export-oriented industrial development, and at the same time strengthen and expand a broadly based national infrastructure-cum-potential, including industrial plant and firms for economic development. This option was highly viable given the country's virtual achievement of universal primary education and high literacy rate. Development of equipment industries, increased external competitiveness and rapid modernisation of agricultural production required not only a vigorous national development policy, and the mobilisation of the population, but also more and better trained middle- and high-level professionals. Strong political will and sustained efforts were deployed towards these development ends.

To finance the HRD effort, ever greater shares of the GNP were allocated to education, and industry increased its contribution by financing vocational and technical education. To ensure the suitability of the HRD effort to an economy striving towards high-level technological development, science education was enhanced, upper secondary levels were diversified (vocational and trade high-schools flourished alongside the general secondary), high-level professionals, especially engineers, were produced in impressive quantities. In line with its efforts to build up high-skill/high value-added industries, R&D personnel were concentrated in the productive sector.

* * *

Twenty years later, the achievements of this country are recognised worldwide, doubtless in large measure because of its highly skilled human resources. The dedication of societal forces to a common goal in education and training and the unyielding will to develop human resources adequate to the demands of modern technical progress must be considered as the crucial elements from which could progressively be built an internationally competitive economy.

These four 'country parables' illustrate the importance of an integrated policy approach, but also of the economic and social context in the choice and determination of educational priorities and strategies.

3. The context of future educational development - some major trends and constraints

Among the many factors which necessarily influence educational decision-making and planning in developing countries, demographic trends, cultural factors, technico-scientific progress and the economic prospects seem to be of particular importance:

a. Demographic trends

Population trends have changed over the past 20 years; from an increase of 1.86 per cent in world population in 1955-60, and 2.04 per cent in 1965-70, it fell to 1.97 per cent in 1970-75, and to 1.75 per cent in 1975-80. UN demographic forecasts are for five-year increases of under 1 per cent by the end of the century.[22] With all the reserve necessary for projecting long-term trends, it seems certain that we are witnessing a fundamental demographic transition which will be reflected in developing countries. Their progression into a phase of declining fertility, accompanied by declining mortality, like all turnarounds, will take time, and will differ from country to country. Some, notably those of the sub-Sahara, have not really entered this progression; but in Asia and Latin America there are countries (China, Hong Kong, Korea, Malaysia, Singapore, Chile, Uruguay and the Caribbean countries, for example) that are rushing ahead so fast they may reach (some have already reached) zero demographic growth in less time than it has taken many of the industrialised countries -- half to one-third of the time in some cases.

Differentiation in the rates of advance may aggravate differences between the southern hemisphere countries; they will ineluctably result in a redistribution of economic and political resources. While the consequences of these changes are long-term, there are short-term demographic pressures for social services which have already been felt. As regards education, there are demands on the part of girls and women for wider participation, there are demands for the generalisation of basic education and literacy, there are young people who want to be prepared for satisfying working lives, and there are adults who demand retraining, particularly rural to urban migrants. In 1985, Africa's urbanisation rate was 32.18 per cent; Latin America's was 68.9 per cent, and that of Asia was 28.2 per cent. By the end of the century, the projected rates are respectively 42.2 per cent, 76.6 per cent, and 35.7 per cent.[23] Urban jobs must be provided for this influx, and far greater training and retraining efforts must be exerted. Human resource development is more crucial than ever, to more countries than ever.

The authorities of most countries, particularly the developing countries, are seriously preoccupied with the problem of urbanisation, which is worldwide and irreversible; by the end of the century it will affect more than half the planet, and in many cases be quite possibly out of control. Research on urban systems is generally limited to the structures and functions of, and forms of adaptation to, urban life, and to the most disadvantaged sectors of communities; it has not yet adequately addressed the cultures of marginalised and excluded populations, nor those which have developed original forms of organisation and management. Education must contribute to train urban migrants and respond to their particular needs, whether in the modern or the informal sector.

b. Cultural factors

An essential age-old task of education has been to conserve and protect an inherited culture and transmit it to new generations. Today there is the added possibility of opening up broad new avenues of intercultural exchange, with all that that entails in potential for mutual understanding and co-operation, through new communication channels resulting from progress in science and technology. Few cultures have remained or will remain static, and education must pursue its difficult twin function of protecting a cultural identity while increasing access to those of others.

This will require that more attention be given in the curricula to such subjects as arts, environment, geography and history, international understanding, local, national and international languages. Between many pressing needs -- literacy and numeracy, science, vocational subjects, cultural development of enrolees -- the art of planning and decision-making in education is to find balanced approaches.

c. Technico-scientific progress

The technico-scientific revolution -- especially in the fields of information, data processing, communications and the media, biology and physics -- is changing the demand for education and training. As Draper put it: "The goal will not only be to provide training in new technologies but also to ensure participation in the creative process of developing such technologies".[24] Economic success virtually depends on access to knowledge, and all countries to a greater or lesser extent are anxious to improve their systems of education. Disparities in the capacities of countries to profit from technological innovation are very wide, however. In Africa, the number of technicians, engineers, and scientists per million inhabitants was, in 1985, 3,451; in Asia, it was 11,686; in Latin America, 11,758; and in the industrialised countries, 70,452. All regions have seen considerable progress over the past few decades, but unless sustained political will is focused on the issue, the disparities will widen rather than narrow because the retardation of those countries that are behind at the outset will continue to accumulate. Some scientific and technical changes are already well established, and the priorities of a developing country must be set with them in mind.

d. Economic prospects

The economic prospects of developing countries will obviously swing with those of the world economy, particularly as concerns inflation and debt, and world economic prospects are never easy to assess. International discussion of current problems receives a good deal of attention from political leaders, but offers little in the way of guidelines. Consensus has it that low-income countries which began a series of reforms in the 1970s to secure their integration in the world economy, and which borrowed relatively little on the world capital market, were able to maintain fairly satisfactory growth rates, at least perceptibly higher than their rates of demographic growth.

With the exception of a small but growing number of industrialising countries and some lower-income countries, world economic prospects allow little hope that within the next four to five years financial constraints affecting the development of education will be significantly relaxed (and therefore hard choices will be more than ever necessary in many developing countries), or that employment conditions (such as generation of jobs in the public and private sectors, wages, and job stability) are likely to be improved. Education and training for self-employment will move up on the agenda, especially in urban areas, and the importance of non-formal education must not be overlooked.

Growing evidence of the success of modern farming technologies emanating from the Green Revolution in many countries of Asia and Latin America lead us to hope that ratios between population growth and that of food supply may be improved. Education must contribute to this advance through training and dissemination of information pertaining to the modernisation of rural areas.

4. Mapping educational priorities : an illustrative exercise.

Because cultural factors are specific to each country and at the same time an important determinant of the present and future of its educational sector, any exercise designed to establish educational priorities for a region or group of countries must be partial, limited to common core factors, and accepted by readers with the greatest of caution. By way of illustration, the *Map of Priorities* at the end of this chapter attempts to offer guidelines as to where selected countries might be inclined to put emphasis in the coming years, and to sketch out broad priority areas for five groups of these countries, mainly on the basis of three essential criteria:
- degree of development of the educational system as seen in primary, secondary, and higher enrolments;
- income level as seen in GNP per capita;
- size of country, which correlates with breadth of range of priorities.

Some complementary information from various sources (notably Unesco, ILO, national reports) on HRD problems and policies in different parts and countries of the world has also been exploited with a view to identifying specific problems -- such as sex inequalities, rural-urban disparities, particular features or weaknesses in educational financing and management -- that seem to require particular attention in the respective groups of countries.

On this basis, the following exercise groups the countries by clusters: each cluster is defined by what can be presumed to constitute their major common educational concern; from there, priorities are suggested in line with major features and constraints they share.

We repeat the caveat that the actual process of setting the priorities for a particular country will depend upon an assessment of the facts of life of that country alone, and the cultural and political conditions pertaining to it. But these, while significant in all cases, are not sufficient, and must be supplemented at the research stage in such a way that the needs of the country can be considered comprehensively. Demographic growth must be taken into account, along with the already tight financial constraints of the less advanced countries; social pressures on upper levels must be reflected upon and dealt with; the modern-day interest in science and technology must be encouraged and fostered in the proper perspective.

In each cluster of countries the challenge will be to choose from among many pressing demands, but three basic needs appear to dominate in all groups:

- more attention must be given to quality considerations;
- more resources must therefore be devoted to the production of basic didactic materials for all levels and to quality teacher training, especially in subject matters;
- management, administration, and pedagogical supports to the educational systems must be improved.

When moving from cluster 1 to clusters 2, 3, and 4 -- i.e. from the group of the poorest countries with low enrolment rates towards the group of economically advanced developing countries with high enrolment rates at all educational levels -- some of the major issues remain, but are modified in scale, and perhaps in importance. Certainly there is some overlapping. The lack of adequate teaching materials in rural areas, for example, still affects the educational environments in cluster 4, but to a lesser extent than in clusters 1 and 2. The following general descriptions of the clusters are preceded by the priority aim that the cluster has in common.

Cluster 1. Selective expansion. This group is composed of countries which are characterised by an extremely low GNP per capita and considerable persisting problems in the fields of adult literacy and universalisation of primary education. Except for the countries of large land area, these countries had the largest proportions and numbers of out-of-school 6- to 11-year-old children in 1986: a total of 40 million, about 40 per cent of the world's out-of-school children of that age. In these countries policy-makers need to focus on the issue of wider coverage under stringent financial constraints. To reduce these numbers, enrolment growth must outstrip population growth, and this is a tall order. An effective delivery system must be developed, and the fastest way to increase coverage is by exploring the possibilities of radio. Incentives for staying in school (retention) must be found, and this means financing school health and food programmes. School environments must be improved, good teaching materials obtained, good teachers trained. At the same time, efforts must be directed toward reducing illiteracy (rates are high in this group), and toward training for rural to urban migrants, who are likely to increase by 30 per cent in the coming decade. Non-formal education must receive high priority in this group.

Cluster 2. Promotion of equality. In comparison with countries of cluster 1, countries of this group are economically slightly better off and their achievements in enrolment at primary and secondary level are higher. Although some countries of this group will also need to place emphasis on the generalisation of basic education and non-formal education (Botswana and Guatemala, for example), the common concern is the enormous disparity among regions, socio-economic groups, and educational levels. Social demand compounded with the lack of adequate monitoring has made the systems grow lopsided. Measures for improving government regulation -- mainly incentives and examinations, particularly at the secondary level -- must be given priority, along with mobilisation of non-governmental resources to finance education.

Cluster 3. Improvement of quality and teaching-learning conditions. Having attained a lower middle-income level the countries of this group are mostly close to the goal of universal primary education and are characterised by growing enrolment rates at all levels, especially at secondary. Despite the particular attention that they have given not only to quantitative but also to qualitative progress, educational development constitutes an area in which budget pressures are first felt, and where cuts are first to fall, and the results are damaging to general performance and aggravating to the problems faced by policy-makers.

Quality improvement is obviously a concern for all -- including industrialised -- countries. But, in the countries of cluster 3, educational quality in general, as well as in particular fields and sub-sectors, faces problems of consolidation which require particular attention if these countries aim at sustained economic and technological progress in the future. It will, therefore, be crucial for them to:

- improve primary schooling conditions, particularly teacher motivation;
- strike the optimum balance between secondary general and vocational sectors;
- accord to the teaching of science and mathematics the importance they deserve; and
- reassess the priorities of higher education.

Cluster 4. Consolidation and extension of improvements. Despite strong heterogeneity, the countries of this cluster have several important things in common. They have been generally successful in achieving economic growth but also in developing their educational systems, in achieving universal basic instruction, in pushing their literacy rates over 90 per cent, and in training the skilled labour they needed. They are now primarily concerned with adapting curriculum contents and methods, extending scientific and technical training at the secondary and higher levels, promoting co-operative research projects between industry and higher education, and, in common with all other countries, purging inequality of educational opportunity.

Cluster 5. Managing differences in regional priorities. The countries of this cluster cover vast expanses of land, and are characterised by wide differences between the preoccupations of their various regions or provinces, and sometimes between their degree of advancement in HRD. About 40 per cent of the world's out-of-school children aged 6 to 11 years live in these countries; thus their highest priority goes to generalizing primary education and reducing illiteracy. At the same time, the majority of the developing countries' scientists and engineers (65%) -- constituting a fair-sized proportion of the world's R&D scientists, engineers and technicians -- also live here, so that high priority must also go to the education and training of high-level skilled manpower. The challenge is to find, and implement, the right balance.

No adequate data base is available on which to establish priorities for each cluster in non-formal education, but the wide variety of functions, levels, and beneficiaries of these programmes will make it necessary for the countries of each group to select areas to develop. Priority within this sector will be assigned by cluster 1 to basic and functional literacy; by clusters 2 and 3 to post-literacy. All groups will have to give top priority to skills development and transition from school to work. Its flexibility and adaptability, and its subsequent effects of reinforcement and extension on the formal sector, make non-formal education a very practical and effective area to allocate resources.

5. Summary: Priorities for the 1990s

This chapter has highlighted the vital role of education and human resource development in the progress of individuals and societies and hence the priority to be given to education and HRD by government in the allocation of national resources. Also underlined is the need for close interconnection between and synchronisation of HRD and global development policies. Four major areas will affect the prospective trends for education and the development of human resources and should not be overlooked by policy makers: growing urbanisation, pressing cultural requirements, growing dominance of science and technology in the shaping of the future of societies, and the persisting problematic economic prospects. When setting up a map of priorities for investment in education and training, policy-makers must, at the same time, take into consideration the need for (i) correcting imbalances, (ii) reaching the target of universal literacy, (iii) reducing inequalities of access to education, (iv) expanding the coverage, (v) improving the quality, and (vi) increasing efficiency in the use of resources. The same priorities cannot be valid for all countries and cannot be implemented immediately and all at once. It is therefore necessary for each country, in the light of its own practical issues and capacity, to address them and to identify and select its own agenda for action.

Putting these 'principles of action' into practice is indeed very difficult. But it is the real challenge that political leaders face. Part II of this book will provide some guidelines for formulating policy, establishing priorities, and outlining strategies to meet the HRD challenge as strongly as possible with the generally scarce, but often extensible or more efficiently manageable resources in hand.

A map of priorities

	Primary	Secondary	Vocational	Tertiary	Non formal	Management, administration and supervision
Group 1						
Group 2						
Group 3						
Group 4						
Group 5						

Table 3.1 A Map of priorities [Mat.: Materials   Teach.: Teachers   Q: Quantity   q: quality   t: training]

	PRIMARY				SECONDARY				VOCATIONAL			
	Mat.		Teach.		Mat.		Teach.		Mat.		Teach.	
	Q	q	Q	t	Q	q	Q	t	Q	q	Q	t
GROUP 1 Selective expansion	+++	+++		+	++	++				-		-
GROUP 2 Promote equality	+++	++		+	+++	++	++	++	++	++		++
GROUP 3 Improve Quality	+++	++	-	+	+	+		+	+	+		+

Priorities by group and sector

PRIMARY

GROUP 1
- Adopt more health and school feeding programme
- Expand intensive use of radio

GROUP 2
- Reduce regional inequality
- Develop pupils' orientation

GROUP 3
- Put special effort in rural and slum areas

SECONDARY

GROUP 1
- Develop or distance education systems
- Improve female enrolment
- Encourage private financing

GROUP 2
- Reduce inequalities
- Improve examination systems
- Develop private contributions in financing

GROUP 3
- Improve basic, science teaching

VOCATIONAL

GROUP 1
- Consolidate and transfer to non-formal sector

GROUP 2
- Improve coherence
- Diversify fields of study
- Develop collaboration with private sector

GROUP 3
- Adapt to manpower requirements
- Expand certain fields of study and cut others
- Improve collaboration with sector

Group 1
Afghanistan
Bangladesh
Benin
Bhutan
Burkina Faso
Chad
Ethiopia
Ghana
Guinea
Malawi
Mali
Niger
Pakistan
Rwanda
Senegal
Somalia
Sudan
Tanzania
Uganda

Group 2
Bolivia
Botswana
Cameroon
Dominican Rep.
El Savador
Guatemala
Honduras
Ivory Coast
Nicaragua
Paraguay

Group 3
Costa Rica
Morocco
Thailand
Tunisia
Turkey
Zimbabwe

Mat. : Materials   Teach. : Teachers   Q: Quantity   q : quality   t : training

	TERTIARY					NON FORMAL		MANAGEMENT, ADMINISTRATION AND SUPERVISION +++
	Mat.		Teach.					
	Q	q	Q	t				
GROUP 1 Selective expansion		+			• Increase the participation of beneficiaries • Change the output mix (fields of study) • Improve quality	+++	• Extend: - Literacy programmes - Job specific for young workers • Encourage on-the-job training skill development programmes	• Constitute a technical staff for data collection and processing • Decentralize • Improve examination systems • Improve school guidance
GROUP 2 Promote equality	+	++		+	• Expand short-term courses • Improve efficiency • Mobilize private financing	++	• Improve and develop materials • Co-ordinate and unify supervision	• Develop data collection and information • Draw up programmes to improve quality • Unify supervision and control
GROUP 3 Improve quality					+ Develop: - applied sciences - Alternative distance education - Short-term courses	++	• Provide activities for neoliterates especially in rural areas	• Improve dissemination • Create national assessment programmes of quality of education • Rationalise and co-ordinate projects to avoid wastage

( ) No priority
- Reduce resource allocations
  Maintain, if possible increase resource allocations
+ Significant increase of resource allocations
++ Top priority
+++ Areas of particular priority

	PRIMARY					SECONDARY					VOCATIONAL				
	Mat.		Teach.				Mat.		Teach.			Mat.		Teach.	
	Q	q	Q	t			Q	q	Q	t		Q	q	Q	t
GROUP 4 **Improve equality in other**	++	+		+	• Improve teachers' motivation • Reduce repetition • Develop local management • Develop pre-primary		+	+	+	++	• Improve equity in access • Improve methods • Introduce initiation to technology	+	++	+	+	• Diversify fields of study • Develop private financing (beneficiaries and industry)
GROUP 5 **Reduce qualitat. & quantit. disparities**	+++	++		+	Achieve: • Universal enrolment and retention • School feeding and health care		++	++		+	• Develop access for rural pupils • Consolidate and diversify learning provisions in urban areas	++	+	+	+	• Develop certain fields of study (health, agriculture and marketing) • Promote self-employment • Improve enrolment in non traditional fields of study

Group 4
Enrolment rates - > 70% primary
              - > 50% secondary
GNP per capita between 1810$ and 7410$

Algeria
Argentina
Hong Kong
Iraq
Korea
Malaysia
Mexico
Panama
Singapore
Trinidad
Uruguay

Group 5 (large areas)
Brazil
China
India
Indonesia
Nigeria

	TERTIARY					NON FORMAL	MANAGEMENT ADMINISTRATION AND SUPERVISION
	Mat.		Teach.				
	Q	q	Q	t			
GROUP 4 **Improve** **equality** **in other**	++	++	++	++	• Develop short term courses for middle level technicians • Diversify teaching methods, (creativity and not memorization) • Improve management and co-ordination of programmes	++ • Develop education for workers • Co-ordinate programmes and projects for skilled manpower	• Develop information on quality (Tests at all levels)
GROUP 5 **Reduce** **qualitative and** **quantitative** **disparities**	++	++	(+)	(+)	• Improve specialization • Co-ordinate projects • Transform teaching methods, develop science and technology, research • Promote access for women	+++ • Promote systematic adult literacy programmes linked with national goals • Maintain neoliterates skills • Adopt programmes for school drop outs, working children and girls	• Develop long term planning • Decentralise • Improve women participation • Evaluate efficiency

1. F. Mayor, Address to the International Round Table on 'Today's children: tomorrow's world.' Paris, Unesco, 1989, (Mimeo DG/89/12).

2. See, for example, World Bank, *Poverty and human development,* New York, Oxford University Press, 1980.

3. Unicef, *Within human reach.* New York, Unicef, 1985.

4. World Bank, 1980. op cit.

5. A recent review of the question can be found in J.P.G. Tilak, *Education, economic growth, poverty, and income distribution: a survey of evidence and further research,* Washington, D.C., World Bank, 1988.

6. M. Lockheed; D. Jamison; L. Lau, 'Farmer education and farm efficiency: a survey', In: *Economic Development and Cultural Change,* Vol. 29, No. 1, 1980, pp.37-76.

7. Kenneth D. Jameson, 'Education's role in rural areas of Latin America', In:*Economics of Education Review,* Vol. 7, No. 3, 1988.

8. G. Psacharopoulos, 'Returns to education: a further international update and implications', In: *Journal of Human Resources,* Vol. 20, No. 4, 1985, pp.584-604.

9. See the study of urban wage labourers in Kenya and Tanzania: M. Boissière; J. Knight; R. Sabot, 'Earnings, schooling, ability and cognitive skills', In: *American Economic Review,* Vol. 75, No. 5, 1985, pp.1016-1030.

10. A. Peasle, 'Elementary education as a pre-requisite for economic growth', In: *International Development Review,* Vol. 7, 1965.

11. See World Bank. 1980. op. cit.; and World Development Report, 1987.

12. G. Göttelmann, *Stratégies d'innovation technologique et politiques éducatives en France, en République Fédérale d'Allemagne et au Royaume-Uni,* Paris, Unesco:IIEP, 1989.

13. A. Inkeles; D. Smith, *Becoming modern: individual change in six developing countries,* Cambridge, Ma., Harvard University Press, 1984.

14. S. Cochrane, *The effects of education on fertility and mortality,* Washington D.C., World Bank, 1986, (Education and Training Paper EDT 26).

15. *Population Newsletter,* (New York, United Nations), No. 45, 1988.

16. United Nations, *Women's education and fertility relationships in fourteen World Fertility Survey countries. Meeting of experts on factors relating to family and fertility,* Geneva, United Nations, 1981.

17. G. Carron; C. Ta Ngoc, *Reducing regional disparities: the role of educational planning,* Paris, Unesco:IIEP, 1981.

18. Victor O. Ibikunle Johnson, 'Perspectives on environmental education', In: *Mazingra,* Vol. 4, No. 3/4, 1980.

19. Major conclusions of national initiatives as well as of the joint UNEP-Unesco Programme of environmental education run in the 1970s are presented in: *Environmental education in the light of the Tbilisi Conference,* Paris, Unesco, 1980.

20. Christian Souchon, 'Some thoughts on the new approaches to science education', In: *Prospects,* Vol. XV, No. 4, 1985.

21. N.N. Postlethwaite; D.E. Wealey, (eds). *Science achievement in 23 countries: a comparative study,* Oxford, Pergamon Press, 1990.

22. United Nations, *World population at the turn of the century,* New York, UN Department of International Economic and Social Affairs, 1989, (Population Studies ST/ESA/SER.A/111).

23. United Nations. op cit.

24. *Sources,* (Unesco) No. 3, 1989.

Part II

Memo to policy-makers

Every major decision concerning education is a political act --
an authoritative resolution of tensions between competing interests
and purposes, which is necessary to determine a common policy and
to resolve the tensions between the conflicting parties. On the
political level, these tensions are recognised to exist in all countries,
whether or not they are acknowledged in public utterances. There is
rarely doubt in anyone's mind that compromise and the resolution of
tensions are part of the business of government. But where education
is concerned, the tensions inherent in all political decisions are not
admitted. Official statements on educational policy seldom mention
conflicts, even in general pronouncements on the objectives of
education. It is not that there are none, but in moving from what is
commonly thought of as the world of politics to the narrower sphere
of education, the meaning of the words is subtly changed, and some
of the tensions are submerged, to reappear in another guise.

There would almost seem to be an unspoken convention,
common to most countries if not all, that the conflicts and tough
realities of the political world should be filtered before they reach the
hallowed halls of education. Because education is an activity that
completely permeates a society, tensions change their form, go
underground, become harder to detect, and therefore harder to
resolve. But they do not cease to exist.

One problem is that politicians and economists who are
experienced in handling political, social, and economic tensions in
their most direct and obvious manifestations, are not accustomed to
dealing with the ways in which they appear in the field of education.

And educators, who have first-hand knowledge of the schools, hesitate to express doubts too categorically, because powerful political forces which they only partially understand must be manipulated with care and precision if they are ever to come to an uneasy balance.

Since it is from interaction between the two groups that educational strategies are developed and priorities set, it is scarcely surprising that they are often expressed in terms so vague as to give little more than a sense of direction. The composites that finally emerge result either in a laissez-faire policy calculated to offend the fewest possible, or in a compromise that satisfies the short-term imperatives of the politicians but not the long-term needs of the society.

Policy choices which give rise to tensions are of three kinds. The circumstances under which a given policy choice is developed vary widely according to the health of the particular national budget.

Global or *intersectoral* choices are made between the interests of education and those of other social or economic sectors supported by the government in question, for instance between education and health, education and roads, or education and exports. Tensions may become intolerable when the government suffers from inadequacy of resources, even to replicate the allocations of an on-going budget in that of the following year.

Sectoral choices are made among educational objectives, each of which may in itself be unanimously regarded as legitimate, but all of which cannot be achieved at the same time. They may not be mutually exclusive at a given stage, but generally they are. Choices between selectivity and equity, between quantity and quality, fall into this category. So does the parcelling out of limited funds between education and training, between the various specialisations at secondary and higher levels, and more generally, between the various levels and types of education. To the parts of the education sector which are not under direct public control, and this applies to most training schemes controlled by industry, to training in crafts, to non-formal and/or community education, the issue of policy choice may perhaps not apply, because the object of the choice is dispersed among many loci of decision-making. When politicians have to allocate budget surpluses among other parts of the educational system, tensions will emerge, if perhaps more subtly, and implications for the various socio-economic groups in the community may be difficult to foresee.

This is where the planner's job is most complex, and the impact of a given decision may be considerable. If, as is often the case, the task of the political functionary is not to dispose of plentiful resources but, in the necessity of balancing the budget of the public sector, to decide where to make cuts in the appropriations of the previous year, tensions may be exacerbated, and a completely different strategy may have to be developed for the sake of resolving conflicts.

Subsectoral choices settle on the ways and means, approaches, methods, and delivery of services that will best achieve a given objective or target once it has been agreed upon. Here the specialist is in a unique position, because the decisions depend primarily on professional factors, which obviously include the educational, economic, and social. A typical example is the choice between a traditional means of expansion of the capacity of enrolment of a higher educational system and the establishment of an open university to serve the whole young and adult population of a nation. Behind the adoption of the latter alternative lie professional considerations such as feasibility, timing, and cost-effectiveness. Such issues as attitudes in the teaching profession, in the higher educational institutions, systems of evaluation and monitoring, and modes of financing may also arise. These constraints can be missed by an eager politician, and new tensions can arise between groups with different ideas on the speed at which even an accepted change can take place.

This section of the book will deal with policy choices at the intersectoral and sectoral levels, and Part III will treat subsectoral choice, which affects more implementation than policy.

Chapter 4

Policy choices

During the 1960s and the 1970s, as noted in Part I, human resource development in general and education in particular received an increased share in the allocation of the public resources of most countries. Predictably, however, even though HRD might continue to be given high priority by governments, the trend of an increasing share could not go on indefinitely without crippling other public services and dislocating whole economies. The share of education has leveled off in recent years, and in some countries is even declining. This does not necessarily mean that governments no longer view human resource development as important. Rather, the claims of other pressing needs, such as agricultural and industrial development or national security, have grown more urgent. Of course, foreign debt servicing has become an immense consumer of the public revenues of a number of countries. Between 1972 and 1985, the cost of debt servicing rose from 1.5 per cent to 4.3 per cent of the GNP of the developing countries together. Yet the share of education in the allocations of public resources remained reasonably high: between 10 per cent and 30 per cent of the national budgets.

Precisely for this reason, policy choices for government are vital.

1. What should be the role of government?

A key policy issue is what should be the role of government? This actually raises two separate questions:

- Should the government play a more or less active role in HRD?
- What should be the role of government with respect to finance, provision, administration and regulation?

a. What government should do?

General consensus seems to favour requiring government to finance all 'public goods', such as clean air and national defence, which benefit all members of the society. Private interests are not willing to pay for these goods because others cannot be excluded from enjoying them simply because they do not pay. It is therefore self-evident that societies must tax their members and provide these goods and services through mechanisms of government. It logically follows that government does not need to finance 'private goods', which benefit only those members of the society who consume them. Individuals will purchase them without encouragement, and government need not be involved.

Note that we use the word 'finance' and not 'administer' or 'deliver'. Whether or not government is expected to take over the provision of goods or services depends very much on the generality of the belief that the government will do a better job than the private sector -- for example when the private sector is ill-equipped to provide the service, or sees no incentive for sharing responsibility for it. Whether or not it is deemed best that the public sector deliver goods or services, it is generally recognised that government must regulate their quality. Because of market imperfections, quality would deteriorate if consumers were left defenceless. The purpose of regulation of norms or provisions is to impose these norms on both the public and the private sectors which provide public goods.

b. Is education a public good?

And what about education? Education is not a purely public good, nor must it be considered a purely private one. On the one hand, rates of return on private investment in education or in some subsectors of an educational system can be interesting enough to attract individuals to pay without the encouragement of government. On the other hand, for the sake of social justice, education must be provided to those who cannot pay for it. Economically speaking, the social benefits of education often exceed its private benefits. If government does not intervene, the level of investment in education will be insufficient from the point of view of the society as a whole.

It is fairly widely agreed that government has an attribute of 'developer' and 'equaliser'. Government must be responsible for (i) developing the structures, services, and institutions of the society, and (ii) equalising access to social goods, one of which is education. Economists tend to regard education as a quasi-public good, and all societies hold their governments responsible for financing and organising it.

To fulfill its role as 'equaliser', the State is required to finance education and training services for those unable to purchase them on the private market. Because education is 'quasi-public', there is private demand and there are private markets (private schools and informal instruction provided by communities and associations, even in the poorest countries). Government must be concerned with policy not only to ensure the rights of those who would otherwise have no access to education, but also to ensure the rights of those whose resources cannot cover the entire cost of their instruction. This means that it must finance all levels and types of both formal and nonformal education and training for those who want and have the ability to profit by it, but cannot pay for it. Obviously this is impossible. Even if money were no object, there are rarely enough well-trained teachers for the needs of any country, and no administration can expand in all directions at once.

The role of 'developer' requires that government should finance, at least partially, certain levels and types of education and training, because those who could pay for it might not purchase enough to meet the society's needs. Some programmes whose private benefit is not interesting enough to attract individuals but whose social benefits are great, must be encouraged by government to fill urgent gaps in the labour market. Government must arrive at an appropriate mix of financial support that will best promote the interests of all, and of course there is no single optimum mix. Even if there were a perfect balance that could be achieved, based on a perfect theory of public resource allocation, it would not be easily applicable, since the costs of moving from the current arrangements in any one country, towards the optimum might be unbearable politically, because of the likely disputes and controversies about distributional implications. The

expenditures of a country in its efforts to achieve it would certainly
be more than its budget could stand.

2. Guidelines for policy choices

There are, however, guidelines that can be considered in making
policy choices. They are summarised below:

Summary of guidelines on the role of government

Area of action	*Criteria*	*Recommendations*
(i) Financing	Equity/social benefit	• Finance to equalise opportunities; • Finance the most "public", i.e., the highest social benefit;
(ii) Provision	Cost/effectiveness	• Seek partnership between the public and the private sectors;
(iii) Administration	Costs and trade-offs	• Target and monitor public support;
(iv) Regulation	Quality/norms	• Regulate delivery systems; • Limit the consequences of market failures.

The questions of administration and delivery, of regulation, and
of financing should be considered separately:
• Whether the *provision* should be left in the hands of the private
sector to a greater or lesser degree is a matter to be considered on a
case-by-case basis, after having assessed its cost-effectiveness in the
private as compared to public sector. And even if these analyses
indicate that one sector would be more efficient than the other, there
may be advantages in keeping both sectors involved.
Competitiveness, regard to cultural factors, synergism, and spill-over
may all constitute reasons for a government to split the
responsibilities for delivery of the service. And there is still no
'correct' demarcation line between the public and private sectors. In
themselves they are fairly loose conceptions, and when it comes to

deciding where to send the bill for a given educational service, or where the responsibility for the provision of the service should reside, distinctions can become even fuzzier. For instance, when a government establishes a school in an area of low population density and scarcity of teachers, in which all primary grades are taught at the same time in the same place, and regards this education as public goods, and all secondary grades are taught together and regarded as private goods (the same teachers being involved at both levels), a partnership between the public and private sectors in the provision of services may well be the most cost-effective solution. The weight assigned to each will vary from case to case.

• Whether or not the government is involved in providing the service, it must *regulate* delivery to avoid differences in quality from sector to sector -- usually meaning bad services for customers in the public sector, who are poor, and good services in the private sector where customers can pay. It must also limit the consequences of market failures when education is provided by the private sector. The private sector is not likely to provide a loan to a student if those involved consider the chances of repayment to be poor. Here a government must step in to widen access to higher education, even to the extent of providing the loans, or at least to make certain that social principles pertaining to education and training are being respected.

• Policy decisions concerning *administration* and *allocation* of *funds* should be consistent with government's role as equaliser. If access to secondary education depends on the ability to pay, as it does in many developing countries, and access to primary education depends less on the ability to pay, government should be sure to subsidize the access of the poorest segments of the population to secondary education. This points up the legitimacy of government's becoming involved in private activities, because it does not wish to see them restricted on the basis of ability to pay. It can do this either by directly subsidising the poor, or by subsidising private provisions to the poor. Through either option, governments must find ways to target and monitor the services or the subsidies, because they tend otherwise to simply replace private spending by those who can afford it.[1] The cost of targeting and monitoring may be very high, even so high as to discourage a government from attempting them. Practical methods such as means tests for awarding fellowships or exempting a student from fees do exist, but in some societies they are not very reliable and are difficult to monitor. The fundamental policy choice of targeting will always involve trade-offs, but it can safely be said that the less rigorous the targeting, the greater the leakage toward the non-poor and the higher the costs to the public purse. And unfortunately, the more rigorous the targeting, the more difficult it is to persuade legitimate impoverished candidates to benefit from the service, and the more difficult to enlist public support for the policy.

• In *financing* and allocating public moneys, a government must strive to provide those services which are most 'public' -- in economic terms, to achieve the highest social benefit -- through the educational programme to be financed. At one time or another, any level or type of education might become crucial to a society, and deserving of top priority in the allocation of public resources. When the most 'public' of the services also contributes to equalising opportunity, policy choices are facilitated. This is the case in countries where enrolment rates are still low, or where the quality of primary schooling is so poor that it is not producing literate citizens. Primary education for girls obviously fulfills both concerns, because in addition to the benefits to the person concerned, many of the goals of society as a whole, such as the improvement of the health and welfare of children and the lowering of fertility rates are met by better education for women. But when the two conditions do not coincide, when a country with limited financial and human resources must decide between different but equally urgent objectives of its educational system, a government's dilemmas are many and obdurate.

3. Setting intersectoral priorities

a. Two general principles

Governments are obliged to respect two imperatives -- they must achieve consistency and coherence in their policies, and they must encourage sectors which can attract extra-budgetary resources. Their success in reaching these goals is fundamental to the process of development.

(i) Achieve consistency in policies. There is little point in feeding all one's resources into the few sectors that are considered to be critical to development, if support is withheld from sectors which

ought to be considered in an integrated strategy for development and economic growth. It is possible for a country to suffer from over-investment as well as from under-investment in HRD, as has been the case in quite a few developing countries in Africa, Latin America, and Asia, where investments in the education sector produced skilled labour which the economies could not absorb. At the same time, trained labour had to be brought in from abroad to work towards the economic targets of the countries. The art of policy-making is to find the right mix. Investments between complementary sectors must be synchronised to achieve and sustain orderly economic and social development.

(ii) Ease pressures on public budget by (a) mobilising additional resources wherever possible (e.g., by encouraging contributions from the private sector through cost recovery or by diversification of revenue sources, including contributions by industry); and by (b) postponing budgetary proposals for future years.

HRD is certainly an area in which extra-budgetary funds can be attracted, particularly in the field of education. Governments are quite justified in trying to ease the pressures on their budgets, sometimes by postponing proposals for a year or two, sometimes by refusing budget resources to an activity or programme that it cannot afford. But that makes it even more vital to find non-budgetary funding to replace or supplement its allocations.

In making intersectoral choices, government ministers are constantly required to make judgements about relative priorities, but the kind of practical problems that ministers of finance and of education have to tackle and the appropriate responses will vary widely according to the overall conditions of public finance. If public resources are growing, there are many questions of relative priorities to be settled; but when resources are shrinking the choices are posed much more starkly.

b. Policy choices in a context of declining resources.

(i) Management of conjunctural public finance deficits. An unexpected decline in income or an unusual need for expenditure is referred to here as a conjunctural deficit. It occurs one year but is likely to be followed by a surplus situation the following year. The minister of finance is faced with the question of where to cut. Should

the country stop providing electricity to the capital city more than 16 hours a day? Should it postpone payment of the salaries of civil servants? Including teachers? And for how long? Obviously there are no theoretical answers to these short-term dilemmas, and even the criteria used in determining the cuts must be tailored to each situation. By and large, one might say, these choices are determined by political cost. It is, generally speaking, more politically costly to upset a well-organised group of citizens than an ill-organised or unorganised group which explains why a government might make one choice before an election, and another after. Also generally speaking, short-term concerns tend to predominate over long-term concerns. The challenge for policy-makers is to handle pressing short-term concerns while avoiding irreversible or expensively reversible damage to the system, in our case, the educational system. Two principles suggest themselves:

•   In adopting packages of measures to balance public finance accounts, a longer spread of years, even a postponement, of the implementation of an educational programme involving quantitative expansion, and a shift of priority towards programmes concentrated on maintaining quality and good working conditions in the schools may be necessary, even if it is not desirable on equity grounds. For instance, it is a good deal less expensive to protect educational facilities and equipment against deterioration than it is to replace them when they are beyond saving. Many developing countries could have avoided prohibitive expenditure to rehabilitate their school buildings, had they given more attention to the need for funding their maintenance costs.

•   If supplementary resources can be obtained for educational purposes, it is advisable to give priority to activities which would be phased out or whose quality would be dramatically deteriorated otherwise, even when they are financed partly or completely by private sources. This policy is justified by the resulting lower marginal costs of educational services. It is probably often far more justified to finance the operation costs of an existing centre of production of textbooks and/or to subsidise teachers' salaries in the private sector than to purchase (or start a new project on) textbooks, and/or to expand enrolment in the public sector.

(ii) Management of a structural deficit. Long-term structural deficits characterise many developing countries; they have to stand

by and see the best part of their revenues diverted to the servicing of a foreign debt, while at the same time their import capacity is hobbled by terms of trade and domestic inflation. Educational policy choices here are very much determined by economic and public finance imperatives to eliminate the structural deficit. Sometimes a government will simply reduce the public sector through privatisation; sometimes a reallocation of funds disguises budget cuts. Different countries adopt different strategies, but they are not often successful, because the very lack of resources at the outset makes monitoring difficult, and external factors are as hard to foresee as to control. International rates of interest, the imposition of new terms, fluctuations in foreign demand for the country's products, which themselves depend on fluctuating economic conditions in the client countries, all bear heavily on a developing nation's budget. And as long as the budget is impoverished, finance ministers, and certainly ministers of education, will find less flexibility and more difficulty in making rational policy choices. Moreover, in some countries, educational expenditures are not entirely under the control of the government, but established by constitutional law. In Central and South America some constitutions require that a fixed proportion of the public revenues go to higher education.

Obviously, these issues do not affect the education sector alone. Over the past decade they have been felt many times throughout the social sectors, and even in the so-called productive sectors of both developing and industrialised countries, anxiously seeking ways and means to meet both economic challenges and social responsibilities. Economists have argued that the need to provide nutrition, health, education, housing, and employment justifies the expansion of the fiscal burden and the streamlining of the tax-collection systems of certain countries. But the power structures of the countries can be very difficult to budge, and the tax burdens very difficult to add to.

A good deal of the policy debate has centred on the following arguments.[2]

In industrialised economies the need is to reverse the trend of mushrooming public sectors. The share of government spending in GNPs has mounted steadily during the past three or four decades, reaching an average of 47 per cent during the 1980s. Some countries have managed to cut government spending, arguing that public deficits aggravate inflationary pressures and discourage private initiative. Others simply stumble along in the possibility that the best government might be the one that governs least. Still others arrange economic partnerships between the public and private sectors, keeping a modicum of regulatory power in the hands of the government. Some of these strategies may result in lower public deficits, if only by simple shifting to the private sector.

The fewer resources a country has, of course, the less flexible it can be in attempting to reduce its public sector; but while some developing countries have tried to follow strategies such as these, their private sectors are small and they have few mechanisms outside the government for mobilising resources for the social sector. For some, the argument is irrelevant.

The share of central governments in the GNPs of developing countries is comparatively modest. On average, public sector spending represents about 22 per cent of the GNP, as opposed to a 47 per cent average in the industrialised countries.[3] In the long run, assuming even limited income growth, developing countries will probably expand educational programmes gradually, at a speed that can be supported by their public institutions. But as long as structural deficits prevail in public sectors, there is no alternative to short- and medium-term attraction of investment in human resource development; education must be partially supported from private and extra-budgetary sources if it is to succeed at all, and if public sector deficits are to be kept at a tolerable level. The specific directions in which one might work to expand government services without adding to tax burdens are: (i) improving effectiveness in the use of resources and improving public sector management of educational programmes; (ii) reallocating resources between the social sectors and within the education sector and the granting of priority to incentive mechanisms that can generate extra-budgetary funds.

4. Choices within the education sector - choosing between terminal or preparatory education: the cost of ambiguity

Perhaps at the root of most tensions in education is the lack of an explicit statement of the aim of each segment of the system. As affirmed in the introduction to Part II, government tries to avoid taking sides between conflicting elements by having general definitions on which consensus is established, but which leave room for divergences of opinion. The result is a creeping ambiguity which affects the whole system from pre-school to university level, and embraces most non-formal and training programmes -- even in countries which have developed their educational sectors to a high degree.

The most typical ambiguity relates to the purposes of certain classes at various levels in a system. Is the class *terminal* in the sense that students who have completed it leave school? Or is it *preparatory* to the next phase? As permanent/recurrent education becomes progressively common practice, does this age-old question become a bit dated? With few exceptions, it does not. The two principal reasons for this are (i) the persistent difficulty in balancing preparation for leaving against preparation for the next level, in the light of budget constraints and limitations, and (ii) the problem of giving every student a fair chance to compete for entrance at the next level, at the same time preparing the mass of students for the kind of life and livelihood they can expect in the communities in which they will live. Most advanced countries, at some stages of their development, have had schools that were frankly terminal, reflecting a fairly well-accepted élitist concept of education and of society. But it could be argued that there were also valid economic reasons for those policies at those stages.

In principle, no education should ever be terminal. It should always open options rather than close them. It is a question of how specific content should be. If it is very specific, it may close options. The main argument against terminal education is that it does not in fact train for particular occupations and real possibilities.

However, it is for each country to decide whether at its present stage of development the conditions are appropriate for selectivity, and if they outweigh the more generous principle of equality of opportunity. Certainly the extreme of having all students in all institutions prepare for further schooling, which for most of them will never materialise, makes little sense. A compromise of some sort is inevitable. It is the level at which the compromise is set that must be decided by policy-makers, in line with their nations' concepts of quantity, quality, efficiency, and equity. Few examples illustrate the dilemma as clearly as the selection of certain levels as 'terminal' or 'preparatory'.

• To countries with low primary school coverage, low quality of education, low efficiency and scarce resources, it is tempting to construct schemes that focus more on non-formal education and reduced length of primary education -- say from four to six years. The arguments seem reasonable: a good four-year education is better than a bad six-year one; it suffices to meet the immediate needs of the children, and to identify most of those best fitted to benefit from secondary education; the saving or stabilising of costs can help to extend the coverage to a larger proportion of the school-age population, either through the formal or the non-formal system.

Some of the objections to this scheme are educational. The need for skills in literacy and numeracy is basic; the margin for manoeuvering in constructing the broad framework of a grades-one-to-four curriculum need not be great; and some empirical evidence demonstrates that the success of students in non-formal programmes increases with exposure to formal schooling. But the principal objections are political. Government may not wish to give the impression to its own citizens and the outside world that it is willing to reduce the length of primary education. Even when the scheme is presented as having attractive 'technical' arguments, such as dispersion of the population and fulfilment of the particular needs of rural areas, rural parents and children see 'first-cycle primary education' as 'second-class education for the rural population', and only when the 'preparatory' nature of these schools is assured do they become acceptable to their potential users.

• Having greater resources and feeling greater determination to provide universal primary education, many countries have achieved almost 100 per cent primary school enrolment; but very few clearly state that grades 5, 6, or 7 (depending on the duration of primary education) were terminal. Thus the methods and curricula of these grades are firmly oriented towards secondary education. The short-term consequences are obviously lack of space in the first year of secondary instruction, and of a structured network for extra-curricular programmes, which generate frustration, doubts about the value of education, and some turbulence, especially in urban areas where young graduates of primary schools sense a wide chasm between what they have learned in school and what they might do to earn a living. The long-term consequences are uncontrolled expansion of secondary enrolment in urban areas in both the public and private sectors, because only strong government can permit itself the political risks of rationing entrance to secondary education to 12- to 18-year-old primary graduates.

The challenge of balancing the terminal functions of any type of secondary school with its preparatory functions is complex, and unresolved in most countries. Governments try to palliate the negative connotations of vocational schools as terminal by offering at least theoretical possibilities for the best students -- even if only a very few -- to transfer to academic schools at the end of their studies. For a number of reasons, among them the capacity to attract better students, a school might incorporate both terminal and preparatory courses. These 'comprehensive' schools are heavily weighted on the preparatory side, which has more of the atmosphere of the traditional secondary school, more glamour, and much bigger pots of gold at the end of its rainbows.

• Most academic secondary schools are assumed to be preparatory, even in countries with well-established and recognised certificates, and even when the possibilities of access to tertiary education are negligible. Early in their educational careers, therefore, those students with family support must deal with a confusing array of entrance requirements for higher education, at the same time knowing that they will have to compete to get in, and that there is no guarantee of making it.

Entrance requirements vary enormously among departments and specialisations in those fortunate few countries with large systems of tertiary education, with the result that both secondary schools (public and private) and their students are trapped in a system over which they have no control. Curricula, teaching methods, and living conditions in upper levels of secondary schools veer toward the dramatic, sometimes losing touch with anything that education can be imagined to be about. Governments themselves, especially ministers of education, regard examinations such as the Baccalaureat as political issues that require all their energy and attention. It is paradoxical that the ambiguities surrounding the value of the examination and its purpose remain generally unresolved.

If the experience of the more advanced countries is any guide, some of these problems will, in the long run, take care of themselves. When the drop-out rate from primary education dwindles to nothing, when secondary education is guaranteed to all, the terminal functions of primary education can be forgotten. But this may take generations in some developing countries. And meanwhile, intellectually as well as politically, governments are torn between two legitimate objectives. The art of planning and making policy choices is the art of balancing preparation for study with preparation for life without study, with clear-eyed understanding of their determinant effects on a system of education that includes part-time education, non-formal education, and various out-of-school training schemes. If a network of institutions and courses for part-time continuing education is created, enmeshed with the formal school system but partly free of it, the concept of terminal instruction will hopefully be upgraded in the public view. In most cases, unfortunately, parity of esteem between parallel and formal academic instruction, on which parents and children pin their hopes, is not yet a reality.

5. Weighting objectives

Two types of situations illustrate the fairly general concerns faced by politicians who, in trying to reconcile tensions and conflicts, may be forced into decisions that one does not normally think of as related to the functions of government.

a. Equity and growth

The increased contribution of education to economic growth and the principle of equality of opportunity appear at first glance to lie peacefully side by side, the twin objectives of any system of education. Each would appear to reinforce the other, to be in its most cherished interests. Yet the moment one seeks to make policy choices in favour of one or the other, conflicts arise. Most developing countries have pledged and are striving to achieve rapid economic growth and social justice, and the two seem complementary in the long run; but the short-term demands of countries suffering from chronic paucity of resources, and acute pressures of cyclic recessions and austerity measures, tend to minimise the weight assigned to equality of opportunity and social justice in the formulation of policy. Restoring economic growth, which inexorably elbows its way to top priority, still means for many policy-makers the concentration of resources in capital and skilled manpower in the areas where they are most likely to be rapidly effective. Renewed emphasis placed on producing that manpower, skilled in both the modern and traditional sectors, often means concentrating the effort on secondary and tertiary level (technical, vocational) education (both formal and non-formal) in the areas perceived as critical to the economy, with scant attention being paid to the growth or improvement of primary schooling. In getting quick results, it seems logical, however politically unwise it may turn out to be in the long run, to train the best workers in the proven productive areas, where economic progress has already been best promoted. And of course this policy tends to aggravate the very inequalities in educational opportunity that governments are supposed to combat.

If, due to favourable political and social circumstances, the pendulum swings towards resolving social inequalities, attention is turned to expanding the availability of primary schooling; but there can still be strong political forces working to divert the flow towards the door of the secondary institution. No conscientious developing government would deliberately choose either extreme; obviously policy should establish and maintain a healthy balance. But it is easier said than done.

Some of the stickiest problem areas to be kept in mind by policy-makers are the following:
• The inherent difficulty in synchronising the production and use of manpower is seen in the time lag between changes in demand for trained manpower and responses to those changes in the educational system. Except where training schemes have been tailored by teams of employers and instructors, in agriculture, for example, or crafts, sometimes in industry, misfits occur, and graduates may be prepared for jobs that do not exist while the jobs that do exist remain empty or are filled by imported labour. Unfortunately the process tends to be irreversible. Moreover, delaying the integration of scientific and technological advances in curricula, because funds are lacking or because of bureaucratic inertia, results in lopsided mixes of graduates, and in critical gaps in labour pools.
• Demographic expansion (which is about 6 per cent per year in the urban, 2 per cent in the rural areas of many developing countries) can exhaust the margins of manoeuvre of policy-makers, and make both equity and growth problematic. In some countries, primary education budgets have been stagnant for years, which certainly does not encourage equity of access, and generally goes hand in hand with diminished response to the economy's demand for training as well.
• Parental and political pressures for adding school places are difficult to resist, but often lead to imbalances. Some governments, for example, have been forced to extend the duration of compulsory education of children in urban areas to avoid social unrest among

concentrations of unemployed primary school leavers, when their rural areas were still a long way from universal primary education, even for the length of time that was established.

• The benefits from educational investment in terms of economic productivity on the one hand, and of equity of opportunity on the other, can never be simply or quantitatively assessed, and no doubt vary from country to country. Fluctuations in educational priorities in many developing countries over the past three decades reflect the unpredictability of these outcomes.

b. Quantity and quality

Probably the most obvious and widely recognised conflict in policy choice when resources are limited is that between expansion and quality improvement. Do we want more students, more teachers, more buildings? Or do we want improved conditions, more textbooks, better-trained teachers, better-equipped buildings? And if we opt for quality, things are further complicated by selections among new teaching/learning practices: what shall be taught, how shall it be taught, who is to be taught and where? When this conflict arises, and it is ubiquitous, it is too much to expect that a government will make its decisions on purely educational grounds. This is just the point where pressures from parents and students weigh heaviest, and, except at the more sophisticated levels of society, tend to weigh in favour of expansion rather than quality. Putting it differently, the so-called social demand or competition among people for education is much more determinant in the final policy than are the well thought-out decisions of the members of the government.

Here again the differences between conditions of budgetary deficit and surplus are critical in determining the flow of students through the system. In sub-Saharan Africa, where deficits are structural and budgets are ever more stringent, there is no problem of quality versus quantity. It is a fact of life that conditions will deteriorate, that enrolments will decline perhaps as a result of decline in social demand, perhaps as a result of the decline in quality or of phasing out schools or classrooms as teachers lose interest for lack of sufficient compensation. Governments struggle to discover changes that can be brought about without budgetary resources, but which might respond to the pressures for expansion and fill the need for maintaining a minimum standard of quality. Boosting financial support from international organisations is vital.

Where the deficit is not structural but conjunctural, a developing country must consider four factors in slicing the pie between quantity and quality:

- the fact that money is short, and the materials and facilities it can buy are limited;
- the shortages of professionals and the unwillingness of those who are there to adapt;
- the lack of administrative infrastructure;
- the lack of time, which exacerbates the other shortages.

Heretofore the usual complaint has been that the grievous shortage of money and the materials it could buy are so inadequate as to undermine any possibility of improving quality. Yet factors other than money are ignored in considering quantity and quality. Many observers of educational development are surprised to see widely supported educational programmes improperly implemented. Indeed, some funding agencies often express regret and failure to understand the slowdowns in disbursements of the educational loans or grants they provide. The experience of many countries suggests that the main reason for believing that educational progress will be difficult does not lie solely in finance, but in a more subtle group of constraints that do not seem to be immediately responsive to quick injections of money:

- Finance can buy more school buildings, but cannot buy immediate changes in what goes on inside them, nor can it have an immediate effect on students' attitudes to keep them in the buildings long enough to realise the benefits intended for them. It can buy textbooks for every child, but cannot make them quickly relevant to his/her needs or to those of the society; nor can it fill the time the teacher formerly spent replacing the textbook. It can increase salaries, and this is of course essential, but can it increase them to the extent where teachers no longer need to hold two to three jobs to make a living wage? Can it revolutionise the habits and attitudes that have been established over decades? A clearer distinction must be drawn between upgrading courses designed to help individuals to improve their income, and in service courses primarily intended to improve teaching methods.

- If, for lack of transport, supervisors are unable to supervise, will they do so when cars are provided? And what will they do in the classrooms? If, for lack of laboratories, workshops, equipment and expensive specialised trainers, the curricula of a vocational school is little more than a pale copy of those in the prestigious academic schools, will more money, better equipment, and better-trained staff be sufficient to make it more vocationally oriented? Unless examinations are redesigned to give more weight to vocational subjects than to academic, it would seem unlikely.

• If entrance examinations at the university level continue to reward memorising at the expense of reflective thinking and reasoning -- which in some societies correspond to the definition of good education -- they will undercut any attempt to change methods of teaching, even in the traditional subjects, and even in the face of massive financing. Training and recruitment of better teachers, coupled with massive crash programmes of in-service training may not be sufficient to change the style of teaching if the teachers and all the pupils over a certain age have grown accustomed to a traditional way of doing things. Working habits acquired in the early stages of schooling -- over-dependence on memorising, failure to identify symbols as such and to link them with their concrete manifestations, intellectual passivity, and the uncritical acceptance of statements as facts -- tend to stay with a student or a teacher to some degree throughout his or her learning or teaching career.

• The official duration of a school year is about 200 days, but in some developing countries, student and teacher absenteeism reduces the total time of combined learning and teaching to about 100 days. Interactive radio programmes, designed to operate 200 days a year, have been proposed to improve teachers' performance and reduce absenteeism. It has been suggested that teachers be stimulated to take part in these projects by the offer of a free, or nearly free, radio set, and this sort of organisation, being regular and chronological, might work to reduce teacher absenteeism. While there could be merit in this sort of programme, and a possible wide impact from a comparatively small investment, one might wonder if it could indeed produce the benefits expected of it. Absenteeism usually results from the need of a teacher to hold more than one job in order to supplement an insufficient income. It is unlikely that a free radio set could do much to combat this problem.

Nonetheless, governments should seek out those changes that can be brought about without, or with little, additional funding.

Available literature is full of proposals for improving efficiency in the use of resources. We might cite the following:

- it has been suggested that pupil/teacher ratios can be widened, within limits, let us say to 35-40, reducing costs without deterioration in the quality of instruction;
- with a given budget, more school places can be provided by a community where expenditures for transport of building materials and honoraria for architects are lower;
- an increase in the proportion of assistantships for junior staff on the faculties of higher institutions may result in savings which can be diverted to equipment and to the research activities that are so badly needed.

We see that a policy choice is gravely vulnerable if it has not been based on systemic observations and preceded by serious consideration of weights, impacts, and interactions among the components of the system and between the system and the larger environment. The crux of the issue is, of course, to determine the concrete conditions under which these suggestions might be implemented.

6. Summary: policy choices

Indeed, the specialist has something to contribute -- even if the contribution is modest -- to such political decisions as setting balances between growth and equity, quality and quantity, selectivity and open access. But as we have tried to suggest in this chapter, even when the broad political decisions peculiar to education are taken, certain conditions must be met if government is to make realistic policy choices:

(i)   There must be frank acceptance of the fact that, as in all political decisions, educational decisions often represent compromises between aims, which, however worthy each may be, cannot all be reached at the same time. Priorities must therefore be established.

(ii)   There should be a clear distinction as regards the role of government between financing to be defined on both equity and social benefit criteria, provision of services to be defined on cost-effectiveness criteria, administration and monitoring of public support, and regulation to ensure adequate quality of service and limit the consequences of market failures. Conflict among these criteria are not uncommon.

(iii) The formulation of educational policies on the basis of general economic and social policies is a complex operation that calls for both political sensitivity and professional understanding of the ways in which political purposes are altered when translated to the field of education. Educational planning must keep a close and continuous finger on the pulse of economic and social planning entities on the one hand, and on institutions in charge of programming and budgeting on the other. This requires that governments achieve consistency in policies and encourage sectors which can attract extra-budgetary resources.

(iv) Choices within the educational sector should be based on clear definition of the purposes of each segment of the system. Although, in principle, no education should ever be terminal, there may be strong grounds -- including economic arguments -- for a compromise between terminal and preparatory for certain levels of education.

(v) In weighting objectives of equity and growth or/and of quantitative expansion and qualitative improvement, some kind of balance should be sought to reconcile the consequences of shortages of resources and of the social pressures of parents, students and teachers.

(vi) Evaluation and review of policy alternatives demonstrate that qualitative as well as quantitative information must be collected on a permanent basis. Over the past two decades, the stock of educational statistics has been vastly improved, to the extent that the assembly and analysis of quantitative data has become in most countries a fairly routine operation. In spite of some notable progress, gathering and processing of qualitative data has remained more difficult. Efforts are needed in this direction.

(vii) On the basis of appropriate information and cool-headed diagnosis of an educational system, a government can make better policy choices. But this is only a first step. The fact that a major educational decision is a compromise between competing factors makes it a generator of tensions, and unless the latter are recognised by politicians, planners, and administrators, and steps taken to ease them, the application of the policy may be endangered. Special efforts must be exerted to get the government's message across to the consumers and the producers of education, through the good offices of the mass media, provincial and local authorities, community organisations, and above all the schools themselves -- which, unfortunately, are rarely equipped for the task.

(viii) Even when all the explanations have been conscientiously communicated, there will be those whose immediate interests do not tally with the national interests expressed in the official statement. It is of little comfort to parents whose children have been refused entrance to a secondary school to be told that improving the quality of education of those who did get in is in the best interests of the society. The problem cannot be properly solved without alternative and less restrictive forms of education such as part-time instruction, privately managed and/or financed programmes, non-formal systems.

Ultimately, a government's policy will be judged by its results. What will matter is what happens in the schools and the extent to which sacrifices made by parents produce tangible returns. Given the financial and social constraints which limit the capacities of a government to respond to its people's expectations, clear and just priorities must be set, announced in official statements, and maintained for periods of time that are sufficient for their success.

---

1. J. Hallak, *A qui profite l'école ?*, Paris, Presses Universitaires de France, 1974.

2. The centrally-planned economies are not included in this discussion, because reforms of such magnitude have been initiated by countries in this group that it is too early to formulate meaningful conclusions.

3. N. Birdsall, *Pragmatism, Robin Hood, and other themes: good government and social well-being in developing countries*, Washington D.C., World Bank. 1989, Mimeo.

Chapter 5

Priorities

Generalisations and predictions based on long and wide experience must be fitted and adapted to each country's specific situation by the government concerned. Common sense dictates that each sets its own priorities, according to its financial constraints and sectoral conditions, weighting:

- the need to concentrate public investment on 'critical masses' and their impacts against the need for consistency between priorities and the resources required for their implementation;
- those measures that respond to short-term pressures against those that concern long-term, basic needs;
- one sector or level of education against the other segments of the formal system, the nonformal sectors, and training;
- the need to give preference to some groups of beneficiaries, in particular women and girls, to reduce inequalities.

1. Setting priorities

a. Financial priorities

Since quantitative change and qualitative improvement in education are lengthy undertakings, and budgetary increments, when they can be made at all, are small, averaging not more than 5 per cent per annum, key projects that receive allocations must be intended to last for at least a five- to six-year period. Unfortunately, the term expectancies of cabinet members tend to be short, and each comes with his own priorities and proposed new agenda.

"In fact, of course, the decision-maker, in this case the minister of education, is a government agent who himself is the embodiment of a certain political theory, or even ideology. He is therefore bound to remain faithful to the main lines or orientations which have been given to him. But in the light, therefore, of the inertia of the system and the limited duration of his mandate, how far does his real capacity to act upon events reach?"[1]

There is no simple solution to the limitations of capacity of the State to establish and implement sustained priority programmes in education. The following somewhat deterministic comment on the relationships between education and society, and on the preparation and the processing of budgets is offered for the consideration of policy-makers.

(i) Sustainability

Setting educational priorities that society will not allow to be implemented is an exercise in futility. It is desirable that some tensions exist between the ideals of a system of education and the expectations of the imperfect society it serves. But if they become too great, the budget proposals of the educational administrators take on an air of irreality. When this happens, which it does fairly regularly, the cause can be either the internalisation on the part of department directors of the unwritten rule 'the more you ask for, the more likely you are to get some of it,' or the confusion on the part of enthusiastic educators of idealistic long-term objectives with feasible short-term possibilities.

Education is part and parcel of a society. It is established by that society to accomplish certain purposes. Its teachers are ordinary citizens, its students come from ordinary homes. They spend their time outside school hours working to earn a living, playing games, watching television, and with few exceptions, they are trying to fit themselves into the adult life they observe around them. With reflective guidance, and if priorities are rationally chosen on the basis of their relevance, an educational system may have standards that are in advance of those of the society at large. But the gap between them can never remain very wide in a sustainable pattern. In setting priorities for education, a government must at all times assess their sustainability in the society that is expected to accept them.

(ii) Routine versus new budget allocations

A project can be undercut or condemned to an early demise simply through the lack of an adequate budgetary instrument. If appropriations are usually in response to erratic or random pressures, chances are that the framework on which priority is assigned will not last very long. To avoid ad hoc budget decisions, the framework should comport appropriate judicial arrangements, including financial plans covering several years, which will lend stability to the implementation of the projects that have been assigned priority. The challenge is sobering, however. How can one impose the legal structures that guarantee stability without risking rigidity in the management of the budget? How can one plan for adjustments and still keep the key priorities firmly in place?

In many developing countries a distinction is made between recurrent or current and development budget allocations. The latter, often largely dependent on foreign resources, are directed towards the new ventures; the former, which under the best of circumstances can be increased by 5 per cent per year (in real terms), go towards more traditional expenditures. While justified on many grounds, this arrangement can cause serious problems, in particular as regards the assignment of priority and implementation. Many innovative activities cannot be separated from routine activities, even on a short-term basis. Any new activity that has significance on a national scale -- which priority activities of course must have -- will be supported from routine funds in the future. Thus, in many respects, rationality and sustainability will depend very much upon the degree of 'routinisation' that it has been possible to achieve in financing a project.

This budget dichotomy, then, is best avoided. If this proves impossible, it is essential that at the outset it be understood that there will be close working links between the two budgets. Any administrative structure that calls for one group of people to manage one budget, and another group the other, will run into serious trouble, serious enough perhaps to impede the implementation of the projects.

b. Sectoral priorities

Sectoral priorities cannot be established in one segment of an educational system without considering their short- and long-term consequences for the other segments. For example:

• An improvement in higher education may be supported with financial, human, and physical resources, but it will not come about without upgrading the quality and standards of the secondary schools. If their standards are low, as they often are, improvements in the level above them will be limited, and it will eventually be difficult to justify giving them priority in the budget.

• An increase in teachers' salaries could be given priority on the very reasonable grounds that recruitment at present salaries is difficult, that teachers cannot live on these salaries without taking other jobs, which means an obvious deterioration in the quality of their teaching, etc. But if the private sector covers a sizable proportion of the enrolment, as is often the case at the secondary level and sometimes in the primary schools of certain countries, and salaries there are already lower than those in the public sector, a salary increase in the public sector will drain off enrolment in the private sector unless some parity can be achieved in the salaries of the two sectors.

• Automatic promotion at the primary level is justified in some cases on both educational and financial grounds. But the introduction of automatic promotion into a system which has been fairly selective, fairly controlled at each level, with a high proportion of repeaters, will cause a bottleneck at the point of entrance into secondary school that will be very difficult to deal with. It may be necessary to finance expansion of the lower secondary grades and job creation for the school leavers.

• A curriculum is considered to be outdated. Prerequisite to curriculum reform is an assurance of resources adequate to finance teacher training, the modification of textbooks, and student evaluation and certification, plus the adaptation of facilities and equipment. Also, curriculum changes must be provided for and expected at the levels above.

• Say a less formal programme of rural primary schooling is proposed to offer three years of education rather than six. A few years later, priority will have to be given to a follow-up course for the graduates of the rural system, because otherwise it will fail. Planners and managers of literacy programmes know well that post-literacy activities are essential to the success of their projects.

• Children in remote areas or from a less privileged economic group are considered to be in critical need of access to education. The provision of it will cost much more than the average expenditure per pupil would suggest. Reaching the last 10 per cent of the children of school age who have not yet had access to primary education is usually far more expensive than reaching any other comparable group; marginal costs increase rapidly per child, putting the idea out of the reach of most countries. At the very least, it requires complete reorganisation of the school network. Spurious diversion of funds may distort the impact of the policy, to the extent of changing the beneficiary group entirely. And even with adequate controls, it may be impossible for a country to reach these children without providing other advantages, such as school feeding programmes.[2]

The principal conclusion drawn from these examples is that beyond a certain magnitude, a modification of any part or segment of the school system will have consequences on its other components, and that due consideration of these implications must be taken into consideration in planning for changes. This is not at all to say that policy changes must be planned for the whole system at one and the same time, or that all segments should receive equal priority. On the contrary, this would throw the profession into disarray; it would certainly be counter-productive. Given the budgetary limitations, governments have to make difficult choices among equally important areas in allocating educational investment. *Politically,* in some societies, there is the need for transparency, and for wide dissemination of the criteria which have determined choices. One might hope thereby to elicit public support, certainly from the group that will receive the greatest benefit from the priorities set. *Technically,* below the point referred to as the critical mass, investments are unlikely to affect the system sufficiently. Thus the setting of priorities must also involve 'concentration', and accepting the vigorous competition which is a fact of life in democratic societies, but not necessarily compatible with the framework of priorities suggested by the advisers of the ministers concerned.

In education, failure to select among objectives often results in linear or over-determined expansion rather than carefully conceived expansion in the most critical directions. Equally unacceptable is the policy statement that gives the impression that all investment is to go to a single area, for example improvement in the quality of secondary education, neglecting the impacts of an unbalanced decision both upstream and downstream. Both in-school and out-of-school activities are structurally interlinked at the 'user' level, even if they ignore each other at the 'producer' level. And the higher level influences an element as strongly as the lower one, through the imposition of its entrance examinations, and the teachers it trains for lower levels. In short, a balance must be found that reconciles the need for concentration and respect for the critical masses of programmes with the need for consistency and complementarity across the board. It means giving practical answers to practical questions. What should we do now? What level or type of education must be served first? Shall the focus be on quality, efficiency, equity, smoother transition from school to work? Or all at the same time? Different countries have tried different approaches, reached different conclusions, with greater or lesser success. Sometimes their decisions are based on their own experience, sometimes on that of others. While it is impossible to generalise on the practical level, it is of course useful to know how comparable projects have turned out in other countries, when selecting among one's own priorities.

2. Shifting priorities

The last three decades have seen some fundamental shifts in priorities in many societies. We have seen in Chapter 1 that in the 1960s and 1970s both governments and society at large gave a much higher priority to education, both as a human right and as a profitable investment in the future knowledge and skills on which a country's prosperity depends. There have been other important shifts in political and social priorities, and politicians and educational policy-makers must reflect on these when allocating resources and choosing between alternative policies.

Politicians and policy-makers have to shift priorities, rather than simply perpetuate those that have influenced decisions and policies in the past.

a. Overcoming inequalities: the last shall be first

There are many examples of shifts in priorities for education that have been proposed or attempted in recent decades. For example, many countries have attempted to shift priorities away from academic education towards vocational and technical education. Advocates of 'recurrent' or 'continuing' education have stressed that learning should be regarded as a lifelong process and that there should be a shift in priorities away from excessive concern with education for children and initial training for entry into the labour market towards wider opportunities for adults, including literacy classes for those who never had a chance to go to school and retraining or updating of professional skills for those who have already benefited from formal education. Such an approach implies another shift of priorities, away from sole concentration of effort and resources on formal schooling towards non-formal and informal education.

Many of these proposals are discussed and explored in this book. A later chapter considers strategies for developing non-formal education, for example, which imply a shift in priorities between the formal and non-formal sectors. Other shifts in priorities are also looked at, between education in rural and urban areas, or between higher education and professional development and basic education.

Another change that is considered essential in many developing countries is a shift in priority towards those who in the past have been relatively disadvantaged, because of poverty, ethnic origin, religion, language or gender. How can policy-makers promote or put into effect such a shift in priorities? The following section examines how one such shift might be achieved: towards greater emphasis on the education of women and girls in order to overcome the imbalance and inequalities that exist throughout the developing world. Similar strategies may be needed to develop educational opportunities for other disadvantaged groups.

b. Overcoming discrimination: education for women and girls.

(i) The challenge

The extent of female illiteracy and the underprivileged situation of girls as regards access to and retention in school education still remains one of the greatest problems of the world.

Over the last three decades, substantial efforts have been made to expand education of girls and women. Much has been achieved, but much remains to be done to achieve equal participation of girls in in-school and out-of-school education.

At all levels, and in almost every region of the world, the access of women and girls to instruction has improved. The entry of women into the modern employment sector -- which has constituted one of the most important changes in the national composition of human capital -- has certainly reinforced this development. Educated middle-class women have stepped out in increasingly large numbers into the world of work, and the emergence of women teachers, especially in the Arab States and in certain countries of Southern Asia, will have important implications for the school, family, and community development of the countries concerned.

In the developing countries generally, at primary school level (ages 6 to 11), female enrolment increased between 1960 and 1985 from 38 to 66 per cent. The corresponding figures for male enrolment were 57 to 79 per cent. During the same period, female enrolment at ages 12 to 17 increased from 15 to 40 per cent as against male enrolment of 28 to 52 per cent, and for the age-groups 18-23 from 2 to 10 per cent as against 6 to 17 per cent for males. The female-male gap thus narrowed in the 6-11 and 12-17 age-groups, but increased in the 18-23 age-group, and these ratios hint at both the magnitude of the effort of the developing countries, and the resistance they have encountered and must overcome.

According to Unesco estimates, out of 889 million illiterate adults in the world (in 1985) 561 million were women. The female illiteracy rate is particularly high in remote rural areas, where it is more than 90 per cent in several countries in the developing world, most of them in Asia. (See *Table 5.1*)

Table 5.1 Female illiteracy in developing countries

Illiteracy range	Number of countries	
	1970	1985
>95%	20	1
80% - 94%	23	13
50% - 79%	17	29
20% - 49%	24	26
<20%	17	25
	101	94

Source: F. Caillods, *Women's literacy for development: a brief overview of the situation today,* Paris, Unesco:IIEP, 1989.

While the access of girls to primary education has improved since 1970, there is still a gap between female and male enrolment which has not diminished in all developing countries. In Afghanistan, Nepal and Pakistan, it has widened. In the developing countries in general, 25 per cent of all school-aged children are not in school, but for girls it is 40 per cent. Average female enrolment in primary school in Africa is 67 per cent, as opposed to 85 per cent male enrolment, and, in the Arab States, 72 per cent as opposed to 94 per cent male enrolment. In the low-income semi-arid countries of Africa, only 19 per cent of the female primary school-aged population were enrolled in 1983.[3]

The education of girls and women must become a genuine policy priority, not only on ethical grounds but also because of the widely recognised key role of women's knowledge and skills in crucial areas of development -- child education, nutrition, health, agriculture, handicrafts, etc.:

•   Where women are better educated, population control is more effective, and family size decreases.[4] The effect and influence of women's education in reducing fertility in developing countries is three times as powerful as the education of men. Education for women also improves infant survival rates and levels of child nutrition and health: literate, educated mothers have healthier children who are likely to live longer than the children of women who have never been to school. Caldwell[5] demonstrated the major factor of maternal education in lowering infant and child mortality in Nigeria. Education for women is doubly important: not only does the family as a whole benefit, but healthier children will in turn learn more easily.

•   Mothers' awareness of the potential benefits of education for their children obviously encourages school attendance, and indeed influences children's performance throughout their school careers. Studies have demonstrated the positive impact of mothers' literacy on school enrolment and pupil retention in Nepal[6] and on the level of parental expectations regarding their children's education.[7]

• Increased participation of women in the labour force adds to the earnings of a household and to the status of the family, and education enhances their eagerness and ability to work. It raises their earning potential and aspirations, changes their attitudes regarding traditional roles in the household and the workplace, and provides them with the qualifications they need to find work. As they raise their educational levels, they may be able to transfer from traditional agricultural work to the modern service sector and a much wider range of occupational possibilities.[8] An agricultural study found that women's productivity gained more from education than did that of men.[9]

• A study of 96 developing countries from 1960 to 1985 showed that increased primary education affected the long-term economic prosperity of girls more than it did that of boys, especially in the poorest countries.[10]

More resources, and at the same time less orthodox strategies, will have to be deployed to overcome present obstacles and enhance female literacy and female participation in school education.

A review[11] of 80 empirical studies of the determinants of educational participation and achievement of women suggests that family economic levels are more important than school-related variables such as distance from school and availability of sanitary facilities. The poorer the household, the greater the reliance of parents on daughters for domestic duties, and the greater their tendency to reserve whatever investment can be made to educate their sons. To be effective, strategies concerning girls and women must take these various cultural and socio-economic factors systematically into account and seek for new responses to the challenge.

(ii) Overcoming coercive roles and stereotypes

In societies in which the 'intrinsic nature' of a woman is regarded by definition as inferior to that of a man, and in which family and occupational traditions, and subjugation to child-bearing and rearing are imposed from a very early age, obstacles to free access to schooling are formidable. Parents may recognise that up to a point it may be profitable to send their daughters to school, but many believe that this point is reached at the age of 13 to 14. Beyond that age, it is feared that education will interfere with a girl's expected domestic and societal roles.

Educators who aim at eradicating beliefs that go against the fulfilment of women, have a long row to hoe. If political will is strong and sustained, however, integrated formal and non-formal programmes can be initiated, and informal campaigns conducted, which in the long run might obtain results.

In the schools, curriculum content may have to be gradually reoriented, to relax the boundaries determining what girls and boys are permitted and expected to do. This could mean that boys begin to learn to cook or sew, while girls learn mathematics, science or automechanics. Amara reported[12] that a basic science curriculum based on indigenous technologies was introduced into an all girls school in Sierra Leone. It included for example the production of household chemicals in teaching chemistry and biology. It has been eminently successful since 1981. But more will be needed. In some societies school practices and curricula will have to change as a step towards reducing widespread prejudice regarding the 'female nature'. This might involve the redesign of textbooks, so that they no longer portray women in purely passive roles. In the classroom, too, girls can be encouraged to play a more active role and participate in class discussions.

Mothers play an important role in influencing their children's performance in school, their rates of promotion, and drop-out. This is particularly true in non-formal education programmes. The more and better educated the mother, the greater her commitment to education; it is thus incumbent on planners of children's programmes to include sessions for the mothers if at all possible.

Non-formal education can be an effective channel for delivering education to women; its flexibility makes it possible to bring the school to the women rather than requiring them to come to the school. Literacy lessons can be conducted inside the home. Women's organisations can teach income-generating activities, mobilise women for health care and nutrition, make them more self-confident, involve them in the politico-economic life of a community. Governments could encourage these projects by offering incentives to women's organisations and non-formal education.

At the informal level, the role of mass media must not be overlooked. Public campaigns can be organised by educational authorities to promote girls' and women's education, and ministries of education can co-operate with other departments, and with professional and cultural associations to weed out the stereotypes that abound *sub rosa* in the media.

(iii) Rural outreach

Simple increase in the number of school places has been used to expand access of girls, and of other under-represented groups, but the strategy is expensive, and has not always been successful. In Kano State, Nigeria,[13] the construction of 100 new primary schools between 1976 and 1981 quadrupled the enrolment of girls, but their relative share of school places increased only from 25 to 30 per cent.

Multiple-shift schooling, with more intensive use of both teachers and buildings might be better advised as a way of increasing the number of places for girls; the establishment of multiple shifts would permit women teachers and girl students the relaxed use of school facilities. In rural areas, where opportunity costs of education for girls are generally higher than in urban areas, a shorter day might be very welcome. The school year or day calendar could be revised to take into account the agricultural imperatives that limit the attendance of both boys and girls in rural areas.[14]

If schools for girls have female teachers, it is more likely that girls will be permitted to attend. It may also be necessary, in some cases, to build more local schools for girls so that they can live at home rather than in co-educational institutes with male teachers and administrators. In some instances, however, co-educational school facilities may have to be expanded or renovated. In Bangladesh, 71 per cent of the rural schools and 53 per cent of urban schools had no latrines in 1982, and girls' attendance was of course adversely affected.

Ministries of education might offer financial and personal incentives to overcome parental prejudice, and also persuade other departments, non-governmental organisations and women's organisations to do the same. Labour-saving devices have been introduced in Burkina Faso, and while they had no effect on the girls' attendance in formal schools, 50 per cent of the women in the experimental village took advantage of the non-formal training offered, whereas only 7 per cent in the control village took up the offer. Responsibility for younger brothers and sisters often discourages the school aspirations of girls.[15] Day-care facilities would help a good deal with this problem. In urban areas in China, on-the-spot child care at places of employment has been successful in increasing female enrolments. General incentives to promote school attendance among both boys and girls may help, and indeed, in some very poor areas financial incentives may be vital. In parts of Nepal, for example, it costs a family up to 20 per cent of its income to send one child to school. Among the incentives offered in some countries are:

- exoneration from school fees;
- provision of books, uniforms, etc., free of charge;
- direct payments to households for the purchase of materials and uniforms;
- free or subsidised transportation;
- school-meal programmes;
- scholarships.

General incentives may not be enough, however, to overcome prejudice; since places in school are limited and the girls' prospects for employment are also limited, incentives offered to parents may not have the desired effect.

In Pakistan, the 'mohalla' school project reduced cost to families by holding the classes in homes and forgetting about uniforms, and even shoes. The participation of girls shot up. There are other examples of incentives and other efforts to reverse discrimination which have produced results. In Bangladesh, 50 per cent of the primary scholarships given at the end of the 5th year of study are reserved for girls. In some rural areas of China, boarding schools, financial help with books and paper, medical allowances, educational guidance and a publicity campaign directed at parents have been tried as a package, with the result that female participation went up by over 90 per cent.

(iv) Opportunity beyond basic education

High-quality correspondence courses for girls, using radio, television, and other distance learning techniques, have helped to make educational programmes available to girls. But they still have little access to secondary and higher levels, or to science education. Quotas and special scholarships may encourage girls to dip a toe into technology, science, and other areas traditionally reserved for men. Too few women aspire to higher education, probably for the most part because they see no hope of financing their studies. In the Republic of Korea, colleges and universities now offer more scholarships to women than to men; in 1980, 58 per cent of the scholarships went to women, as compared to 38 per cent in 1975.[16]

Women are subject to discrimination at home, school and in the labour market, three areas that are important and interconnected. Reducing discrimination in one of them affects discrimination in the others and hence, overall discrimination. Education could be the central point to break this chain, since it may weaken the negative influence of structural factors on female participation in schooling and social life.

3. Weighting priorities

Political, educational and economic considerations are at play when priorities are set to dispose of budget increments or to deal with cuts. No ideal theoretical solution can be cited as preferable to all others, and indeed the art of deciding priorities lies in combining and balancing judgements, juggling the factors relevant to HRD, and more specifically to education. The time factor must also be considered, and in designing flexible strategies, modifications must be provided for over certain periods.

a. Ethical considerations

Education is generally accepted as a human right. It logically follows that equality must be a determining factor in setting the priorities for investment in education. The crux of the problem is what kind of education, and for how long. The rationale behind the international community's principle of 'providing basic education for all' can be interpreted as reconciling resource constraints with the right to education and the need of a country for HRD. Many countries add 'fostering national unity'. In practical terms, it must be determined what proportion of the population, both young and adult, can actually be reached. Many countries set their goals at 80 per cent. Marginal costs and the demands of other segments of the education system make it prohibitive in some countries to provide access to the most remote 20 per cent. Yet some countries seek to reach the 'last 20%'. Literacy is made possible for adults by setting up appropriate and accessible facilities. For children, several routes are possible. A minimum number of compulsory school years (usually 3 or 4) are set, and attempts are made to avoid the problem of 'lapsed literates' by following up this formal programme with out-of-school services. Either six years of primary schooling are regarded as compulsory. Or, in some countries, a few years of secondary education are compulsory.

b. Political considerations

From a political point of view, the weight to be given to a benefit seen to be a human right may depend on the power of a government to resist those well-organised groups of citizens who struggle to capture the lion's share of public resources, when a large part of the population is still denied access to primary schooling. The ultimate shape of the budget will reflect the priorities set by the government, as well as the relative strength of producer and user groups in the society. Where they are well organised and strong, the share of the education budget that goes into literacy and adult education is generally modest and rather ineffective.

c. Economic considerations

Where economic considerations are paramount, primary education should receive high investment priority. Primary education is the most 'public' sub-sector in the education sector. A recent study[17] covering 30 developing countries (9 in Africa, 8 in Asia, 5 in Latin America, and 8 across-the-board middle-income countries) and 14 industrialized countries, indicates that:
- the social return on investment in primary education is the highest in the sector, whether it is provided publicly or privately;
- the social return on investment in secondary and in higher education varies with the country. In 12 of the 30 developing countries for which data were available, the return on investment in higher education is higher than that in secondary education;
- social returns from investment in education are generally higher in developing than in industrialised countries.

Some criticism has been directed at the methods used for calculating rates of return on investment in education, and there is of course difficulty in generalising results coming from different countries. Taken in conjunction with other methods and criteria, however, they give indicative guidelines for weighting priorities.

d. Educational considerations

Where due regard is given to the human right principle, educational considerations are determinant in shaping the budget. It is logical to start 'increasing coverage and improving quality' at the lowest levels, and to assume that they should have priority. The performance of the secondary level will obviously improve with better graduates from the primary schools, who will then go on to improve the higher institutions, and thus the whole system benefits. But history does not always confirm the wisdom of this approach. Experience has shown that expansion of primary education is a long job, and increasing the literacy level of a population even longer. One must talk in terms of decades rather than years. One of the reasons for this, which is often ignored by specialists and planners, is that the higher the proportion of adult literates, the easier it is to expand primary schooling, and vice versa. Thus, in purely economic terms, it is probably less expensive in time and resources to share priority between the primary and adult literacy programmes, provided they serve the same families in the population.

Experience also shows that higher stages influence those below so heavily that there may be justification in serving the apex of the system first. Improvement of quality at the tertiary level, in function with national needs, and limiting access according to the training needs of the economy and the financial resources, so that higher education sets the norms for the secondary sector, and thence for the primary, is a surer way of seeing to it that educational priorities fit graduates to the needs of the society. Moreover, because expansion of enrolment is controlled at the secondary and tertiary levels, more funds are available to finance UPE. Arguments against this approach are many, however, and perhaps the most cogent is that there is no easy way for government to control student flows, or to see to it that equity is preserved in the operations. Under such a policy it may be forced to downgrade the importance of fair access. And there is certainly consensus on the need to place higher priority on primary education.

While no clearcut guidelines can be offered for dosing the resources of each component of an educational system, the very fact that education does need to be dealt with in a holistic way, and not piecemeal, makes it essential that the possibilities and choices be examined. Let us now turn to the question of dosing.

4. A menu of priorities

Little attention is generally paid to pre-school education by ministries of education. Few children are concerned, usually in the private sector; little public finance is involved (often less than 5 per cent of the education budget); cultural tradition has heretofore established the division of child care between the family and the outside world very clearly, and pressure groups of distraught parents are not yet organised to fight for nursery schools. Yet it has been incontestable for decades that this period of life is critical in educational performance, and that chances of success at the primary level can be substantially improved through the implementation of pre-school programmes, particularly for children of four to five years of age.[18]

a. Early childhood care and education

Children in good physical and educational condition perform far better than children suffering from malnutrition, poor health, and lack of introduction to basic knowledge. As one specialist[19] expressed it, "the principal determinants of any real equal opportunity in educational, occupational, and social terms are for most laid down in the years between birth and five or six years of age".

The vast majority of mothers in developing countries -- whether their contexts are rural or urban -- are full-time workers outside the home. Even among the 'better-off', part-time work is attracting mothers away from the traditional stay-at-home patterns. In some countries, the extended family system is eroded or even replaced with the nuclear, in which many children must be taken care of by two overwrought parents, and sometimes only one. The upshot is a demand for pre-school services which is already enormous, growing fast, and well beyond the economic and educational capacities of most countries.

It is precisely in the developing countries, where children suffer most from malnutrition, health problems, and poor educational environments, that HRD efforts at the pre-school level are likely to be most needed. Data are not available, but it is also probable that investment at this level will produce the highest payoff. Indeed, many private foundations, multilateral and bilateral projects are turning their attention towards it. UNDP and Unicef programmes illustrate the concern of the international community in this area. At local country levels, it is more difficult to sensitise the public at large to the dramatic conditions of the families concerned, and to explain the challenge presented. Government mobilisation is crucial. Even if budget priority must be directed elsewhere, this is certainly an area where a multisectoral, integrated approach is required. Ministries of education, of health, of community development, of labour, and as many non-governmental organisations and social groups as can be enlisted, must become involved in addressing the needs of this group of children; 0.5 to 1.0 per cent of a country's GNP should be adequate[20] to make significant inroads into the problem, and it need not necessarily come from ministries of education or health.

Few government resources are necessary, but political will and enthusiasm are vital, to (i) provide education to parents (thus equipping them to fill their children's needs); (ii) mobilise private, local, and foreign support for the provision of health, nutrition, and educational services to children under six, and (iii) encourage local communities, associations, guilds, and the like, to assume the responsibility for managing and administering these services.

b. Basic education

The official entry level, and the cornerstone of most educational systems, this sub-sector usually accommodates more students than all the other components of the education sector combined. The definition of basic education is flexible enough to cover a wide range, and can mean: (i) a minimum number of years of education in which a beneficiary is expected to achieve a level of numeracy and literacy which can be maintained through out-of-school services after graduation, or (ii) the maximum number of years that a government can afford to provide for all or most of its citizens. It is assumed to be three to four years, but in more economically fortunate countries it may consist of ten to twelve years.

'Basic education for all' is the number one priority of the international community today. Four major international agencies, Unesco, UNDP, Unicef, and the World Bank, and a number of bilateral donors involved in co-operation in educational development are preparing a world conference on education for all, to take place in Thailand in 1990. This exceptional event will undoubtedly affect the economic prospects and boost the HRDs of the developing countries concerned. But it is the attitudes of governments, their budgetary efforts, and their ability to attract international support that will determine its degree of success.

(i) Quantitative expansion

Experience has shown that with few exceptions, governments can make substantial inroads towards the target of basic education for all. Indeed, dramatic advances in primary school enrolment ratios in most countries were responses to priority given to primary education, and the allocation of large shares of budgets (more than 60 per cent of the sectors' budgets in some cases) to the purpose. The average was 36 per cent in 1960 and 75 per cent in 1985. Statistics concerning 84 countries show that in spite of wide differences in their efforts, adult education activities were effective in benefiting populations aged 15+ in some countries of Africa, Asia, and Latin America.[21]

Economic recessions followed by austerity programmes and budget cuts obviously curtailed the resources available for primary and lower secondary education, where stagnation and even decline in enrolment ratios were observed. However these events did not significantly change the ranking of countries by closeness to the target of basic education for all. Of the 41 countries whose gross primary enrolment ratio was over 100 per cent (because of late entries and repetitions) in 1980, only one -- because of a civil war -- fell below that ratio. The ten developing countries whose enrolment ratios were below 50 per cent in 1985 had been below that percentage in 1950 as well, but some of them had made some progress. Partial adult education statistics for Africa show that, with the exception of three countries, enrolment rates rose until 1979 and then went into a decline, probably at least partly due to budget cuts.

Many countries have tried, with greater or lesser success, to adopt complementary non-formal programmes. Data on NFE programmes are incomplete and rarely reliable, and usually insufficient for comparing formal activities with non-formal. But the general indications are (i) NFE programmes established by decentralised initiatives in response to lack of clear policy directions regarding basic education, are successful as long as they remain modest in size and do not conflict with the formal system (for example, Burundi), and (ii) NFE programmes established by governments as part of a combined approach to expand services to the remote rural areas (which teachers normally shun) manage to impart to a fairly large number of school-aged children an equivalent to basic education. These programmes have been successful, for example, in India, Indonesia, Burkina Faso, and Kenya.

Perceptible increases in primary school enrolment, and especially in the literacy rate of a population, take much longer to bring about than one expects at the outset, and must be spoken of in terms of decades rather than years. Designing, building, and equipping schools, training and recruiting teachers, developing curricula and selecting materials are all lengthy jobs, and governments must plan enough time for them. Sometimes a country will try to save time by first mobilising funds, or perhaps by focusing on the inputs which take longest to develop, such as teacher training, in the meantime hiring foreign teachers. This was recently done in Yemen. Often, even in rural areas, the selection of sites takes time. Some countries have tried to accelerate the process by dividing plans into stages, say, starting with 4-year universal primary education or introducing a 3- or 4-year first cycle in an already existing 6-year primary school. Where universal primary education is already established, a 3-year third cycle might be added to the basic education agenda. An issue that must not be forgotten here is whether to stress the 'terminal' or 'preparatory' attributes of each segment.

In considering the financial, physical, and human resources needed to expand the coverage of basic education, attention must be paid to the perceptions of parents. It is well known that the better educated the parents, the greater the demand for instruction and the better the outcome. If a government intends to waste no time in getting basic education into the hands of all, it must give adult and literacy programmes enough priority to make a difference in the educational environment of children, and to boost the demand. The Unesco approach to eliminating illiteracy is justified not only by human rights considerations, but by economic and social considerations: parallel efforts aimed at adults and the young in the same strata of the population are without doubt, and for very good reasons, synergistic, and much more effective than focusing on primary education at the expense of that of adults. One reason why adult literacy programmes sometimes fail is, in fact, that they sometimes serve populations in which most of the children do not benefit from primary education.

With few exceptions, those countries that have not struggled very hard to equalise educational opportunity between the sexes are those that find themselves falling behind in expanding basic education. There is a good deal of evidence to support the opinion that the more educated, and the more literate, the women, the faster and more sustained the participation in education, and the better the outcome. Education for women is justified on the grounds of human rights considerations, but also on the grounds of cost-effectiveness of a strategy for providing general basic education. Placing priority on education for women will require targeting budget allocations in tandem with solid mechanisms for monitoring and control. Costs may be high, but the returns must clearly outweigh them.

Where there is no deliberate, sustained, and structured policy of priority allocations for minority ethnic groups, the target of basic education for all must be considered to be receiving little more than lip-service. Reluctance is justified in some countries on the grounds that fairness means equal opportunity (and priority) for all; but in making a foot-race fair, it would seem that one first has to see that all runners start from the same point. The positive discrimination implied in placing priority on minorities and otherwise marginalised members of the society is in practical terms the means of bringing them to the point where an opportunity can be considered to be equally available to them.

Most attempts to provide educational services to minority groups of different languages have suffered, indeed failed, sometimes because of insufficient planning or resources, sometimes because of resistance on the part of majorities. Here again the time factor is vital; money can go a long way, but it cannot cut short the time required to change mentalities in a society, to break down prejudices, even to be ready to widen socio-cultural interests in the groups which constitute the rich tapestry of the human community of the future.

Marginalised children, the number of whom is never precisely known, have no links with employment and have no education or training of any kind; they are thus very difficult to deal with. The principal issue concerning them is more socio-economical, perhaps even more cultural, than educational. The only initiatives that have had any success in integrating these children have been *ad hoc* local groups, and this may be the best way to deal with this problem.

The ruralisation of primary school curricula have tended to create dual systems of education, which is counterproductive to some of the aims of basic education as perceived by children, and by parents. Obviously the curricula of rural children should be adapted to some extent to their environment, i.e. centred around agriculture, and these curricula would concern the majority of the school-age populations (68.5 per cent of children and 63.4 per cent of the youth)[22] of most of the 'less-developed' regions.

But the systematic ruralisation of curricula and integration of preponderant agricultural studies that some countries have adopted cannot succeed without supplementary support and follow-up programmes. Both parents and children in rural areas hope that attendance at school will mean a way out of the difficult conditions of rural life, and preparation for migration to the city.[23]

(ii) Improving quality and increasing efficiency

Output must receive as much attention as input in the allocation of scarce resources. Cost-effective investment in basic education for all means allocating resources to those initiatives which are likely to produce the greatest benefit in terms of educational outcome. It is not suggested that piecemeal, blinker-visioned approaches be adopted, or that inputs be directed towards some sub-sectors while ignoring others. Nor, on the other hand, is it our feeling that one sub-sector may not require priority over the others under circumstances of strategic value or opportunities for improved cost-effectiveness. Consistency and complementarity must remain the rule.

A plethora of national and international studies evaluate the effects on quality and/or efficiency of various combinations of resource allocation, from which useful guidelines might be drawn.

The reservation to be kept in mind is that data limitations on this front have forced researchers to compromise on methods of quality measurement. School quality is usually measured in terms of teaching/learning indicators, such as average expenditure per pupil. But such statistics would conceal the fact if inputs had simply been wasted. A better way of measuring the quality of a school is by assessing indicators of outcome: what the student has actually learned. The school that produces more learning on the part of the students for the same input is probably the better school.

Investment in teachers, in their training, support, conditions of recruitment and status, is so vital, and their role in implementing educational policy so crucial, that no government can seriously consider improving quality and efficiency without according them high priority.

The fact that the largest item among the recurrent costs of primary education is teachers' salaries is no guarantee that their priority is high enough in the overall allocation of resources. But considerations of quantity versus quality aside, it is clear that the feasibility of expansion and improvement is tightly contingent on what is done to attract a stable, well-trained, motivated and accountable teaching force. And if it is financially impossible to attract a battery of good teachers, then one must try to combine various approaches to reach the objective. One might, for example, offer incentives in the private sector -- help it to expand its coverage and improve its teachers -- all the while keeping an alert eye on quality standards.

Pedagogical inputs such as textbooks and writing material constitute another priority area for investment. The acquisition of didactic materials for both students and teachers, and seeing to it that they reach the schools and are indeed used, will of course raise achievement and retention rates, much more quickly than for example the reduction of pupil/teacher ratios. Where resources are not available to provide a textbook for each pupil, alternative low-cost materials such as loose-leaf files have proven viable.

It is common today to give low priority to school buildings among the investments in primary education. But experience indicates that a school building (and the equipment for it) is a sure investment when funds are available, it does justify expectations that what goes on in the classroom will be improved, and may reduce drop-out rates in the early grades where overcrowding, dreary surroundings and getting lost in massive classes add up to a cheerless introduction to the adventure of education. The worst buildings, those which make good modern teaching impossible, should be replaced, and sometimes as many as 50 per cent of the others should be improved and expanded. Multiple use of buildings is still necessary, most often in urban settlements, in which case, the buildings should be specifically planned with secure storage and facilities for co-operation between the various sets of teachers using the classrooms.

Incentives, financial and non-financial, may be effective in reducing repetition[24] and drop-out,[25] but for many countries these problems will remain for long years to come. In addition, efforts should be exerted to increase the time a child spends at school and doing homework. The greater the length of time spent studying, the more a child learns. But here again the factor of time must not be overlooked. It should not be forgotten that in Massachusetts, USA, it took 80 years to go from 100 to 200 school days per year, and in France it took a century.

(iii) Co-ordination of basic with other types of education

Keeping in mind that it is imperative to consider the education sector holistically, and not piecemeal, 'basic education for all' must be considered with an eye to its context. Upstream, related priority must be assigned to pre-school level HRD; downstream, to post-basic. As enrolment in basic education expands and exceeds a critical level, post-basic pressures will increase, and if planners are not prepared for them, the top blows off their system. They must expect, and cost, compromises between the inevitable demand for more places in secondary schools on the part of the graduates of basic education, and the speed at which they want to make the basic level universal. It may be necessary to accept trade-offs in order to maintain the possibility of raising standards, and avoid complicating their problems with, for example, the educated unemployed.

c. Other priorities

(i) Education versus training

Some conceptual overlapping occurs between the areas of general education and training. The former includes the development of rote memorisation (common to all countries), understanding, internalising processes, mental capacity and creativity, and the application of knowledge to problem-solving. The latter develops understanding and its application to the performance of tasks, and knowledge and its application to problem-solving, but also includes mental development and the stimulation of creativity. General education is not usually thought of as relating to the needs of the labour market, whereas training is; and this is where criteria for setting priorities diverge. For our purposes, general education will be defined as focusing on the cognitive and affective, and training as focusing on the acquisition of skills. No government can afford to ignore the needs of any level or type.

Considerations of economic efficiency and educational consistency indicate the wisdom of supporting continued investment in secondary and higher education. Arguments are particularly valid and convincing for science, mathematics and technology education at both levels. But scope and magnitude of expansion have probably been determined rather on grounds of political expediency, for example dealing with the pressures of primary and secondary school leavers. This fact of life is amply illustrated in the shares of educational budgets that go to these two sub-sectors, and in the much faster increase in enrolment of the past three decades.

(ii) The secondary sub-sector

Secondary priorities are set on the basis of the existing conditions, the needs of the secondary system, and policy choices concerning its future. In most democratic societies, the central problem is devising a system of schools that will cater to the varied interests, abilities and future needs of a wide range of students without creating social and intellectual schisms. Crucial to all this is deciding what makes a good structure on which to build a system.

There can be no consensus on a universal set of criteria, but there are broad points on which agreement might be reached. A good structure should:[26]

- fit into national geographic, political, social, cultural, and economic conditions. In many of the formerly colonised countries, the colonial structure is still eminently visible. The extremes are those countries which have inherited and still maintain two separate secondary school systems, sometimes with different curricula, different languages of instruction, and even different examination systems;

- be as cost-efficient as possible, making the fullest possible use of specialised buildings, equipment, and staff, and avoiding the absorption of a disproportionate share of the administrative funds available. Population dispersal in a number of countries has made most of their secondary schools too small to be cost-efficient. On the other hand, large-size schools offering the variety of facilities and staff needed, may require heavy costs for boarding and transportation of students and teachers. Cost-effectiveness analyses should be used to address the issue of school size;

- be capable of preparing some students for further education, and others for immediate entry into the world of work. Neither function must predominate to the detriment of the other, and ways must be found to avoid social distinctions between the students. Many efforts have already been made in this direction;

- ensure entrance to any course on the basis of ability, and provide for cross-transfer of students who have embarked or been guided towards what turns out to be the wrong channel. Every student in a terminal programme, and every drop-out, must be given the assurance that he or she can resume studies if willing to make the effort. These principles are seldom respected. Cross-transfer between institutions in particular is not easy, and continuing, out-of-school, and training opportunities for school leavers are far from adequate;

- encourage experimenting with curricula and methods, especially to allow the gradual transformation of heavily-weighted arts curricula to give more grater emphasis to science.

Most developing countries are having a good deal of trouble satisfying these principles in the short run, except perhaps for the first, which like it or not, they are obliged to deal with. The dominant consideration in setting priorities is and will remain monitoring and control of quantitative growth and qualitative adaptation.

Strict selection at entrance to the secondary level is unlikely to be successful, and the problem arises as to what kind of education should be provided. Political bodies are often forced to give priority to secondary education; how rational can decisions be under these circumstances? Supported from strained finances, and limited by considerations of equity, secondary curricula have to be 'cheap,' and most poor countries cannot afford traditional secondary education even if it is cheap. Some, such as Rwanda (see *Inset 1*), have been able to establish legal structures for shorter programmes in locally-managed secondary schools.

For several reasons, scientific learning is an area that merits high investment priority. This area has suffered budget cuts so severe that in many countries laboratories cannot be maintained, scientific equipment has not been replaced, materials for experiments are woefully inadequate. Students are merely taught about science rather than getting scientific learning. It is pointless to try to strengthen scientific learning at the higher education level, a vociferously touted target in many countries, if students start off with inadequate grounding at the secondary level. In a context of economic uncertainty and rapid technological change, HRD policy must seek to improve the quality and flexibility of manpower. Experience shows that this is more easily achieved when students have benefitted from long and solid basic science training.

(iii) Higher education

The higher education sector in general, and the university in particular, are the object of a good deal of criticism. But the expenditures and the growth rates in enrolment of the past twenty years fully demonstrate that this sector is given very high priority. They demonstrate, too, how difficult it is to discourage social demand for tertiary education.

It is not always possible for government to impose and monitor allocations to higher education. The loci of decision-making are dispersed because of the tradition of autonomy of higher institutions, and the present-day economic constraints suffered by governments. Where possible, it is advisable to:

123

Inset 1
Rwanda: Rural and craft-integrated centres double the capacity of matriculation of primary school leavers

The per capita GNP of Rwanda is US$300 annually; demographic growth is 3.7 per cent per year, and the population is largely young and dependent (55 per cent under 20 years of age). Shortage of land and incapacity of absorption of the population in agricultural activities places burdens on the already meagre financial resources of the government. Secondary and tertiary educational institutions are nonetheless expected to produce manpower for the labour pool.

The transition rate from primary to secondary is less than 10 per cent. Unit expenditure per pupil is high, and the civil service, the principal employer of secondary school graduates, is limited. It has therefore been difficult to finance, or justify financing, the expansion of secondary schools from the point of view of employment. At the same time, social pressures for more schooling have been strong and increasingly difficult to put off.

In 1982, the government established a new type of post-primary institution called 'Centres for Integrated Rural and Craft Education'. Local authorities manage and finance their operations to a great extent. Curricula are 70 per cent practical with a large proportion of required agricultural courses (21 per cent), specialisations in masonry and carpentry for boys and sewing for girls. Courses are on a 3-year basis as compared to a 4/6-year secondary cycle. The system has had great success; with the 340 centres operating today, almost all of Rwanda is covered. Transition rates from primary are twice those of transfer to the traditional secondary programme, and quality is quite comparable with these.

Unfortunately, when the first batch of graduates arrived on the labour market, they were unable to find jobs, either in sectors normally reserved for secondary school graduates, or in other sectors. This caused a decline in enrolment at the centres. Perhaps supplementary measures could facilitate transition from the centres to employment opportunities: for example, contractual arrangements with employers, craftsmen, artisans and local communities or parents for training graduates; financial support could be offered to graduates to encourage self-employment; structural modifications might help to prepare for the arrival of newcomers to an already saturated labour market.

For the time being, social demand for secondary education persists. The problems of the graduates of the centres and the financial difficulties of the government, have prompted the burgeoning of private secondary schools. From 12 in 1985, they have mushroomed to 57 in 1987. But growth in the private sector will do nothing to alleviate the problem of aggravated unemployment of all secondary level graduates.

Source: E. Gakuba, *Diagnostic de la ruralisation de l'enseignement post-primaire au Rwanda de 1982 à 1988*, Paris, Unesco:IIEP, 1989, (Mimeo).

• *Give priority to those institutions that contribute most to the society.* In a world characterised by rapid scientific and technological advance, the disciplines which should receive priority from governments and other funding agencies are technology, engineering, and the basic and applied sciences. Unfortunately, average expenditures per student tend to be far higher in these streams than in the arts and humanities. Funding agencies may be torn between the need to give priority to areas of higher social return in the long run, and satisfying social demand for higher education under stringent budget conditions. Governments sometimes solve this dilemma by developing open institutions and distance-learning alternatives, which have proved reasonably cost-effective in other countries. Another possibility is to attract private support. But these are never enough in themselves. The 'developer' role of the State requires that it fulfill its responsibilities: in mobilising specific resources and building the structures necessary to produce needed professional cadres -- technologists, researchers, and managers; that it provide training in less prestigious areas of specialisation that are easy to neglect; and that it should generate the knowledge necessary for the various sectors of the economy to advance.

• *Invest in quality control and incentive mechanisms.* If the State is unable to provide higher education to all who desire it, the high private benefit attached to it will stimulate private initiatives, which will mushroom to satisfy the social demand. A vital area for government investment lies therefore in the regulatory and incentive mechanisms (including efficient diffusion of information on the costs versus the output of various institutions) to reconcile the need for adequate standards with the need to avoid interfering in a way that might be counterproductive if it discouraged initiatives for innovation and for private provision of higher education services.

• *Under some circumstances, give priority to alternative approaches* in the provision of tertiary education. For instance, a need for qualified technicians, who are often critically scarce, and other professionals might be met by offering shorter tertiary programmes -- say of two to three years rather than five to seven -- in polytechnical institutes, community colleges, and open universities. Terminal programmes have proved effective when concentrated on highly specialised fields through which graduates found easy access to the labour market.

- *Invest in under-represented groups* such as women or students of rural origin. The 'equaliser' role of the State demands that a sizable portion of its investment be targeted on these groups in order to balance the participation of the population as a whole. The resulting national unity and spirit of social justice are major goals in all countries.
- *Accord investment priority to career guidance and counselling* at the upper secondary level to acquaint students and their families with the prospects for educational and professional careers at the higher level. By contributing to more rational individual choices, a government can bring about a more effective co-ordination of expanded tertiary education with prospects for employment.

(iv) Training

Experience in setting training priorities emphasises four essential elements:

(a) *Versatility.* Ministries of education have been debating the inclusion of skills development within the formal system for thirty years, and the problem has certainly not been resolved. Opponents refer to the 'vocational school fallacy'.[27] The problem lies in the difficulty of forecasting with any degree of accuracy the requirements for specific skills in an economy. Predicting technological change, even one year ahead, is not an easy task; little wonder that long-term forecasting should fail. Pre-employment vocational training on a full-time basis should impart broad general skills that can be applied to any of a variety of work situations, implying that instructors with both academic background and work experience must be brought to the task. These are hard to find and expensive both in terms of salaries and working conditions. Rigidity of salary scales in the public sector suggests that the private sector has the advantage, and the best way for a government to go would be to solicit its active participation in middle-level professional training.

(b) *The need to generate 'non-modern' employment.* The limited absorptive capacity of the modern sector in many developing countries, and the high unemployment rates, suggest that government should place higher priority in the technical and vocational area on the development of personal initiative and entrepreneurial attitudes

126

and the preparation of students for self-employment. Employment is less dependent on training than on the pace of economic growth, the success of agriculture, and the progress of industry and services.[28]

(c) *The need for an effective network of technical and vocational institutions.* For many developing countries, vocational schools represent the sole possibility for training workers. The production sector is generally poorly organised and small. When an employer lacks the technical expertise to direct training or finds it uneconomical to employ a training specialist, the only recourse is to a training school; but the effectiveness of the training found there will also depend on the quality of the relationships between schools and employers, and between them and the government authorities. The stronger these links, and the greater the degree of involvement of employers, the better the chances of the schools being effective, and of their producing graduates who are employable. The lack of employer organisations reduces the real possibilities for developing such links in many developing countries, and even in many industrialised countries, and weakens the arguments in favour of rapid development of the technical/vocational sector.

(d) *The need for cost-efficiency.* As might be expected, given the requirements for specialised equipment, numerous specialised trainers, and large service staffs, the costs of vocational schools and training centres are very high. Substantial savings might be made by increasing the size of the schools, lengthening the school day and/or year, and by cautious and monitored opening of the schools to the community for evening classes. Incentives might also be offered to students, staff, and other participants to maintain their own facilities and equipment. Income might be generated and benefit the training units by encouraging the production and sales of goods by the schools themselves, also of course necessitating proper organisation and arrangements, careful monitoring, and incentives. The trade-off is between the incremental costs of introducing the schemes and the benefits accruing to the users, and must be decided on a case-by-case basis.

On-the-job training is perhaps as large and effective a source of training as developing countries enjoy. It may develop skills from the lower operational to the managerial. There is little for

127

government to do here, except perhaps offer incentives to employers to pool their efforts when their enterprises are too small to make on-the-job training economical.

Privately owned autonomous institutions, regulated by government, provide training that combines the formal in the classroom with the practical in the workshop, and varies in duration with the needs of those served. Trainees are usually selected by their employers. These schemes (SENA, SENAI, SENAC, ITB, and others) are popular sources of training in most Latin American countries, and evaluations of their programmes indicate that although the costs are sometimes high, they have been successful in training, retraining and upgrading workers to acceptable standards of efficiency. Their experience may be useful to other countries that are trying to address the need for cost-effective continuing training of workers. The direct investment of governments need not be great; indeed costs to ministries of education are likely to be minimal. But indirect investment, legal structures, tax deductions, monitoring and quality control are all areas in which government involvement is necessary.

5. Summary: Priorities

In setting educational priorities, appropriate juridical arrangements should be made, including financial plans covering several years, to give stability to the implementation of programmes to which priority is assigned.

Sectoral priorities should be established after due consideration has been given to their short- and long-term consequences for all segments of the education system. Beyond a certain magnitude, a modification of any part or segment of the system will have consequences on its other components.

There seems to be broad consensus about the need for shifting priorities in the allocations of educational resources to reduce inequalities and discrimination, in particular concerning women and girls. To achieve such a shift requires a package of measures both at the formal, non-formal and informal education levels.

In weighting educational priorities, ethnical, political, economic and educational factors should be considered. *More than 'where to start?', the issue for policy-makers is 'how to dose?'*. Education does need to be dealt with comprehensively as a system and not piecemeal; and it is therefore necessary that attention be given to all levels and types of education; though particular emphasis would have to be put on 'early childhood care and education', 'basic education for youth and adults', the definition of which depends on the conditions prevailing in the country concerned, and on the co-ordination of basic with other types of education. Other priorities may be to improve the structure of secondary education, to monitor allocation and improve efficiency of higher education and of those training programmes more likely to respond to the needs of the labour market and generate 'non-modern' employment.

1. S. Lourié, *Education and development: strategies and decisions in Central America*, Paris, Unesco:IIEP, Stoke-on-Trent, U.K., Trentham Books, 1989, p. 91.

2. B. Levinger, *Malnutrition, school feeding, and education performance*, Paris, Unesco/World Food Programme, 1989.

3. F. Caillods, *Women's literacy for development, a brief overview of the situation today*, Paris, Unesco:IIEP, 1989.

4. S. Cochrane, *Fertility and education*. Baltimore, Md., Johns Hopkins University Press, 1979.

5. J.C. Caldwell, 'Education as a factor in mortality decline: an examination of Nigerian data', In: *Population Studies*, Vol. 33, No. 3, November 1979.

6. P. Kasaju; T.B. Manandhar, 'Impact of parents' literacy on school enrolments and retention of children: the case of Nepal. In: G. Carron; A. Bordia (eds.) *Issues in planning and implementing national literacy programmes*, Paris, Unesco:IIEP, 1985.

7. C. Muñoz Izquiero, 'Factores determinantes y consecuencias educativas de la perseverancia de los adultos en los círculos de alfabetización', In: *Revista Latinoamericana de Estudios Educativos*, Vol. 15, No. 3, 1985.

8. A.C. Smock, *Women's education in developing countries*, New York, Praeger, 1981.

9. P. Moock, 'The efficiency of women as farm managers', In: *American Journal of Agricultural Economics*, Vol. 58, 1976, pp.831-835.

10. A. Benavot, 'Education, gender, and economic development: a cross-national study', In: *Sociology of Education*, Vol. 62, 1989, pp.14-32.

11. N. Stromquist, *Empowering women through knowledge: policies and practices in international co-operation in basic education,* Paris, Unesco:IIEP, 1988, (International Working Group on Education, IIEP/IWGE/88. Mimeo).

12. J.M. Amara, 'Indigenous technology of Sierra Leone and the science education of girls', In: *International Journal of Science Education,* Vol. 9, 1987, pp.317- 324.

13. B.J. Callaway, 'Ambiguous consequences of the socialization and seclusion of Hausa women', In: *Journal of Modern African Studies,* Vol. 22, 1984, pp.429-450.

14. World Bank, *Improving the quality of primary education in developing countries,* Washington,D.C., World Bank, 1989, pp.105-108.

15. Ibid.

16. J.B.G. Tilak, *Female schooling in East Asia: a review of growth, problems and possible determinants,* Washington, D.C., World Bank, Population and Human Resources Department, 1989, (PHREE background paper series, No. PHREE/89/13).

17. G. Psacharopoulos; M. Woodhall, *Education for development. An analysis of investment choices.* New York, Oxford University Press, 1985.

18. The development of education in industrialised countries demonstrates that when universal lower secondary education is achieved, a significant and growing proportion of 4- to 5-year-olds attend pre-school institutions. For many developing countries, this is still a distant target, especially when finances cannot even cover universal primary education unless the number of years of instruction is reduced, or the age of entrance is postponed, sometimes to as late as ten years of age.

19. A. Heron, *Planning early childhood care and education in developing countries,* Paris, Unesco:IIEP, 1979, (Fundamentals of educational Planning, No. 28).

20. This is a very rough estimate, presuming the following rates: US$50 per child per year, for 200,000 children of 4-5 years of age in a population of 10 million with a per capita GNP of $500.

21. R. Carr-Hill; J. Lintott, *Comparative analysis of statistical data on adult education for 84 countries,* Paris, Unesco, 1985, Mimeo.

22. United Nations, *Selected demographic and social characteristics of the world's children and youth,* New York, United Nations, 1986.

23. However, findings sometimes indicate that the productivity of small farmers is improved by ordinary general education. See for example: World Bank, *Agricultural research: sector policy paper*, Washington, D.C., World Bank, 1989, and A. Figueroa, *Productividad y educación en la agricultura campesina de América Latina*, Rio de Janeiro, ECIEL, 1986.

24. We are not considering automatic promotion which of course reduces repetition but leaves unresolved the problem of achievement.

25. Incentives may not apply to dropping out that is due to the poverty or ignorance of parents and thus not directly dependent on government decision. Government might, perhaps, invest in public information campaigns targeted on parents from marginalised social groups, but there is little evidence that such campaigns reduce drop-out rates.

26. C.E. Beeby, *Assessment of Indonesian education: a guide in planning*, Wellington, New Zealand Council for Educational Research and Oxford University Press, 1979.

27. The term originated with Philip Foster, who, in 'The vocational school fallacy in development planning', In: C. Arnold Anderson; Mary Jean Bowman (eds.), *Education and economic development*, Chicago, Ill., Aldine, 1965, brilliantly discussed the inability of vocational and technical schools to train middle-level skilled manpower.

28. J. Hallak; F. Caillods, *Education, training and the traditional sector*, Paris, Unesco:IIEP, 1981, (Fundamentals of educational Planning, No. 31).

Chapter 6

Strategies

Let us say that a government has decided exactly what its policy choices and priorities for education are; it still faces three problems in setting its strategies for bringing about the desired development. First, we are far from fully understanding the complex relationships between political and economic objectives, or being able to make the changes in the educational system that are most likely to reconcile them. And even had we been, specific educational objectives are distorted by changing socio-economic conditions over time, so that conflicts arise and public support is undermined. It is thus dangerous to be simplistic or univocal in stating what the country should do: hardheaded determinism confuses the profession and can have lasting effects on the economy of the country as well.[1] It rather looks as if any educational strategy must be integrated, or at least related, to its general economic and political context, and set forth with caution so that it can be adapted as and when its application points up its shortcomings.

Second, consumers of education who have strong opinions about what education should be -- students, parents, employers -- may organise political pressure or simply subvert portions of an educational system which the planners devote to a purpose they do not support. Assume for example that a legal arrangement has been made for an internship programme for untrained school leavers. The idea is to give them another chance at training on the job, at no cost to the employers, for a limited period of time. The government has perhaps even subsidised the programme to make it more palatable to the employers, and to facilitate the transition of the trainees from school to work. Unless there is fairly tight monitoring, and serious attention to social demand in designing the schemes, employers may subvert the scheme, profit from the work of unskilled, and unpaid, labourers, and not bother to train them to do anything.

Third, producers of education -- the teachers, school supervisors, and administrators through the highest levels -- may have views on the way things are going and the way they should go, which differ not only from those of the consumers, but among themselves. The most powerful groups will have determinant influences on the volume and organisation of the education supply. Let us consider the practice of admission into secondary schools via a quota system. The views of primary school teachers may not be the same as those of the secondary school teachers, and rural teachers' views may differ from those of urban teachers. Rural primary teachers may support the quota system because it favours their pupils, and increases enthusiasm for the school on the part of the parents. Urban primary teachers, whose pupils lose out to make room for a proportion of rural primary graduates, may tend to resist. High-school teachers in both contexts are not likely to be in favour of the system, as the experience of Papua New Guinea shows. They believe the system lowers the academic backgrounds of the students entering. They resent what they see as conversion of their institutions into remedial primary schools, or at the very least, the widening of ranges of ability to extents that are not compatible with effective teaching and learning.[2]

And one must not overlook the special type of inertia which is peculiar to education. In designing education strategies, inertia and resistance to innovation must be combated with real and effective incentives, and student flows through examinations must be carefully controlled if policy objectives and priorities are to be attained.

Once again, while no single strategy is valid for all societies, there are simple, general principles which may be considered in formulating them.

1. Multiple-phase strategies and the time factor

Strategies which call for introducing changes into a school system, however small they may be (we are not talking about massive reforms here), must include a patience factor to give the changes time to work their way in. The technique of dividing an innovation into phases may constitute the means of giving an educational entity the time it needs to break with established patterns.

It may also make it easier to adjust to unexpected change in the larger context and facilitate the orchestration of concurrent changes in the educational, economic, and political spheres. A principal, a supervisor, a regional administrator, each at his or her own level and for different reasons, will choose to encourage or retard a process, and some districts or provinces always stand out in adopting new, officially-backed practices before the rest of the profession. Even more significantly, in some fortunate cases individuals will introduce their own innovations. Added to these irregularities are the unique blends of influences -- political, religious, cultural, etc. -- peculiar to each locality, which bear on the educational system. The line of advance of any policy will be ragged, and short of using authority to control what is going on in each classroom, there is no way to tidy it up.

The attitudes of a country towards this uneven line of advance go far in determining its strategies for execution of policy. If variations are looked upon as undesirable deviations from the norm, they will either be ignored by the administration or attempts will be made to iron them out piecemeal, usually by endowing the laggards with special assistance. What appears to be a better solution is to accept the broken front as inevitable, and even, within limits, as a sign of health and vigour, and to provide for differences when designing the strategies. The strategist should seek ways of encouraging the natural innovators and the most dynamic components of the system to blaze new trails for the less able or more timid. But care must be taken to see that the innovators in the system are not trapped within the system they create. A *laissez-faire* policy would not offer any such defence. One might offer incentives, and these will be discussed later in this chapter. Another way is to divide the implementation of a strategy into more than one phase, usually two, but sometimes three or even four. The approach is the same; an 'experimental component' is provided for at every level and for all types of education, through which new ideas can be tried out. Let us examine the simplest.

In two-stage strategies, there are two operations that overlap. During the first phase, which is programmed to accommodate limited changes throughout the system, an experimental or pilot sector is selected to fully implement the policy change decided upon. The second generalisation phase follows as soon as the lessons have been drawn from the first, amendments introduced, and the policy adapted to the conditions that apply. Two specific examples of circumstances in which multi-phase projects are seen to be appropriate are (i) in the introduction of changes in existing primary and secondary curricula to streamline transitions between education and work, and (ii) in reorganising higher education to shift emphasis to small-group work in preference to amphitheatre-scale lectures, for example, to introduce modular organisation, or to completely revamp a curriculum.

As an example of the former, we might consider the pre-vocational studies which a number of Asian countries have introduced into curricula. In the initial phases, the countries called upon the bulk of the profession to introduce only such changes in practice as the average teacher could be expected to manage with the in-service training and supervision that they could realistically be offered. Concurrently, particularly able teachers were selected in certain areas of the country (preferably both rural and urban), to experiment with a second generation of methods and materials and to introduce more sweeping changes in the curricula. The wider programme was generalised as and when the bolder innovations had been tested and amended, a cadre of teachers experienced in applying them had been built up, and the innovations had become established in enough schools for other teachers to see them in practice under conditions not too different from their own.

But even then the line of advance is not regular, because in a healthy system there will always be conservatives resisting change and pioneers eager to break new ground, with or without assistance.

To illustrate the second type of experiment, successful elements from 'experimental colleges' might spread throughout a system of higher education if they prove appropriate. When it is hard to find such colleges among existing institutions, and wide-scale changes are bound to be resisted by the system as a whole, some countries -- such as Venezuela, with its 'Universidad Nacional Experimental de Guyana', or the United Kingdom with its Open University -- might find it more convenient, even if not always easy to finance, to establish a new institution.

Two-stage strategies are never simple to administer, even when the proposed change is modest, that is, not actually affecting the system at its roots. The principal difficulty lies in the difference between the conditions likely to encourage the most dynamic part of a system to change its practices and the conditions required to make the other parts want to emulate the changes. Freedom and a few additional resources might suffice to release the drive of some who are ready to implement government policy, but may only confuse those who are content with the old ways. Yet the same regulations and administrative mechanisms must apply to both. They must be loose enough to allow the dynamic elements in the system to progress and take some risks, but firm enough to offer support to the uncertain, stimulation to the sluggish, and to control the erratic or irresponsible. This is easier said than done. The main advantage of two-stage strategies is that they make distinction between these elements clearer and easier to deal with separately; but there is the ineluctable danger that they might be consolidated, that rolling reform might be institutionalised so that some segments of the system are always ahead of the others.

The question may also arise as to whether two-phase strategies are even possible in the many developing countries in which the majority has opted for a centralised system of organisation. The main advantage of such a system is that it makes it possible for massive operations to be carried out more rapidly and efficiently than would be possible with a multitude of autonomous personalities. Its weaknesses tend to lie in identifying the growing points in the system, and in allowing enough flexibility to stimulate initiative and a sense of commitment on the part of individuals of varying capacities. These qualities may not always be easy to find in a decentralised system, either, where pilot projects might be well worth considering.

There are a distressing number of pilot projects, in rich countries as well as poor, that have never piloted anyone anywhere. They may fade into obscurity, or they may remain as showcase pieces -- objects of national pride or of controversy. When this happens one might suspect that at the outset insufficient attention was given to the possibility of their application to the whole system. Perhaps a project has sprung up spontaneously as a result of a perfectly commendable local initiative; in such cases, it is for the government to judge whether or not the project has more than local significance, and if it has, to see that its possibilities are diffused. But something more systematic is required of projects which originate officially and are set up to improve or expand educational systems in new directions. If these are to come to life, those responsible for them must co-operate with administrators and planners early enough to foresee their generalisation throughout the country. And it is precisely at this point that our knowledge is scanty, and might be improved through better systems of monitoring.

Generally speaking multiple-phase strategies are a good idea. But resources must be mobilised to finance (i) careful planning and programming of each phase; (ii) diffusion of information on the strategy adopted and its intended implementation; (iii) experimentation and innovation at each step in the implementation; (iv) incentives to promote initiatives and to execute government priorities; (v) wide diffusion of the modalities recommended to each sector or sub-sector concerned; (vi) evaluation and adjustment of the experimental phase; (vii) monitored transition from one phase to the next.

2. The need for integration

a. At the macro level

Over the past three decades, a good deal has been written on the need for integrated planning strategy. In practice, however, this sort of strategy is not easy to implement, or indeed to adopt. The term has come simply to mean that either one expands the educational system according to social and political needs and leaves it more or less at the rhetoric stages, or co-ordination must in fact be streamlined among the various ministries concerned with education. The latter has remained little more than a pious hope. Needless to say that in countries where three different ministries are appointed to deal each with one level or type of education -- and this type of organisation is not uncommon -- the lack of integration has severely crippled the implementation of policy. Sometimes co-ordination of ministries has meant rather that clear distinctions must be made between the targets of universal primary education on the one hand, to be struggled for on socio-political grounds such as national unity, social justice, equity and human rights, and of manpower needs of the economy on the other, which is sometimes possible and sometimes not. Sometimes expansion and improvement of the system of education is planned primarily on economic grounds, that is to say, depending principally on the financial, human, and material resources that the government can provide. In these terms it is difficult to interpret the trends in educational expenditure of the past three decades, which have been cyclic. Stages of increased shares in government resources have been followed, in some countries, by declines, in some instances as a result of 'good integrated planning', that is, the ability to tailor the strategy of education to the evolution of the availability of resources.

b. At the sub-sectoral level

Virtually any modification of even a single component of an educational system should be considered within the broad economic and political framework of a society, but seldom is. Policy-makers tend to consider that problems, issues, factors, and obstacles that are outside their own area of direct concern will either be addressed by those who are concerned, or will disappear spontaneously without much affecting their policy choices and priorities. Educational strategies thus tend simply to ignore them, and this explains their frequent failure to address the entirety of the pertinent issues. The classical example of failing to consider the big picture occurs in the attempt to adjust teachers' salaries.

(i) The need for priority. In many countries, the main obstacle to improving the condition of teachers is the impact of any rise in their pay on the government budget. Because teachers are members of the civil service, an increase of x% of the teachers' remuneration means an increase in the entire salary bill of a government by x%. Ministries of finance therefore usually resist pressure from ministries of education to raise salaries, and in the best of circumstances suggest special allowances. If parity of salaries across the board is respected, the effort to attract and keep good teachers is held down, meaning that any strategy which provides for a perceptible increase in the quality, quantity, or sustainability of teachers' service is doomed to failure.

(ii) Spill-over effects. Once every ten years or so, after a significant change in the political outlook, a government may decide to substantially adjust the salary scale of educational professionals. The gesture is perfectly justifiable on both educational and economic grounds, but unless its consequences on the whole profession, in both the public and private sectors, are examined and assessed, unforeseen

outgrowths may abort the whole purpose of the strategy. The experience of Haïti is particularly interesting in this regard.

In 1986 and 1987, after many decades of stagnation during which primary education was for the most part ignored, the Haïtian government projected two significant salary increases for public school teachers, and put forward the cost savings that would finance them. In addition to satisfying the legitimate needs of the teaching force and attracting better teachers, the intention was also to contribute to expanding primary school enrolment. The strategy was well planned and well implemented, but it did not take into account the spill-over effect onto the private sector. The private sector -- highly heterogeneous in denomination and in quality -- enrols more pupils than the public sector, and its teachers' average salaries are far below those of the public sector. After the salary increase a number of primary teachers left the private sector for the public (this was not a stated purpose of the salary increase), and some left the teaching profession altogether. The result was a decline in enrolment in the private sector. Classrooms, sometimes even schools, were phased out, and the ministry of education had to initiate negotiations with representatives of the private sector to supplement teachers' salaries -- experimentally -- in the private sector. It is obviously not our opinion that teachers' salaries should not be increased; simply stated, each government must reflect on the possible ramifications as thoroughly as possible, and all contingencies must be provided for.

c. At the micro level: enrolment and child labour

Some children manage to organise themselves to make time for school in a working day, but in many countries government's biggest obstacle to expanding enrolment, and limiting absenteeism, repetition and dropping out, is the bleak necessity of child labour. Children either do not attend school at all or their attendance is limited because they have to work for their living. Moreover, children leave school because their parents cannot pay for school uniforms, transportation, even paper and other fundamental equipment, although tuition itself may be free. But if parents are already paying these fees, they may be able to continue, and in some cases the government might recover some of its outlay by charging them for tuition, say, at cost. Where parents are too poor even to pay cost fees, they must be subsidised, or they simply will not send their children to school. Partial but convergent statistics indicate that these costs can be far from negligible,[3] and this fact must be kept in mind in looking for cost-recovery at lower levels of education.

A small-scale study undertaken in a village in Central Java, Indonesia, shows that both children and their parents are prepared to make great sacrifices to see that at least part of a child's day is devoted to being educated. But when hours at school are added to those spent on household chores and on productive work, 6- to 8-year-olds work for a total of about six hours, 9- to 11-year-olds seven to eight, and 12- to 14-year-olds eight to eleven hours per day.[4] Even excluding China, it is possible that 50 million school-aged children, or more, cannot spare the time to go to school at all. The problem is particularly acute in Brazil and Southern Asia, but is certainly not limited to those areas.

In designing strategies to expand and improve primary enrolment, attention must therefore be given, as for example in Bangladesh (see *Inset 2*) to the special needs of working children, who need flexibility. The best way to provide schooling to those whose workload is too heavy to allow a normal school day may be to accommodate them in non-formal programmes.[5] Integrated intersectoral approaches that give proper attention to non-educational factors may be the answer. The watchword here is *adapt schools to children, and not children to schools*

Attendance might be improved, and drop-out due to heavy workloads decreased, in the formal schools as well, by making timetables and calendars more flexible, allowing children to choose morning, afternoon, or evening schedules. Awareness of the proportion of working children in a class, and in a school, is a vital prerequisite to being able to take special care of them. It is important, too, to take advantage of their experience rather than ignore the fact that they work; to ask them to explain their jobs, and what it takes to do them well. Of course, a teacher may encounter problems in singling out working children in a group where non-working children predominate. Trade-offs between positive discrimination and the benefit of the group against tact and *esprit de corps* must be assessed in making these decisions.

Inset 2
Bangladesh: Underprivileged Children's
Educational Programmes (UCEP)

Established in 1972 with the help and co-operation of the ministry of manpower development and social welfare, UCEP aims at bringing about improvements in the economic, educational and social status of working children without causing a disruption in their working and socio-economic environment. Its primary focus is on provision of education and technical training. UCEP children continue to work even after they have been enrolled in UCEP schools and therefore learn as they earn. The programme has expanded in both size and scope. It now covers both boys and girls, and its activities also include the provision of subsidised nutrition and health services. UCEP started its first school in Dhaka in 1973 with an enrolment of 60 boys. (It also started a similar project in 1978 in Kathmandu, Nepal).

The specific objectives of UCEP include the following: to provide basic education and training in different trades; to promote self-confidence, self-reliance, proper socialisation and a sense of responsibility; to provide ancillary services, such as health care, supplementary nutrition and recreation; and to provide information and counselling to parents and adult students on family planning.

UCEP schools operate a shift system. Most schools run three shifts a day; each shift is of three hours' duration and students are required to attend only one shift. The schools run two sessions throughout the year: January to June and July to December. They usually take children between the ages of 10 and 14. There are a total of 20 schools catering for 9,260 students: ten schools in Dhaka, six in Chittagong, and four schools in Khulna. Educational materials and uniforms are provided free once a year. There is also free medical care and students are given one full meal a day at a subsidised rate (Tk 0.50). According to UCEP, the fact that children pay for services, even if they are subsidised, ensures and reinforces their commitment to the programme and the philosophy and practice of self-reliance.

For the child to be enrolled, permission is required from the guardian because school attendance may result in the child being able to earn less money each day and from the employer because the child may need time off work in order to be able to attend classes. UCEP social workers make these initial contacts and, once established, close contact with the guardian and/or the employer is maintained throughout the six years a child may be in project schools.

In Bangladesh, four out of every ten children never attend school, more than half of those who do never get beyond second grade and more than three-quarters do not complete primary level. Fewer girls than boys attend and more drop out. In UCEP schools the drop-out rate is only about 10 per cent.

Source: *Conditions of Work Digest*, (ILO), Vol. 7, No. 1, 1988.

3. Levers for influencing social demand

The determinant ingredient in the recipe is social demand. It is therefore vital to keep a finger on the pulse of the student's needs all the way through the system, and to keep closely in touch with the society's views on education. Examinations, for example, must be designed in harmony with those views.

a. Regulation: moving from selective to open systems

At the two extremes are the highly selective systems and the open. Typically, the former use 'directive' pedagogical methods. Teacher-learner relations are strictly defined and formal; repetition rates are high, especially at the end of each cycle, and access to the upper levels is determined on the basis of manpower needs. The advantage of such a system is that it is easy to manage where budgetary constraints are tight. Its drawbacks are well known: they ignore social demand for education, and can operate only under authoritarian political regimes; education at the lower levels is 'preparatory', and its quality is conditioned by the requirements of the upper levels.

The pedagogical methods of the open systems are 'participatory and active'. Teacher-learner relations are friendly and informal; repetition rates are average to low; access to the upper levels is relatively easy and determined on the basis of social criteria. Examinations tend to become tools for orienting students as well as evaluating their achievements and justifying certification. The drawbacks of these systems include the fact that they are difficult to manage where budgets are tight, and they may generate frustration among underqualified school leavers when they find that job openings in the labour market are limited.

The position of a country between these two extremes obviously corresponds to its values and its conception of education. Generally speaking, the formal systems fall closer to the selective extreme, the non-formal and out-of-school systems closer to the open. Examinations, which determine whether or not a student is qualified, must distinguish qualifications that are important to the society. The excellence of an examination will be reflected in the quality of the preparation for it and, if adequately administered, will help to keep track of student flows. Examinations are thus a key element in regulation.

b. Improving the quality of education

Social demand for education depends to a great extent on the quality of the education offered, which varies in turn with sector (public or private), segment (general, vocational or technical), and cost (high or low). It determines the degree of satisfaction of the student, and therefore the rate of re-enrolment after each completion, and also largely determines his or her career and social prospects.[6]

While examinations are often, sometimes legitimately, condemned as barriers to progress, experience shows that standardisation of examinations, for example, along with localisation of curricula and well-conceived systems of student evaluation, can be very helpful in improving the quality of instruction.

(i) *Standardisation of examinations.* In decentralised developing countries such as Kenya, as well as industrialised countries with long-standing traditions of centralised administration such as France, the standardisation of secondary entrance or exit examinations appears to be an efficient way to improve outcome, especially when combined with supportive evaluation and guidance services for teachers. Because they strongly stimulate repercussions (reactions to perceived positive or negative teaching practices), standardised examinations can encourage the concentration of effort on certain crucial subjects such as languages or mathematics via an increase in weight on the tests, which of course results in an upward levelling in these areas overall.[7] General cognitive aptitudes can be encouraged by including questions which test more complex and higher-level cognitive skills, e.g. shifts from descriptive (recall) items to explicative, observational, and reasoning exercises.[8]

(ii) *Localisation of curricula.* Many developing countries have been attempting to link examination reform with the introduction of curricula which are more closely related to the life of the majority of the population. Experience, for example that of Sri Lanka,[9] shows that these attempts often encounter the resistance of parents who are convinced that academic education is the only kind that offers the possibility of access to higher education and to upward mobility.

Sometimes, in fact, the test items introduced have not resulted in better performance, especially on the part of students in rural areas, perhaps because they reflected insufficient knowledge of the actual living conditions of the students. This appeared to be the case in the very good example of Kenya's primary school certificate reform during the 1970s (see *Inset 3*).

(iii) *Evaluation.* Great improvement in the quality and outcomes of educational practices can be made through systems of control and evaluation. Swaziland[10] has recently experimented with this approach by developing guidelines for teachers and manuals for supervisors and school administrators, and by running training schemes for these groups, with the result that students' performances in standardised examinations have improved to a significant and surprising extent within a few years. The active participation of local or regional networks of schools on the one hand, of experts and authorities in the assessment, adjustment, and development of further action on the other, has proved a precious support to initiatives of this sort in the OECD countries.[11]

c. Management of student flows

A number of developing countries have tried unsuccessfully to limit access to secondary and tertiary educational institutions on grounds of financial constraints, and sometimes on the grounds that white-collar employment prospects are limited.

Yet the examination systems often put more emphasis on criteria for access to upper levels than for access to the labour market. Changes in national examination systems, especially when combined with guidance services and tight policies for control of the expansion of the educational supply can help steer people in realistic and satisfactory directions. Initiatives described by various countries open up promising avenues, notably in certain African countries. For African countries. For example, the Côte d'Ivoire[12] has successfully taken steps to increase the selectivity of entrance examinations to public secondary schools and university. Strong social demand has often led to parallel expansion of the private educational sector, however. Access to higher levels of academic education can be limited only if entrance and exit examinations in the private sector are standardised -- as they are in many Western European countries -- and alternative pathways to employment developed.

144

Inset 3
Kenyan examination reform: goals and modes of action

The Kenyan reform concerning the Certificate of Primary Education, launched in 1973, was aimed at achieving, through changes in examination questions and the introduction of an information feedback system on examination results, the following goals: an increased minimum level in the quality of primary education, increased relevance of examinations and curriculum to the local environment, and reduced quality differences among schools/districts. It was believed that a progressive shift of test items towards higher-level cognitive skills would provide for more efficient selection/allocation of secondary school places, and that rural biases in examination questions could help make it more equitable.

Steps were taken to develop a team of testing, evaluation and research specialists. 'Incentive information', consisting of school performance lists, as well as 'guidance information' (via a CPE Newsletter in particular) based on detailed analyses of the test candidates' performances, was provided to teachers and heads of schools with a view to stimulating and supporting their active engagement in the improvement of the quality of primary school teaching.

As a result of the efforts deployed since 1974, one can see, by 1981, a general upturn in the schools' performances, including those in districts with previously weak performance records. Although inter-district disparities had not been reduced to the desired extent, improvements in examination results were spectacular in districts where adequate professional and administrative support had been provided (teachers' advisers, education officers, new supervisors and intensive in-service courses).

A progressive shift towards test items requiring higher-level cognitive skills has been achieved over the years, but it has proved difficult to improve the chances of success of children in rural areas through changes in test items only, without strengthening the school support systems.

Source: H.C.A. Somerset, *Examination reform in Kenya,* Washington, D.C., World Bank. 1987. Also: 'Examinations as an instrument to improve pedagogy'. In: S.P Heyneman; I. Fägerling (eds.), *University examinations and standardised testing,* Washington, D.C., World Bank, 1988.

Pressures on the upper levels of an educational system relax with improved conditions of access to employment in the public services (the largest modern employment sector in the developing countries). Until recently, the public administrations of Zambia and Gambia[13] recruited middle-level personnel on the basis of a series of aptitude tests, without asking for a secondary diploma. Special training courses were given before subsequent appointment to administrative positions. In-testing of trainees of varied educational backgrounds has also proved successful in Sierra Leone[14] as an alternative to selection for training as instructors in agriculture, and a study[15] comparing the experiences of Sri Lanka and Kenya concluded that the more generalised the access to jobs -- through job-related testing and training -- the lower the pressure on the higher levels of academic education.

Concentration of the efforts towards selecting the contents of vocational/pre-vocational and technical public training, and towards facilitating transitions from school to job-related training, on the part of educational authorities with those of potential employers, added to the establishment of rules and standards, has proved helpful in improving the employment perspectives of holders of non-academic certificates in the Federal Republic of Germany, and in the overall regulation of student flows.[16]

A mix of university selection through standardised national entrance examinations with selection by internal assessment has been tried with a view to overcoming biases against students from agricultural backgrounds. Under certain conditions, internal assessment has proved to be effective in recruiting secondary school leavers from underprivileged areas who, even if they have had initial difficulties in competing with recruits that have passed the entrance examination, generally overcome their handicap, and often out-perform the others.

The principal conditions of success, according to the Indonesian experience[17], are (i) strict selection of schools benefiting from the privilege of participating in the scheme; (ii) effective control of the performance of students thus recruited and regular comparison of their university performances with their schools' assessments; and (iii) confinement of this alternative path to less popular courses. Extension to sought-after courses would make the system unmanageable and neutralise efforts towards equity.

146

d. Administering examination systems

Combining examinations and testing with student guidance as a means to effective monitoring of educational demand and supply works only where adequate institutional capacity and operating rules apply. The guiding elements might be summarised as follows:

- transparency of content and respective weight of questions in standardised examinations;
- transparency of the correction and administration of examinations, as well as the measures aimed at avoiding cheating and corruption (for example, professional -- and properly paid -- teams of designers and correctors of examinations, computerisation of test correction, etc.);
- administering tests under financial circumstances adequate to ensure their professionalism and independence;
- back-up of test evaluation and educational guidance services: institutional units specialised in research and information on testing/evaluation and in educational career guidance, with comprehensive (if possible computerised) information systems; these units may be part of or associated with university research centres competent in educational research;
- consulting and negotiating mechanisms involving educational authorities and employers to facilitate transition.

4. Levers for influencing the producers and consumers of education: the role of incentives

Incentives include both the rewards and the penalties that involve resources, and they may or may not be intentional. When planners and advisers of political authorities contemplate the adoption of policy, or set priorities, or decide upon strategies, they rarely recognise these elements. Yet incentives can affect what students are taught, how well they learn, how efficiently their time is used, and whether or not the sector will grow in productivity. Incentives can eliminate or create obstacles to the adoption of a brilliant innovation in a pilot project. They may be necessary to the success of a financial reform, say, a cost-recovery scheme for higher education or a modification in the system of grants to private schools, to the mobilisation of funds from employers to support school-to-work programmes, to generate support for or against a certain type of education. They can be used to stem or divert a flow of students into an area that would otherwise appear unattractive, to reduce repetitions, or multiple matriculations at the university level. They can be useful in encouraging non-formal programmes, apprenticeship schemes, and other out-of-school training, post-literacy, continuing education, and others.

If a system of education requires stimulation, or one of its components is lagging, incentives can be targeted on the various groups concerned. Sometimes changes are required in the behavioural patterns of a group or several groups -- consumers or producers. Incentives can change the attitudes of communities that are lethargic about what is going on in their schools. They can encourage the choice of a method to achieve a desired outcome, stimulate the degree of involvement and co-operation among teachers and other personnel, spark enthusiasm for new instructional methods and individual experimentation.

Incentive can be simple financial rewards to a particular target group, individual, or institution; to children, to parents, to employers, to teachers, to a select type of personnel. They may be legal arrangements which encourage or discourage activities organised outside the public sector. Other non-financial rewards may bestow status, or public recognition -- awards, affiliation with prestigious associations, investitures, medals. They should be introduced and phased out according to needs; otherwise their cost-effectiveness will be short-lived, and their interest may wane as well. They need not be centralised, and should be adapted to their purposes and targets.

a. The value of incentives

An incentive system is designed to contribute to the accomplishment of objectives set by the policy-makers:
- it improves cost-effectiveness;
- it generates supplementary resources;
- it reduces inequalities;
- it enhances efficiency of outcomes;
- it increases the productivity of graduates.

Obviously, no single incentive system will wipe out all the tensions and conflicts that policy decisions evoke, and because governments are torn in many directions the inconsistency of their decisions makes it impossible for one incentive to contribute to the achievement of all of them. *If, as is often the case, objectives and priorities are in contradiction among themselves, no incentive system will be very effective.* It is only when conflicts can be resolved, when policies and priorities are balanced and harmonious that incentives can be designed to give emphasis to certain elements and help them to get off the ground. The challenge then is to alter existing incentives -- they are always there, some implicit, some explicit, reflecting societal values and traditions -- to make them more consistent with policies and priorities. An arduous task under the best of circumstances.

Incentives can be used selectively, however, to accomplish specific objectives when policy inconsistencies are minimal. As illustrations we might cite:

- the recruitment of female teachers to increase the attendance of girls in the rural areas of some societies;
- allowances of various sorts for teachers and other personnel as rewards for expanding their services to well-targeted users such as rural children and inhabitants of border areas. Where such allowances have been introduced they have usually been too small to be effective;
- free distribution of midday meals to children who attend morning classes in slum areas;
- free establishment of schools, without permits, and their operation over a period of perhaps three years, in areas not served by any sector, and not likely in the short run to be reached by the public sector;
- authorisation of headmasters to mobilise local contributions to improve the functioning of their schools;
- the allocation of fellowships to all applicants who have the ability and desire to enrol in a study course whose facilities are underutilised and for which there is a shortage of graduates entering the labour market;
- tax exemptions for employers who provide needed training;
- weighting of practical subjects in secondary entrance examinations to help reconcile the terminal/preparatory duality of primary education;

- use of the mass media to announce free distribution of new textbooks to the pupils of a given geographical area, to increase their chances of reaching the targeted pupils;
- aiming services at minority groups (as, for example, in India - see *Inset 4*).

b. Guidelines for improving incentives

In modifying an established system of incentives, one might consider the following four steps:

(1) *Diagnosis:* analysis of the incentives heretofore offered in the context of the functioning of the educational system. This step is generally inadequate, and needs a good deal of study and research.

(2) *Goals:* examination of the intended change, and consideration of the appropriateness of the incentive in bringing it about.

(3) *Information and feedback:* costs may not always be justified by the results expected.

(4) *Careful programming:* (a) design and experimentation (perhaps in multiple phases); (b) publicity (public campaigns if necessary); (c) budgeting; (d) implementation on a wide scale; (e) built-in evaluation.

Let us consider the difficulties in designing good systems of incentives, in the light of the objectives to be attained. We wish to improve efficiency in the use of resources. There may be a host of possibilities, each of which addresses a different problem. If school supervisors receive allowances on the basis of the number of schools they have visited rather than the number of schools in their district, for example, they may become more effective. We wish to generate extra-budgetary resources. Consider for example the 'plan tripartido' in Guatemala, where local communities were prepared to contribute, in cash and in kind, to the design, construction, and implementation of primary school buildings in collaboration with the ministry of education. We want to attack the problem of inequality. A frontal attack with incentives may prove complex, and difficult to implement. Empirical evidence sometimes indicates that attempts at political equalisation are delicate, and may be more successful if they are directed at other problems, such as equalisation of geographic or intergenerational opportunity, which encounter fewer direct obstacles, and manage to achieve the political objective indirectly.[18]

Inset 4
India: incentives to increase participation
in Industrial Training Institutes (ITI)

Equity in education is regarded as a most important policy objective. In an attempt to ensure equality of opportunity to the two most educationally deprived groups -- the scheduled castes and scheduled tribes -- a number of incentives and facilities have been provided at various educational levels.

Vocational and technical training is considered important to improve the productivity of these groups. Places are reserved for them in the institutions imparting such training, and eligibility conditions waived. Various other incentives are also offered. As a result, the enrolment percentage of the scheduled castes in the total enrolment in the ITIs went from 6.9 per cent in 1961 to 13.3 per cent in 1981, and that of the scheduled tribes from 1.1 per cent to 3.7 per cent over the same period.

The major incentives are stipends, free equipment and uniforms, flexibility in marks, and places in general hostels and in special hostels for the scheduled tribes in the tribal areas.

Reservation was practised in all the States in varying degrees, but implementation was mechanical, and did not permit due regard to the abilities and aptitudes of the students.

Stipends were available to all of these students in the ITIs, but rates were different between the tribal and general ITIs. In fact, the amount was too meagre to provide any meaningful relief to the scheduled groups, whose poverty is abject.

Long and complicated procedures for the release of grants to the various ITIs resulted in considerable delays in the disbursement of the stipends, and meant considerable hardship to students who were forced by financial difficulties to leave training without completing it. The main reasons for the delay in stipend disbursement seemed to be bureaucratic procedures and lack of sufficient and committed staff. The stipends were released to the institutions only after students had attended classes for at least one month, and their names and applications were received and examined by the awarding agencies. The money was often disbursed by the regular staff of the institutions, who gave priority to other administrative matters. It is suggested that the money be placed at the disposal of the principal before the start of each session, as soon as the students are admitted. Subsequent amounts can be tagged to regular attendance. Additional office staff may also be assigned if the number of scheduled-group students is large. Besides stipend money, incentives such as equipment, uniforms, etc., should be provided in time.

Source: Kusum K. Premi, *Scheduled castes and scheduled tribes in industrial training institutes: a study of five States*, New Delhi, National Institute of Educational Planning and Administration, 1989.

Where the aim is to increase productivity, incentives are very difficult to design, given the extreme complexity of relationships between the producers and the consumers of education. In the short run, the greater the input of the users in the design, the more productive the system is likely to be. In the longer term, there needs to be a much wider vision of the aims of education, and a clearer idea as to how to produce 'modern manpower' which could promote social and economic changes. Our limited knowledge in this area suggests that a good deal of study, research, and experimentation will be necessary before meaningful incentive mechanisms can be designed.

In attaining the goal of increased educational efficiency, incentives should be tailor-designed and thoughtfully applied to specific situations, directing the activities of teachers and students towards educational accomplishments that are important to the community. Learning outcomes must be accomplished with the resources available to the schools; incentives may be used to upgrade teacher qualifications through in-service training, to improve the attitudes of supervisors, to reduce teaching loads through better class organisation. To be effective, all incentives must be based on thorough preliminary evaluation.

Some ambitious projects -- usually in industrialised countries, and in particular in the USA -- intended to control the behaviour of teachers and change the educational outcome by relating it tightly to a system of incentives, may prove ineffective. Schools are complex, living entities whose activities cannot be measured economically, and on which administrators and other outsiders face grave difficulties in trying to impose efficiency. It is no inexpensive matter for administrators, politicians, and the public to find out about the most educationally significant activities of students and teachers and to ensure that they are carried out.

One peculiarity of the teaching profession intensifies the difficulty of getting teachers, through incentives, to improve their work. Teaching is a solitary business. Except in still very rare situations where team teaching is practised or schools are on 'open plan', teachers do not normally see each other at work. When closed off in a room with 30 to 60 pupils, a teacher is as central to those he or she teaches as is any other teacher in a system. The relevant characteristics of his or her way of teaching are intangible and difficult to evaluate, and only the most observable aspects of the work -- the number of hours spent in the classroom, manner of handling discipline problems, regularity of attendance at meetings, and number or absence of criticisms from parents, students, or colleagues -- are available to serve as criteria. These fuzzy indicators do not always correlate well with teaching efficiency or communication. Simplistic approaches to the concept of incentives such as 'merit pay' are not likely to be successful, and may be counterproductive.[19]

Incentives targeted not on individual teachers but on schools or groups of teachers may prove more effective, and may be easier for teachers' unions to accept. While no actual evidence of success is available, this idea has been considered to be worth exploring by a number of ministers of education.

5. Summary: strategies

The design of strategies for implementing policy choices and programmes to which priority is attached should be based on a few general principles:

(i) The need to take into consideration the time factor. Introducing changes, however minor they may be, requires time because of the very nature of the education system (e.g. it concerns, at any time, a large number of cohorts of students and several age-groups). It is suggested that multiple-phase strategies be adopted; these may constitute the means of giving the education system the time it needs to break with established patterns. In general, multiple-phase strategies are not simple to administer and require careful planning, programming, experimentation, and evaluation of each phase, as well as arrangements for monitoring transition from each phase to the next.

(ii) The need for integration of the education system at the macro, sub-sectoral and micro levels. In practice, policy-makers should (a) accept to tailor the strategies of education to the availability of resources; (b) reflect on possible ramifications of decisions and provide for all contingencies in the elaboration of the strategies; and (c) give proper attention to non-educational factors in designing the strategies.

(iii) The need to influence social demand. Because of the dominant and determinant role of the social demand factor in the evolution of the educational system, strategies should include means for regulating its evolution, improving the quality of education and managing student flows. The role of examinations is crucial; they should be designed and administered in harmony with the purpose of the strategies.

(iv)   The need to influence producers and consumers of education. Inertia and resistance to innovation are typical and peculiar to education. These are partly due to the delicate blend of influences -- political, religious, cultural, etc. -- that bear on the educational system. In designing strategies, inertia and resistance to change should be combated with real and effective incentives, which should be used selectively, however, to accomplish specific objectives when policy inconsistencies are minimal. Otherwise, incentives may prove to be unsuccessful and even counterproductive.

---

1. It is fashionable today for planners to reject requests for investment in technical/vocational education and training on the grounds of: (i) high unit costs; (ii) low effectiveness; (iii) lower social rates of return than the more academic branches. One cannot disagree with the validity of the arguments, although the rate-of-return approach has been questioned. But then what is the alternative? The production sector cannot take the responsibility for training because it is not equipped to provide it .-- especially at the middle level. Sending people abroad for training can be even more expensive than funding domestic training, and far less effective. It may well be that there is no choice but to improve the effectiveness of whatever system of technical/vocational training exists, which need not necessarily be restricted to the department of education, until training capacity in the country's production sector is made adequate.

2. See Mark Bray, 'High school selection in less developed countries and the quest for equity, In: *Comparative Education Review*,, Vol. 29, No. 2, 1985.

3. According to R. Carr-Hill, in 1986 they represented 7.6 to 16% of GNP per capita in Benin; 12.2 to 18.8% in Mali; and 7.2 to 14.4% in Togo.

4. B. White, 'Child labour and population growth', In: *Development and Change,* Vol. 13, No. 4, 1982.

5. In some countries children under 15 are not allowed to attend literacy classes, and are not offered evening classes. If their presence is considered defeating to adults who are enrolled in these classes, one might consider establishing such classes specifically for them. Ideally, for reasons of cost, flexibility and adaptability, they should be integrated; but if adults resist, literacy and evening classes should be offered to children.

6. See G. Göttelmann, *Examens et 'management' de l'éducation,* Paris, Unesco:IIEP, 1989, Mimeo, (IIEP/Prg.GG/89.18).

7. Experiences in the USA are reported in H. Dickson Corbett; Bruce L. Wilson, 'Raising of stakes of Statewide mandatory testing programmes', In: Jane Hannaway; Robert Crowson (eds.), *The politics of reforming school administration,* London, Taylor & Frances Ltd., 1986. For the results of similar experiences in Singapore, see William Bingham (ed.), *A cross-cultural analysis of transition from school to work.* Paris, Unesco, 1986, (Report Studies S.132).

8. See H.C.A. Somerset, *Examination reform in Kenya,* Washington, DC., World Bank, 1987, for a discussion of the Certificate of Primary Education.

9. K. Lewin; A. Little, *Examination reform and educational change in Sri Lanka, 1972-82: modernisation or dependent underdevelopment?* Brighton (UK), Institute of Development Studies, 1982.

10. Unesco/SIDA, *Final evaluation report of management development seminar-workshop on institutional leadership and accountability in education,* Mbabane, Ministry of Education, 1986.

11. W.G. Van Velzen, et al, *Making school improvement work: a conceptual guide to practice, (OECD International School Improvement Project),* Leuven (Belgium), ACCO, 1985.

12. See Annie Perrier, "Vocational guidance in the Côte d'Ivoire", In : William Bingham (ed.), 1986, op cit.

13. ILO, *The paper qualification syndrome and unemployment of school leavers,* Addis Ababa, ILO/Job Skills Programme for Africa, 1982.

14. Ibid.

15. J. Oxenham, *Education vs qualification.* London, Allen & Unwin, 1984.

16. M. Maurice; François Sellier; J.J. Silvestre, *Politique d'éducation et organisation industrielle en France et en Allemagne: essais d'analyse sociétale,* Paris, PUF, 1982.

17. H.C.A. Somerset, *Secondary education, selection examinations and university recruitment in Indonesia,* Brighton (UK), Institute of Development Studies, 1983.

18. See L. Cerych; P. Sabatier, *Great expectations and mixed performances,* Stoke-on-Trent, U.K., Trentham Books; Paris, European Institute of Education and Social Policy, 1986.

19. See S.A. Hoenack, 'Incentives, outcome-based instruction, and school efficiency'. In: D.H. Monk; J. Underwood, (eds.), *Microlevel school finance*. Cambridge, Ma. Ballinger, 1988.

Part III

Memo to practitioners

In the spring of 1989 six ministers and former ministers of education were asked[1] what had been the single most important lesson they had gleaned from their experience at the head of the education structures of their nations. All of their answers had to do with implementation:

1. to be regularly involved in routine management and to interact with senior staff of the ministry and universities;

2. to avoid announcing intentions to change established procedure in the ministerial departments too early;

3. to find practical solutions to sensitive political issues which will otherwise fail, however good the intentions;

4. to convince, with professional arguments, senior staff and the teaching profession of the value of proposed policy changes;

5. to programme the adoption of new approaches, delivery systems, examination and selection procedures with care;

6. to establish co-ordination with other ministries, other levels of responsibility, and the other partners involved in the future of the country's educational system.

It is quite natural that these officials be concerned with implementation, and that they measure their success by the policies they applied, the options that worked, the strategies they executed -- in short, with what they actually got done. There is a large body of specialised literature on public administration and management, but in the last analysis it is the amount of direct control an administration can exercise over the implementation of change that makes the difference, and no universal guidelines can create this sort of control.

In developing countries it is easier to introduce quantitative change than qualitative classroom reform, but it can still be very difficult. Experience may be more useful here than theory, but there may be value in discussing certain approaches to (i) the management of resources (the teachers, teaching materials, technological tools and buildings) critical to the transformation of education and (ii) serving priority groups. In Chapters 7, 8 and 9 we deal with the resources that can be brought to bear, i.e. teachers, educational technologies, buildings, equipment and materials; Chapter 10 treats a long-neglected area of concern, the case of non-formal education.

The minister of education of a developing country wishing to make changes as rapidly as possible will usually find it necessary to decide early on whether to use the existing structures of the ministry or try to devise new mechanisms and start from the ground up. He or she may hope for a more imaginative project if new, fresh minds, uncluttered by routine, are set to the task. Surely the results will come faster; but the price may be high if the routine officers in the central departments and regional offices feel no involvement in the new practices. The whole administrative machine may be pressed to move faster than it was ever intended to move, and both quantity and quality may be sacrificed in the end. In Chapter 11 we discuss various approaches to administering change and maintaining continuity and examine priorities for management and administration.

---

1. Personal interviews were generously accorded to the author by Mr. Paul Yao Akoto of the Côte d'Ivoire, Mr. Reuben H. Harris of Antigua and Barbuda, Mr. Anwar Ibrahim of Malaysia, Mr. Abdelsalam Atallah Majali of Jordan, Mr. Luis Manuel Penalver of Venezuela, and Mr. Iba Der Thiam of Senegal.

Chapter 7

Teachers: priorities for planning teacher supply and demand

Three areas are crucial to policy regarding educational personnel: finance, training, and administrative and pedagogical support. Policy-makers must be willing to confront these three responsibilities; otherwise the future development of educational systems from primary right through tertiary levels will be limited by the critical constraints of teacher-related factors and because the quality of the education depends on the quality of teachers.

1. Salaries

a. The trends

Finding funds for education is one of the most difficult and contentious problems that developing countries face. Teachers' salaries are the biggest item in the education budgets: from 65 to 95 per cent. In many countries, teachers represent the largest group of salaried workers, and in virtually all countries they are the largest group of public employees.

While a few countries have managed to pay their teachers reasonable salaries, in relation to GNP per capita, most of those for which data are available have not, and even the poor salaries of yesteryear have dwindled to catastrophic lows, notably in North and sub-Saharan Africa since independence[1] (see *Table 7.1*). In Latin America and Asia, except in countries such as Colombia where teachers' unions are well organised and powerful, decline has been

Table 7.1 Average teachers' salaries expressed as percentage of GDF

	Primary (1)				Secondary (2)				High level (3)			
	1970	1975	1980	1985	1970	1975	1980	1985	1970	1975	1980	1985
Togo	17.9	13.7	12.0	11.0	29.4	22.4	19.6	18.0	-	-	-	-
Zambia	4.6	4.7	4.4	3.5	8.6	8.1	8.0	5.0	11.0	10.1	9.9	6.3
Ivory Coast	-	16.2	10.3	9.9	-	20.3	13.7	13.2	-	44.6	30.2	28.9
Congo	12.2	6.0	3.4	1.6	16.1	7.8	4.4	2.0	-	18.6	10.5	6.6
Colombia	3.0	3.1	2.1	2.4	3.0	3.1	2.1	2.4	-	-	-	-
Mexico (1)	-	2.7	1.3	1.2	-	4.8	2.6	1.6	-	-	-	-
Indonesia	-	3.8	1.5	2.0	-	5.4	2.0	2.8	-	7.1	2.1	3.0

1. Most highly qualified primary teachers
2. Qualified teachers of upper secondary
3. Post-secondary professors.

Source: C. Tibi, *Les salaires et les enseignants*, Paris, Unesco:IIEP, 1989, (IIEP/PRG.CT/89.97), Mimeo.

particularly acute through the 1980s. Many education sectors are finding themselves no longer able to attract qualified personnel. In those countries for which we have data, all except for the Congo, the Côte d'Ivoire and Togo have lowered qualification requirements to make their minimal salaries acceptable, with the result that unskilled and qualified salaries are compressed, and it hardly pays to struggle to acquire skills. In some respects -- in particular on equity grounds -- this compression is desirable; but it does suggest less attractiveness for the teaching profession and may produce 'negative selection' and deterioration in the qualification of the teachers.

The situation is even more critical in rural areas where it is more difficult to attract and maintain qualified teachers. Teachers' remuneration policies are either national or regional; they may be related to public/private differentials in pay; they are generally tied to national civil service regulations; thus any change in pay scales will profoundly affect the educational budget. The quality of service deteriorates because of the demotivation of the teachers; absenteeism rises; perhaps also a growing number of public sector employees, including teachers, have come to depend on income supplements from other employment, sometimes outside the public sector, for survival. In a country like Tanzania for example, "the economic recovery programme has brought about a considerable divergence between the formal salary structure in the civil service and the effective structure of the nominal earnings of civil servants. ... Civil service salaries have come to have two components: an official salary set by government or parastatal directive, and an unofficial salary composed of various allowances and supplementary payments. In practice, it is these allowances and supplementary payments within the public sector that provide the bulk of a civil servant's income, and not private entrepreneurial activities outside the public sector."[2]

b. The options

Salary increases are possible in some countries in which economic growth has relaxed the squeeze on the overall budget and/or the fiscal system can be improved and public income increased through taxes. Theoretically, taxes can be increased, particularly in Latin America, where the tax systems are inefficient and evasion is rampant, and the ratio of government income to GNP is very low. But in practice it has proved consistently difficult to do it, and possible only where political conditions are very nearly ideal.

Even where economic and fiscal conditions are appropriate, there must be (i) policy options in the budget to cover the increases; (ii) a process of revision of teachers' salaries to avoid automatisms and discontinuities in adjustments which may generate at the same time inflationary tensions. Obviously, the issue can be dealt with only on an individual country basis, and only without jolting its traditions. Japan, for example, in 1974, designed a system of periodic evaluation of teachers' salaries which has succeeded in protecting parity with comparable professions in the private sector without introducing rigidities into the salary management, or bureaucracy into a profession considered to be 'seishoku'(sacred).[3] Other countries might follow its example, and experiment with processes of salary adjustment that are financially feasible and reflect the intention of the government to maintain a quality teaching force.

In trade-offs between increases in salary and new job offers, governments tend to favour recruitment to meet the needs of new enrolment, leaving salaries constant in nominal (but not real) terms. Improvement in managing student flows, that is in controlling enrolment expansion by level and type of education, makes it possible to give preference to salary increase. This policy concept cannot be applied in isolation. It must be considered in the light of the overall changes taking place in a public sector, and must involve:

• *Close monitoring of the salary budget to eliminate 'ghost' teachers,* who have died, retired, or left for other employment, or who have been appointed but never taken up their positions, but whose names remain on salary schedules. Haïti successfully reduced the number of ghost teachers in 1986-87, and the savings helped to finance a respectable increase in the salary scale.

• *Streamlining of the administration at central and regional levels.* Too many teachers are in fact working as administrators, and being paid from the teachers' salary budget; staffs are sometimes padded and unwieldy. Paring them would result in savings which could be used for other purposes.

• *Transparency in recruiting practices and salary schedules,* to control ascriptive recruitment and promotion within and outside the public sector. Incentives might be offered to promote adherence to rules and discourage corruption in the management of public funds.

• *Adaptation of conditions of recruitment in the public sector to the needs of all levels:* local communities, districts, regions and central ministries. A side effect might be an increase in flexibility in managing the resources of the public sector as a whole, so that a greater part is devoted to teachers' salaries. But equity might be impaired, and disparities aggravated between teachers of different skill levels, as has been the experience of some of Brazil's municipalities and States.

c. Incentives

The teaching profession can be made more attractive in a number of different ways.[4] In many countries there is a glut on the unskilled labour market, and a desperate demand for certain skilled personnel, such as secondary science teachers for example. This is to some extent due to wage policy, which puts teaching out of competition with private demand for the same skills, and might be corrected, in some countries, by selective adjustment of salary scales, accelerating promotion, and combining seniority credit with the reduction of salary differential with the private sector. Technically, although formulae tending in these directions have been proved to be feasible, a good deal of experimentation and local testing is required before they are safe to adopt on a large scale; politically, they may be anachronistic, or applicable only after negotiation with teachers' unions, or useful only as an element in an overall reform of the civil service.

In remote rural areas, the profession needs to be trimmed and stabilised. Some countries have tried, with more or less success, (i) to make rural areas more attractive by granting accelerated promotion to rural teachers; (ii) to achieve better integration of teachers into the communities they serve by recruiting locally, and/or directly involving the communities in the day-to-day operations of the schools; and (iii) to make teachers accountable for a fair day's work by encouraging communities' participation in providing incentives to reduce absenteeism and turnover: free housing, improvements in working conditions, loans, allowances in kind. One country may be able to profit from the experience of another in deployment of resources, provision of special allowances and other supplements, and accelerated promotion for teachers who accept rural service.

2. Training

a. The trends

Partial evidence[5] suggests that the general tendency is toward uniformity: primary teacher training institutions are tending to require preparation which approximates more and more closely that of secondary and higher instructors. As of the 1970s, we observe the extension -- albeit uneven, from country to country -- of compulsory education, which requires higher levels of teacher preparation, and some governments are tending to accept the case put forward by unions for enhancement of the professional status of teachers. In Vietnam the number of compulsory academic years is seven; in Korea it is twelve. And the length of the specific professional preparation of primary teachers goes from two to four years beyond completion of the general cycle. Most countries require secondary teachers to complete twelve years of general education plus four years of professional preparation.

However, the distinctions between pre-service, in-service, initial and continuing teacher education have become blurred with the introduction of work/study schemes, distance training, and school-based professional development. Teacher training today can no longer be limited to a two- or three-year course of study prior to entering the profession. As in any other profession, in-service training is an important element in the process of professionalisation, and is compulsory in some countries. Principle No. 6 of the Unesco *Recommendations concerning the status of teachers* states: "Teaching should be regarded as a profession; it is a form of public service which requires of teachers expert knowledge and specialised skills, acquired and maintained through rigorous and continuing study."

The necessity for recruiting untrained teachers is and will continue to be a problem for many countries. The rapid universalisation of instruction in countries such as the Côte d'Ivoire, and later Bangladesh, have led to chronic teacher shortages and the recruitment of large numbers of untrained teachers. And those teachers, once recruited, remain forever, becoming major obstacles to improvement in quality, and increasingly difficult to adapt to the growing expectations of better educated communities. Some countries no longer suffer teacher shortages (Malawi and Sri Lanka for example), but many of their teachers are not qualified to teach the subjects they teach, nor at the levels at which they teach them. Normal colleges and university departments of education have long been centrally concerned with the pre-service preparation of teachers. As numbers of untrained and unqualified teachers have been recruited to meet expanding requirements, the institutions have found themselves increasingly involved in qualifying serving teachers. But training needs have been too great to be met by these institutions, and other approaches have had to be found.

Some evidence suggests that in-service training of unqualified teachers has been inadequate because (i) programmes are poorly designed, and their contents are lacking in relevance to the courses the teachers are expected to teach; (ii) they are overly theoretical and inapplicable to the workaday needs of the teacher; (iii) the tutors who dispense them are not themselves familiar with pedagogical innovation; (iv) their schedules are irregular and fail to consolidate learners' knowledge or upgrade their skills and competence appreciably; (v) they impose too heavy a workload on already hard-working teachers, who are thus discouraged to take on the courses; (vi) they benefit too few teachers and do not reach beyond the tip of the iceberg of untrained teachers in the profession; and (vii) they do not materially affect performance because the poor conditions under which the teachers are labouring in the classrooms -- inadequate facilities, lack of teaching materials, and absence of pedagogical support -- persist.

b. The outlook

Expected growth in enrolment at the primary and secondary levels will generate demand for the training of new teachers. Existing teacher training structures and higher institutions will be more than adequate to cope with the demand in some countries, but most will need to expand, and to phase out or redeploy the institutions that are ineffective. University training may be preferable because students generally support the opportunity costs of their studies, i.e. university fees and/or income foregone of students' time. Data are not available as to the cost-effectiveness of the various alternatives: where to train, how long to train, and what to study are questions to be answered on a case-by-case basis in function with costs, cultural and social factors, and relevance to the society's needs.

(i) What to study

But there is broad consensus that primary teachers should master the information and skills generally accepted as basic in the country, and have the ability to teach under varying conditions. When the basics are established, they need not be necessarily acquired through formal certification, as uncertified people may very well master the basics and be qualified. Some flexibility in the criteria and methods of recruitment is advisable. While experience and training in pedagogy obviously contribute, ability to teach is not a quantitatively measurable skill, and certification may be less relevant to the coming demands upon a teacher than acquired information and the innate ability to transmit it.

The academic-versus-vocational choice which is posed at the post-primary turning point must be addressed. Once the academic education deemed necessary has been acquired, emphasis should be placed on vocational training; one must not fall into the trap of believing that achievement in academic disciplines automatically means the ability to teach well. Industrialised as well as developing countries have often suffered from making this assumption. Vocational (i.e., pedagogical) training is essential to teachers at all levels, in all styles and vehicles of instruction.

Teachers must start with self-knowledge, and a desire to innovate and improve their teaching methods. Added to this, the best possible imagination of the process from the student's point of view, knowledge of the psychology of motivation, and acquaintance with working methods through which information is transferred. Third, the talent for good human relations that promotes the transmission of information and enthusiasm for it. Fourth, training in planning instruction, analysing content, preparation of teaching material. Fifth, alert and sensitive communication, followed up with monitoring of the learning process and evaluation of the result. And lastly, sensitivity to the relationships between the educational function and its environment.[6]

(ii) Where to train

The issue of pre-service and in-service training must also be addressed. To be effective, in-service training programmes should be designed to fit the pre-service level of the teacher's training. Yet, like other professionals, teachers need continued in-service training to keep up to date and perform properly. The programme which would produce the 'profile' of a structured and organised set of skills should theoretically include the following:

- relevance to learning objectives;
- comparison of an initial and a completed profile, and coherently planned steps leading from one to the other;
- financial feasibility;
- interfacing between pre-service and in-service training.

On occasions when it is necessary to recruit teachers whose pre-service training has not been adequate, the target profile, established after due consideration of the financial resources available, might serve to define in-service training needs. In-service training might be provided through 'modules', each consolidating already acquired knowledge with the new skills and aptitudes offered, and associated with a certificate of completion. Incentives, both financial and moral, would have an important place in the scheme.

The heterogeneity of teaching forces cannot be eliminated overnight. New recruitment of unqualified or underqualified teachers may be made necessary by straitened circumstances, and requirements for recruitment will be lowered; the persistence of serving teachers who are un- or underqualified will tend to keep them low; requirements due to increasing uniformity in the pattern of preparation of teachers will tend to raise requirements, and in-service training must be fitted to all levels. Financial, educational and organisational resources must assure the consideration of a wide variety of factors:[7]

- educational aims of the curricula and examination requirements;
- flexibility and rigidity in the demands on teachers;
- degree of knowledge of curricula on the part of serving teachers;
- teaching conditions -- textbooks, materials, pedagogical support;
- legal and traditional teacher-pupil relationships;
- school calendars;
- roles of school heads;
- school/community relationships.

(iii) How to train

Assessments must be made of each training institution's adequacy in the way of staff and facilities. Key personnel such as school supervisors and headmasters may be assets or liabilities, but they cannot be ignored. Unconventional arrangements such as distance teacher upgrading in Kenya, multi-media delivery systems in Zambia, 'cascade' training in Malaysia (see *Inset 5*), mobile teacher training in Bangladesh or in Lesotho (see *Inset 6*), master teacher programmes in Papua New Guinea, teachers' centres in India (Calcutta), and workshops in Guatemala might be deemed appropriate after careful review of local conditions, needs, and targets.[8]

Programmes should be targeted toward priority groups, and policy set to determine where to start. It is often suggested that priority go to the least trained and qualified group among the serving teachers, but 'cascade' training starts with the better trained so that they, in turn, can disseminate their knowledge and skills among their less qualified colleagues.

Inset 5
'Cascade' training in Malaysia

In Malaysia's programme of 'cascade' training, messages flow from experts and specialists through several layers of personnel to teachers. Small groups of specialists are brought together to train larger numbers of middle-level personnel, such as college lecturers and school supervisors, who in turn train teachers at local levels. An important feature of this technique, which has been used to improve teaching methods and curricula in Malaysia, is the provision of follow-up to training at the school level, through which teachers receive support and assistance in solving practical problems.

Inset 6
Mobile teacher training in Lesotho

Two arguments favour the use to which the government of
Lesotho has adapted a mobile teacher training strategy. The cost of a
few trainers moving from place to place, rather than movements of
large numbers of teachers to distant facilities, is relatively low; and if
well done, it can help teachers to gear training to their own contexts
and problems. On the practical level, of course, very few countries
can form entire frameworks of mobile trainees with particular skills
and transport them throughout their areas; Lesotho is a fortunate
exception and has successfully created an In-service Education for
Teachers programme (LIET), encompassing a correspondence-with-
contact method of training unqualified teachers.

Induction, in the sense of planned and systematic support to new
teachers in a school, is widely acknowledged to be an important type
of in-service provision. It can help to consolidate and make up for
deficiencies in initial training, help new teachers to overcome
unfamiliar teaching and classroom management problems, and reduce
feelings of isolation and frustration. Done well, it can make a
substantial contribution to reducing teacher wastage. But there are
practical problems in organising and financing induction training,
such as the need for co-ordination between training, recruitment and
deployment. Resources must be concentrated on training institutions,
since induction is labour-intensive and time-consuming. And legal
problems may arise if trainers are not then recruited.

(iv) How to increase supply

Salary systems which make the teaching profession unattractive
will very probably continue to aggravate deficits of teachers in some
subjects, such as science, mathematics, English, French. Only a
package of complementary actions that addresses the issue of
shortages from different angles could possibly make a significant
dent in this problem: actions should seek to increase supply of
specialists, improve the use of specialists, and make teaching more
attractive.

• An increase might be achieved in the teacher 'supply' by increasing the number of graduates from higher institutions in relevant subjects, through appropriate incentives such as fellowships, and early, but conditional, recruitment of teachers by offering financial or moral incentives such as affiliation in prestigious professional associations to specialists, cadres, and other non-teachers who agree to fill part-time teaching posts or to take on one-time teaching assignments, particularly at the tertiary level. It can be most rewarding to high-level specialists to work part-time at a university.

• Improvements in the use of specialists could be brought about by introducing changes in the organisation and use of staff, by using assistant heads of departments (when the size of the school makes it feasible) to relieve specialist teachers from administrative tasks, thus encouraging them to devote their time to teaching subjects that are in heavy demand.

• When shortages are acute and severe, early recruitment could help; in such cases it might be advisable to offer contracts on the basis of a minimum number of years of civil service. Within limits, the longer the duration of pre-service training, the less costly the recruitment for the education budget, because the opportunity costs of teachers' in-service training time accrue to the public budget, and those of pre-service accrue to the individual in training. Yet most countries try to shorten pre-service training in the face of financial crises, and end by providing in-service training, which may be unsuitable because inadequately funded, or much more expensive than normal pre-service training would have been.

For countries that can afford it, 'sandwich' training, combining training sessions in educational institutions with on-the-job training is a very attractive formula. For a three-year sequence, for example, the first year would consist of training in an institute, the second an internship in a classroom under the supervision of a 'master teacher,' the third in the institute. Effective application of this formula (see the experience of Zimbabwe - *Inset 7*) requires:

    • monitoring of the progress of each trainee, and formative evaluation of both general education and specific training;

    • selection of master teachers and their institutions, and particularly the seeking out of co-operative heads of schools;

Inset 7
Zimbabwe Integrated
National Teacher Education Course (ZINTEC)

The ZINTEC is a multi-media initial teacher training programme for primary teachers. Its objective is to be professionally equivalent to the conventional training course, and efficient in its use of scarce educated manpower. Devised to confront the teacher shortage, especially acute in rural areas, and to increase the number of trained teachers to meet the needs of school expansion, the four-year course combines face-to-face contact and distance teaching.

The curriculum is similar to that of the conventional training course. Phase 1 is a four-month college-based residential programme which provides basic training in classroom skills. Students are graded at the end of the term. Phase 2 is school-based. Trainees are placed in rural areas and given full teaching responsibilities, and are assigned four correspondence modules and two written projects during each of ten terms. They attend seminars every other Saturday, and two-week vacation courses at the end of every other term. Field staff, education officers and school principals offer school tutorials and lesson supervision, and there are weekly radio broadcasts to supplement correspondence materials. During the last two terms of Phase 2, trainees are examined in teaching practices. Phase 3 is a consolidation phase -- a college-based residential course -- followed by a final written examination which leads to certification by the University of Zimbabwe.

ZINTEC can accommodate classes of about 2,400 per year, divided into three promotions of trainees accepted at four-monthly intervals. Trainees receive a salary which rises by the end of the course to the starting salary of a qualified but uncertified teacher. They are bonded for three years after qualifying. The drop-out rate is negligible, and it is reported that the programme is so attractive as to draw trainees away from the conventional three-year course. Mobility between the staffs of ZINTEC colleges and conventional colleges has resulted in cross-fertilisation, and over a period of four years (by 1985), 8,000 teachers graduated from the programme and were posted in rural areas. At present, a secondary teacher training programme, which builds on the experience of ZINTEC, has been initiated.

- compensation agreements -- financial, in kind, etc. -- with master teachers and profiles of their relationships with the trainees and training institutions;
- stable financial provisions, -- this may be difficult given the distinction between recruitment and training and the risk of drop-out of newly trained teachers before appointment.

3. Administrative and pedagogical supports

Two important aspects of teacher development policy relate to the everyday conditions under which teachers operate: administrative and professional support. Needless to say how important it is to the morale of a teacher to work under decent conditions and to have proper materials and equipment. Highly motivated teachers are often discouraged because they do not have the wherewithal to do a proper job of teaching. Authorities can recognise these problems by developing the financial responsibility of principals and enabling them to purchase items (both didactic and administrative) needed in the operation of the school.

The two main challenges here are, first, to create flexibility in procedures for supply and distribution of services, materials and equipment so that local initiative can fill gaps when routine procedures break down; rigorous mechanisms of accountability must be evolved; second, to create effective channels of communication between administration and teachers. Lengthy bureaucratic procedures that deliver late, or not at all, disillusion even the most energetic teachers.

a. Principals and heads of departments

Evidence is accumulating to indicate that the first line of professional support of a teacher is the school principal. Of course, a lot depends on the size of the school: a one-teacher primary school is not organised along the same lines as a multiple-stream secondary school. But it cannot be over-emphasised that special in-service school-based training of principals in teacher support would be highly cost effective.

The profile of a typical primary school principal is that of a man or a woman two to five years older than the typical teacher, with a few years of classroom experience and about the same socio-economic background as the teacher. In expanding systems, he/she may have less education and more experience. Rising to this level is at the individual's own expense, and typically involves determination, ambition, and perhaps aptitudes above the average; but some of the authoritarianism of the system has rubbed off on the principal by the time he/she arrives at this position, and principals are inclined to look for guidance from upper levels. Their fragmented general education is likely to form a block against the mainstream of modern thought in education, and to make them somewhat ill at ease in initiating changes that can easily go beyond their knowledge of educational thinking and practice.

Secondary school principals and heads of departments generally differ more widely from 'average' secondary teachers; but, except in the case of very small schools, they tend to spend a good deal of their time in managerial tasks for which many of them are not trained, and some in supervisory duties for which they do not always have the technical backdrop to carry them out effectively. School principals need not conduct the training themselves, but they should develop it as part of an overall staff development strategy.

These ideas may appear sound enough, but they are workable only in an environment of real responsibility, in which adequate resources devolve to principals, and in which they enjoy real managerial autonomy. Otherwise no amount of in-service training will produce much in the way of results.

Especially at the secondary level, and in large primary schools, in-service training of school principals and headmasters and headmistresses is perhaps more important than ever before. The responsibilities of schools towards their pupils and the communities are greater and more complex than ever before. In countries where management is in the process of decentralisation, principals are required to learn new skills. The ideology of professionalism enables the principal to take the lead in school-based curriculum activity and the professional development of teachers. The same philosophy places greater reliance on principals' performance reports on which promotions are decided, and on the need for training in evaluation techniques. It has been shown[9] that training is provided for those principals who already hold posts rather than for those being prepared for them. Programmes range from one-day sessions on limited subjects, such as the management of filing systems, to one-year agendas on training teachers in classroom management.

b. Inspectors and supervisors

While situations vary widely among developing countries, it would appear that rural teachers receive virtually no pedagogical and administrative support, and urban teachers sometimes very little. At the primary level there is often wide discrepancy between what is expected from a school inspector and what is delivered. Funds for transportation, motivation and incentives are often lacking, both for serving the schools and for serving the ministry, and consequently district inspectors often devote most of their day to routine administrative duties such as collecting statistics, inspecting buildings, accompanying visitors, and attending official events. Rarely do they visit the schools, even those which are not difficult to reach; rarely do they see teachers at work, make suggestions, or offer advice.

The plight of the secondary school supervisor is in some ways more difficult. The supervisors live in a provincial capital, but they work at a much greater distance from their schools and have to rely on slow and unreliable public transport. There are far too few of them. It would be a good idea in most cases to try several ways of financing additional supervisors: offering a basic salary, making allowances based on measurable criteria such as number of schools visited or time passed in dispensing services (problems of management and control might be dealt with on a case-by-case basis). Since most supervisors lack training, and in some countries know very little about what their assignment entails, a profile might again serve to clear up misconceptions:

• A well-designed programme of training should be based on the principle of gradual improvement in performance of administrative tasks; it might start simply with field seminars, where groups of inspectors establish common administrative job descriptions and discuss methods of applying the principles;

• One supervisor has to perform advisory, inspectorial, and evaluative functions, and must be trained for all of them. Some, of course, would argue rightly that these functions should be separated. But, in actual fact, scarcity of resources and the prevailing conditions 'in the field' in most developing countries suggest that even to get all schools and teachers properly staffed with inspectors is a challenge for education authorities. *Table 7.2*[10] indicates what might be offered in a training course for school inspectors with 'multiple functions'.

Table 7.2. The education of an educational inspector.

I.   A review of the regulatory system

II. Versatility
     • in-depth exploration of subjects for assisting teachers
     • identification of subjects and the most appropriate methods for each

III. Psychology and sociology
     • understanding children and their living and working environments
     • student teachers and their problems
     • the objectives specific to primary teachers
     • the social, economic, and political context of the school

IV. The history of the school

V.   Observation of the individual environment, after the above detailed investigation of the context
     • the working environment or organisation of a given school or class
     • behaviour and methods

VI. How to evaluate the work of a teacher or a trainee
     • evaluation of an exercise
     • training in communication
     • conducting meetings
     • conducting personal interviews

VII. Regulating the educational system or training programme

VIII. Developing awareness : inter-personal relationships and teamwork

IX. Training for research, experimentation and action

X.   Demarcation of responsibility: finding one's own place in the responsibility flowchart.

---

c. Planning, management, and research

The goal of improving the competence, professionalism, and effectiveness of educational personnel seems to transcend all the boundaries of specific national priorities and problems; striving towards it, too, appears to take the same form in the various diverse contexts. Countries must formulate long-term, sustained policies and programmes; they must organise management and co-ordination; and they must carry out research on priority needs within the teaching service.

These issues cannot be addressed piecemeal. Plans and policies which recognise the inter-relations among the components of productive change -- such as, for example, the need for change in the recruitment of teachers -- must be devised in function with the resource implications in materials, in-service training, revision and innovation in examinations, salary increase, etc. Cost implications of medium- and long-term strategies must be closely examined, and policies formulated that:

- take into consideration institutional options for pre-service and in-service teacher training;
- leave room for changes in duration of academic versus vocational education;
- define profiles and project the improvement to be realised;
- consider staffing conditions and deployment of teachers;
- remain open to innovative means of financing teaching services, through the central government, the local communities, public and private interest groups, etc.;
- provide incentives to make teaching a more attractive profession.

The complexity of factors at play, and the crucial importance of the time factor make it necessary to accompany policy development with action plans which spell out clearly what is to be done, how it is to be done, when it should be done and by whom. Many of the failings in developing countries' teaching services can be traced to inadequate management machinery. Unless long-term strategies for education recognise the human resource component of this labour-intensive activity, it is unlikely that the critical qualities of commitment, morale, and resourcefulness will be developed. The long-term aim must be to develop the capacity to train and support teachers, professionally and administratively, throughout their careers. Strategies that recognise all aspects of the well-being of teachers, which manifest an understanding of the value of a well-managed teacher service commission, of interlinked research units, professional associations, and central ministry machinery, are the strategies most likely to succeed.

Unless a country can avail itself of a certain minimum in the way of research capacity, its planning and management are not likely to operate effectively. A number of areas merit priority; we shall name but a few:

- The effects of teacher support and supervision;
- The cost-effectiveness of various methods of staff recruitment;
- The feasibility of various in-service training delivery services;
- Evaluation of innovative experiences in mobilising the resources of families and communities, and their effectiveness in stabilising teaching forces;
- Teacher wastage and absenteeism.

Developing strong research capacities should be among the top priorities of developing countries' education ministries, and the scope, degree of sophistication and mode of organisation of each should be carefully established according to the specific conditions of each. Policy-makers should examine ways in which university personnel, educationists, and specialists in related fields might be encouraged to collaborate with schools, to their mutual, and their considerable, benefit.

4. Summary: priorities for planning teacher supply and demand

Three priority areas should be considered by planners and practitioners:

(i) Finance

There is a need for improving the salary and income conditions of the teachers and making the teaching profession more attractive. Even if economic conditions are appropriate, there must be policy options in the budget to cover the increases and regulate mechanisms for revision of teachers' salaries to avoid the risk of bureaucratising the teaching profession. When economic conditions are not appropriate, there should be a balanced approach which reconciles the need for salary increase with recruitment, treats the teachers' salary issues in the light of overall changes in the public sector and improves administration of the salary budget. The role of incentives should not be overlooked: there may be room for introducing more flexibility in the salary scales in some societies; there may also be room for making rural areas more attractive, in particular by achieving better integration of teachers in the communities they serve.

(ii) Training

The necessity for recruiting untrained teachers is and will continue to be a problem for many countries; therefore, the demand for training has to be addressed. Teacher training today can no longer be limited to a two- or three-year course of study prior to entering the profession. Consequently, there is a need for establishing training strategies to meet educational objectives and society's needs. Where to train, how long to train and what to study are questions to be answered on a case-by-case basis; this requires (i) assessments of the cost-effectiveness of various approaches to training; (ii) design of training programmes that will produce the 'profile' of a structured and organised set of needed skills, and, perhaps, (iii) the adoption of unconventional arrangements to deliver training.

(iii) Administrative and pedagogical supports

The improvement of everyday conditions under which teachers operate is crucial to the morale and motivation of teachers. The role of supervisors and inspectors should not be minimised. Two sets of actions could be undertaken: (i) the creation of flexibility in procedures for supply and distribution of services; and (ii) the creation of effective channels of communication between administration and teachers.

Here, as in other areas, practitioners should accompany policy development with action plans, with programmes, for organising management and co-ordination, and with projects to develop institutional capacities to address research priority needs within the teaching service.

1. C. Tibi, *Les salaires et les enseignants,* Paris, Unesco:IIEP, 1989, (IIEP/PRG.CT/89.97), Mimeo. See also Edward A. Cox, *Teacher compensation in less developed countries,* Washington, D.C., World Bank, 1987, (Paper prepared for the conference on cost and effectiveness of teachers, 20 April-1 May 1987).

2. J. Samoff; M. Wuyts; B. Morhander; K. Flodman, *Swedish public administration assistance in Tanzania,* Stockholm, Swedish International Development Authority, 1988, (Education Division Documents No. 43).

3. J.F. Sabouret, "La 'revalo' à la japonaise", In: *Le Monde,,* 20 April 1989.

4. J.B. Gunerio; R.M. Ibañez, *The education of primary and secondary school teachers: an international comparative study,* Paris, Unesco, 1981.

5. L.A. Dove, *Teachers and teacher education in developing countries: issues in planning, management and training,* London, Croom Helm, 1986.

6. See M.L. Goldschmid, 'The training of teachers in higher education: sample curriculum', In: *Senior educational personnel: new functions and training, Vol. II,* Paris, Unesco, 1987, (Educational studies and documents No. 55).

7. N. Chiappano, *Politique et stratégie de formation des enseignants dans les pays en développement,* Paris, Unesco:IIEP, 1989, Mimeo.

8. L.A. Dove, 1986, op. cit.

9. J. Greenland (ed.), *In-service training of primary teachers in Africa,* London, MacMillan, 1983.

10. See R. Mélet, 'Establishment of a national training centre', In: *Senior educational personnel: new functions and training, Vol. II,* Paris, Unesco, 1987, (Educational studies and documents No. 55).

Chapter 8

Delivery systems: priorities for selecting educational technologies

In 1982, at its Twelfth World Conference, the International Council for Correspondence Education changed its name to the International Council for Distance Education. DE is a new concept which has emerged as an outgrowth of education by correspondence as a consequence of the development of electronic communications.

Governments have rarely been much concerned with education by correspondence, which was generally in the hands of private (non-profit or commercial) organisations whose students were required by exceptional circumstances to study specific courses by mail. In the 1920s, countries with scattered populations and isolated communities, such as Australia, Canada and New Zealand, developed programmes as second-best solutions for families that even the rural schools could not reach. They were set up on classroom models, and classroom teachers, often already overburdened, were assigned the correction of the lessons. Parents of the students often had little or no formal education, but they were enlisted -- especially the mothers -- as home tutors, receiving and dispatching the materials, supervising the pupils and seeing that they worked regularly. In the 1930s, because of shortages of university professors, correspondence education was developed in the USSR, and there are still around 1,200 institutions serving 1.5 million students -- about 30 per cent of the total number in the higher levels.[1] Public correspondence education was developed in France during the Second World War to provide primary and secondary schooling for refugees. Ad hoc extramural and extension courses have been provided for minorities

180

of working students throughout the western countries. But overall, correspondence education has been viewed as much inferior to classroom instruction, and has had only a marginal impact on the provision of education.

1. Which media?

For decades, radio broadcasting has been a well-established and essential educational tool the world over, often for non-formal or rural audiences. *Figure 8.1* indicates the weight of educational radio and television broadcasting in the total broadcasting hours of over 50 countries. It can be seen that developing countries devote a good deal of broadcasting time to education: 1,000-2,000 hours per year, or 3 to 6 hours per day. In the developed countries, with the exception of Japan, Turkey, and the Eastern European countries, much less time goes to education.

But without follow-up, learning through educational programmes is not very effective, and links between broadcasting organisations and educational authorities remain for the most part sporadic.

In the 1960s, under pressure for both quantitative and qualitative improvement, educational decision-makers and planners began to show interest in using the media. Government-sponsored organisations in both developed and developing countries took initiatives in areas formerly dominated by the private sector. In 1967, for example, Unesco and its International Institute for Educational Planning published *The new media: a memo for educational planners,* together with three volumes of case studies under the title *New educational media in action: case studies for planners.* In the intervening 20 years, a good deal of awareness of and experience in DE, and an appreciation of its potential, have been acquired.

Distance education recognises the fact that rigid requirements in place and time are not essential to the learning process, provided communication links can be established between teacher and learner. As long as a communication network is accessible, an entirely rational, objective approach to teaching, including an efficient division of labour -- course design, production of materials, tutoring, and assessment -- is possible. DE institutions sometimes contain warehouses, printing presses, even broadcasting studios, in the place

Figure 8.1(a)   Educational radio and television as percentage of total broadcasting hours, 1983-1985, Africa

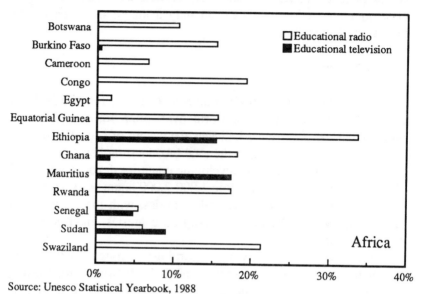

Source: Unesco Statistical Yearbook, 1988

Figure 8.1(b)   Educational radio and television as percentage of total broadcasting hours, 1983-1985, Americas

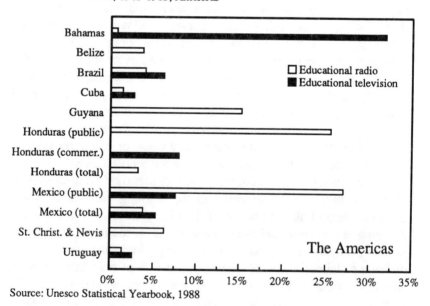

Source: Unesco Statistical Yearbook, 1988

Figure 8.1(c)   Educational radio and television as percentage of total broadcasting hours, 1983-1985, Asia

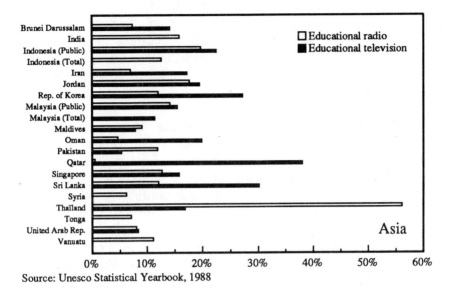

Source: Unesco Statistical Yearbook, 1988

Figure 8.1(d)   Educational radio and television as percentage of total broadcasting hours, 1983-1985, Developed countries

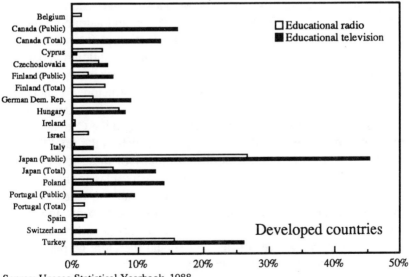

Source: Unesco Statistical Yearbook, 1988

of lecture halls, laboratories, and dormitories; Keegan[2] lists the primary characteristics of DE as:

- separated rather than face-to-face learning;
- independent study rather than institution-influence;
- the use of technical media for communication;
- two-way communications channels for interaction;
- occasional rather than set meetings, for purposes of both education and socialisation;
- industrialised form.

The phenomenon is no longer marginal. It is a modern and effective mode of delivery, which readily solves certain real and ubiquitous problems, but as the problems are local and individual, it is difficult to trace the development of DE precisely. Initiatives cover vast ranges of national and local institutions, private and public, at all levels and in all types of instruction. In 1984, the International Centre for Distance Learning (ICDL), created under the auspices of the United Nations University, conducted a questionnaire survey of 1,070 institutions in 88 countries. Of these, 304 responded.[3] Their present (1989) data bank includes up-to-date records on more than 800 programmes in around 500 institutions, a few of which pertain to Eastern European countries.[4] *Figure 8.2* shows the percentages for the various levels. Only 7 per cent of the programmes are primary; two-thirds are post-secondary and adult. These programmes require a good deal of motivation and autonomy on the part of the students, and the physical deprivation of interaction of a pupil with teacher and peers presents problems for children under 15. Australian correspondence schemes provide for teacher substitutes. In other cases, DE is integrated with classroom structures, conducted through interactive radio, as in Papua New Guinea for example (see *Inset 8*), dispensed via educational television (as in the Côte d'Ivoire) or organised in non-formal reception groups, such as the rural forums and radio schools in Latin America. In many of these schemes the DE component is temporary. After some years, classroom teachers master the content of the programmes and are able to teach on their own without these appendages, which are no longer useful. In-school broadcasting, for example, is considered a success when it is no longer necessary. Devices of this sort should therefore be planned to adapt to other needs when the time comes.

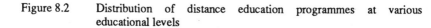

Figure 8.2   Distribution of distance education programmes at various educational levels

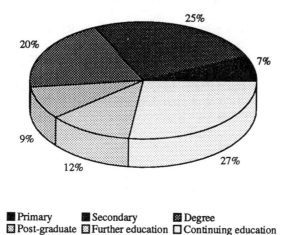

■ Primary   ■ Secondary   ▨ Degree
▨ Post-graduate ▨ Further education ☐ Continuing education

Source: Based on data from ICDL data bank, In: A. Kaye, *Distance education: the case of the art,* 'Prospects', Vol. XVIII, No. 1, Unesco, 1988.

Distance education has not been a successful tool in combating illiteracy, very possibly because of the degree of autonomy required of the student. An important problem in illiteracy lies in the fact that a person who has not learned how to read cannot benefit from distance education. Unit and opportunity costs of higher and adult education are high in traditional settings, and more economical alternatives are attractive.

About 40 per cent of the institutions reviewed in the ICDL survey were intentionally set up to provide DE; of the 'dedicated' institutions, the Open University in the United Kingdom is an example. A further 35 per cent were dual-mode institutions -- conventional structures containing a DE or extension component, for example Australian universities such as Deakin. And 25 per cent were conventional, having DE programmes but no specific administrative structures for them. The average enrolments of dedicated institutions were estimated at 12,500, and about two million in all types together. A recent country-by-country survey calculates a total of four million students in the tertiary level, "of which three million are in four countries: China, the Republic of Korea, Thailand, and the USSR."[5]

```
┌─────────────────────────────────────────────────────┐
│                      Inset 8                          │
│          The Radio Science Project, Papua New Guinea  │
│                                                       │
│     The Radio Science Project addresses two of the most important │
│  educational issues in Papua New Guinea today: quality and        │
│  efficiency. At a time when the standards of educational are perceived │
│  to be declining, the project aims to develop a method for providing │
│  systematic, high quality instruction in primary science - a subject for │
│  which many teachers consider themselves inadequately prepared.   │
│  Another aim of the project is to maximise the cost-effectiveness of │
│  distance education in Papua New Guinea - a critical goal because of │
│  severe budget cuts and rising enrolment rates.                   │
│     The radio programmes are based on the official community (rural) │
│  school curriculum in science, plus aspects of health, agriculture and │
│  community life. The lessons teach the core science curriculum; they │
│  are not designed as supplementary material. The radio science lessons │
│  for grade 4 were broadcast in 1988, grade 5 in 1989, and grade 6 will │
│  be broadcast in 1990. Each week, for thirty weeks, children have two │
│  lessons of 30 minutes duration. Each lesson consists of a 20-minute │
│  radio broadcast and a 10-minute post-broadcast period. During the │
│  broadcast, the classroom teacher participates in a supportive role. │
│  After the radio portion of the lesson, the teacher conducts specific │
│  complementary post-broadcast activities, as outlined in a teacher's │
│  guide. Both the broadcast and post-broadcast portions of the lesson │
│  are supported by worksheets and science materials.               │
│     The radio science lessons are based on the concept of interactive │
│  radio instruction that calls for maximum student participation during │
│  the broadcasts. The lessons are presented in a lively and engaging │
│  fashion that hold the children's attention and stimulate them to │
│  participate in the lessons. The scripts for the lessons are written │
│  specifically for the children using Papua New Guinean writers, actors, │
│  sound effects and examples; however, adaptation of these lessons for │
│  use in other countries should not be difficult.                  │
│                                                       │
│  *Source:* USAID. Education Development Center, Newton, Ma., (USA). │
└─────────────────────────────────────────────────────┘
```

This figure represents about 7 per cent of the total world tertiary enrolment. Some of the national dedicated institutions are large, especially in the Asian region. Unesco[6] reports the enrolments of five major Asian DE institutions, four of which are tertiary, as percentages of total national tertiary enrolments, as follows:

- China Central Radio and Television University (640,000): 44.3 per cent of the total;
- Sukhothai Thammathirat Open University of Thailand[7] (152,000): 13.6 per cent;
- Universitas Terbuka of Indonesia (69,000): 7 per cent;
- Indira Gandhi Open University of India (37,000) 0.7 per cent, two years after its foundation. (Note that Andhra Pradesh Open University in Hyderabad has an enrolment of 40,000 and that by 1982 Madras University had about 450,000 students enrolled in correspondence courses).

Other sources report enrolments of 150,000 at the Korean Air and Correspondence University;[8] 65,000 at the Allama Iqbal Open University in Pakistan,[9] and 32,000 at the Universidad Nacional Abierta in Venezuela.[10] The largest primary level experiment, the Instructional Television Programme in the Côte d'Ivoire, reached 15,635 primary classes, 652,000 pupils, and 84 per cent of the primary enrolment in 1979-80, two years before it closed. Of the non-formal projects, the Satellite Instructional Television Experiment in India reached 2,330 villages in 1975.

These large-scale applications of DE methods enjoy a good deal of visibility, but the other side of the coin is that only 35 per cent of the dedicated institutions have had more than 10,000 students, and 25 per cent had less than 1,000; also, 1 per cent of conventional institutions with distance services had 10,000 students or more, while 60 per cent had less than 1,000. There is a divergence in the development of DE, one element of which has set up large-scale national institutions of the open university type, the other local and community institutions using local area networks and operating outside the educational systems. In industrialised countries, the latter model is represented by the radio schools for adults such as Acción Cultural y Popular in Colombia and Radio Santa María in the Dominican Republic (see *Inset 9*), both church owned. In developed countries this approach is used to provide highly specialised training to limited and specific populations, (or upon request) large firms, branches of the civil service, the armed forces, etc.

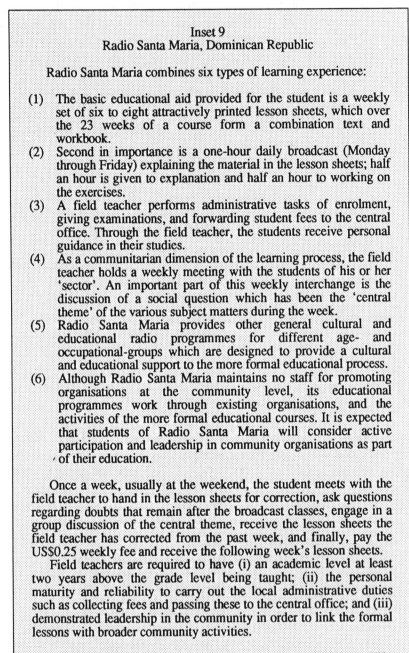

Inset 9
Radio Santa Maria, Dominican Republic

Radio Santa Maria combines six types of learning experience:

(1) The basic educational aid provided for the student is a weekly set of six to eight attractively printed lesson sheets, which over the 23 weeks of a course form a combination text and workbook.

(2) Second in importance is a one-hour daily broadcast (Monday through Friday) explaining the material in the lesson sheets; half an hour is given to explanation and half an hour to working on the exercises.

(3) A field teacher performs administrative tasks of enrolment, giving examinations, and forwarding student fees to the central office. Through the field teacher, the students receive personal guidance in their studies.

(4) As a communitarian dimension of the learning process, the field teacher holds a weekly meeting with the students of his or her 'sector'. An important part of this weekly interchange is the discussion of a social question which has been the 'central theme' of the various subject matters during the week.

(5) Radio Santa Maria provides other general cultural and educational radio programmes for different age- and occupational-groups which are designed to provide a cultural and educational support to the more formal educational process.

(6) Although Radio Santa Maria maintains no staff for promoting organisations at the community level, its educational programmes work through existing organisations, and the activities of the more formal educational courses. It is expected that students of Radio Santa Maria will consider active participation and leadership in community organisations as part of their education.

Once a week, usually at the weekend, the student meets with the field teacher to hand in the lesson sheets for correction, ask questions regarding doubts that remain after the broadcast classes, engage in a group discussion of the central theme, receive the lesson sheets the field teacher has corrected from the past week, and finally, pay the US$0.25 weekly fee and receive the following week's lesson sheets.

Field teachers are required to have (i) an academic level at least two years above the grade level being taught; (ii) the personal maturity and reliability to carry out the local administrative duties such as collecting fees and passing these to the central office; and (iii) demonstrated leadership in the community in order to link the formal lessons with broader community activities.

Source: H. Perraton, *Secondary education at distance*, Cambridge (UK), International Extension College, 1983.

The future needs of continuing education at the post- graduate level will probably stimulate the further development of diversified and specialised services, and 'narrowcasting' will supplement broadcasting for these purposes.

It is not within the scope of this book to provide guidance for the establishment of a DE service, but two highly specific and unprecedented aspects of course development and media selection have bearing on the efficacy and costs of such a system. A good deal of effort is devoted to the development of quality course materials for DE as opposed to extension, which is primarily constituted of mimeo reproduction of lectures. DE course materials are designed and developed to enhance and facilitate learning, to stimulate thinking, and also to foresee and sidestep difficulties that the learner may encounter. Courses themselves should be developed according to knowledge of student achievement, and this sort of development can take upwards of two years. *Table 8.1* estimates the time it will take to prepare the various components of a learning package;[11] the time involved must be considered as a capital investment that is to be amortised. Great savings in human and material resources can result from the adoption of a modular system, and inter-institutional co-operation should be actively encouraged. *Inset 10* may contribute one or two appropriate suggestions. The increasingly strong regional DE associations, especially at the tertiary level, should provide frequent bases for this type of co-operation.

Table 8.1 Academic input time for various educational methods

Teaching method	Input time[1]
Lecturing	2-10
Tutoring	1-10
The following also need support staff:	
Audiovisual	10-20
Teaching text	5-100
Broadcast television	over 100
Computer-aided learning	over 150
Interactive video	over 200

[1] Typical ratio of man-hours per student hour of work generated
Source: R. Smith, "Growth and scope of distance learning", In: *Distance education,* Vol. 1, Asian Development Bank, 1987.

Inset 10
Regional collaboration in course development

There have been at least three such programmes, all of them small-scale, for highly specialised groups, and concerned with professional personnel development. In West Africa in the early 1970s, modern mathematics of an agreed form was being introduced in a few English-speaking countries, Liberia, Ghana, Nigeria and Sierra Leone, in co-operation with the West African Examinations Council. There was an immediate need to train teachers in modern mathematics instruction, but the tutors at the teacher training colleges were themselves still uninitiated.

A correspondence programme was therefore developed at Cape Coast University in Ghana and taught to all mathematics tutors in teacher training colleges in the four countries, and linked to travelling super-tutors and national seminars.

A second programme, which is still running, is the African Curriculum Programme run from Kenyatta University for the East and Central African region. In this programme, senior curriculum development officers from all countries undergo an advanced postgraduate course, partly by correspondence and partly through residential seminars.

A third project is being prepared and is soon due to be launched. This is a joint Youth Programme, for Central Africa, to take place in Lusaka for Botswana, Zambia and Kenya. It will also be run by correspondence courses linked to national seminars.

Source: Commonwealth Secretariat, *Commonwealth co-operation in open learning: summary report,* London, Commonwealth Secretariat, 1988.

The most frequently used medium in education is the printed page. *Table 8.2* suggests uses of media in DE programmes based on information from the ICDL data bank, which observes that many of the programmes combine printed material with other media, and claim to be multi-media programmes; a few rely on print alone. Audio-cassettes are used more often than radio broadcasts; television is still a prestige medium, serving as a flagship and generating public recognition. Most of a DE package is printed; standard textbooks may be supplemented with study guides, coursebooks, booklets or worksheets developed by the institution. Materials are distributed through the postal services, and time must be planned for distribution, especially where these services are less than reliable. Sometimes study materials appear in the local press (see *Inset 11*).

Table 8.2 The use of media in distance education programmes

Type of institutions[1] (Number of programmes)	Number of distance education programmes using:						
	Print only	Print + other	Radio + other	TV + other	Audio + other	Video + other	Kits
Type A (317)	20	297	80	60	113	64	63
Type B (291)	26	265	41	35	143	59	47
Type C (231)	30	201	26	31	110	56	41
Overall percentage (n = 839)	9	91	18	15	44	21	18

[1] Type A: Institutions set up to teach at a distance
   Type B: Conventional institutions with distance-teaching departments
   Type C: Conventional institutions with some distance-teaching programmes, but without a special distance-teaching department
Source: Based on data from ICDL data bank, In: A. Kaye, "Distance education: the state of the art", *Prospects,* Vol. XVIII, No. 1, 1988.

The above-mentioned Unesco survey in Asia[12] compares the importance of the various media in DE programmes. At Universitas Terbuka in Indonesia, printed materials represent 96 per cent of the total material that a student receives; this is supplemented by material on audio-cassettes (2 per cent), television (0.5 per cent), radio (0.5 per cent), face-to-face tutorials (0.5 per cent), and satellite television (0.5 per cent). At Sukhothai Thammathirat Open University in Thailand, text is supported by audio-visual materials and home experiment kits, but there is a problem of limits on air time allocated to educational programmes, which is usually available only in the morning or late at night. It is estimated that only 10 per cent of the students have access to the programmes.

Air time is a problem which is common to all projects that use broadcasting for education. The general public comes first, and the air time left over for education shrinks as public demand expands. In the mid-1970s, Chicago Television College had to make a transition to video-cassettes, and it is now using the home cable television service inside the city.[13] There is somewhat less pressure on radio time, because there are more stations, especially on the FM band. If students are assigned cassettes it is implied that they will have access to machines, at home or at a centre, and to maintenance. Availability, accessibility, and cost criteria narrow the media options, and in the end it is the price of the technology that determines the teaching strategy.

Inset 11
Newspapers and Distance Education

The concept of newspaper courses is designed to meet the needs of a diverse learner population. Newspapers provide a medium of greater flexibility than the typical teacher-student face-to-face situation.

The objectives of 'Courses by Newspapers' (CbN, for example, the series developed by the University of California, San Diego), are:

(1) To offer new features on significant and timely subjects that will provide millions of readers with solid information on subjects of great concern.

(2) To offer the readers the opportunity to pursue additional subject matter in greater detail by purchasing educational materials developed in conjunction with each course. These could include a list of readings, study guide, and source book.

(3) To offer a credit or non-credit course for those readers who want a more structured examination of the subject for college credit in a convenient home-study programme.

The course provides for 15 weekly articles prepared by CbN to appear in a local newspaper. Students read a course text which takes the form of a reader containing articles by experts in the field. The articles are co-ordinated to the different sections of the text, and are intended to introduce and highlight the section to be studied during that week. A study guide is also provided primarily for learners taking the course for college credit. It summarizes the contents of the newspaper and text articles, reiterates important concepts, and provides questions on the course content.

Participating newspapers receive free of charge all course materials including the weekly articles, photographs and promotional advertisements. The newspapers are then required to print the articles without editing and to inform readers how to enrol for credit and how to obtain the other course materials.

Each participating institution agrees to provide an instructor who meets with the students for a minimum of two contact sessions. The reader and study guide are to be used by the instructor.

The structure of the course is the prerogative of the educational institution. The institution selects the instructor, compensation, credit hours, fee structure and appropriate academic area.

Since 1973, CbN courses have been conducted in over 1,800 newspapers nationwide having a total circulation of 16.5 million readers for one single course. Between 37 and 65 per cent of these readers actually followed the CbN newspaper articles.

More than 80,000 students connected with over 1,000 colleges and universities nationwide have taken advantage of these innovative resources for continuing adult education and other non-traditional programmes.

The last CbN courses were offered in spring of 1982, when the funding was cut.

Source: N. Knaper Reid, 'Teaching by newspaper in the USA', In: *Distance Education*, Vol. 17, May 1988.

---

2. Structures

For educational, psychological and social reasons, DE systems must provide students with support services, channels for interaction and feedback, opportunities for practical work, and assessment. Where students can be enrolled in groups, in schools or community centres, interaction is built into the system. Where they cannot, the system must provide for it. The organisation and management of student services is certainly among the most difficult and sensitive of the problems that DE institutions have to solve. Resources are usually found in the local environment of the student: local educational institutions and their staffs and facilities are used for tutorial sessions and laboratory work, community facilities for practical work and on-the-job training. Secondary distance education sometimes uses primary school facilities as study centres; their teachers serve as tutors, and are given extra pay.

The amount of time spent in face-to-face sessions varies with the institution: 30 per cent of a student's time in the USSR (where study is combined with work), 5 to 10 per cent at the United Kingdom Open University, and 0.5 per cent at Universitas Terbuka. These arrangements are much easier in countries where education is developed, but in developing countries where there are few public libraries, few retired professionals, etc., the learning environment is generally poor. Transfer of DE systems from North to South must be undertaken with great care, and the systems must be carefully adapted. The Sukhothai Thammathir Open University has created a national network of supporting centres through co-operation with other educational institutions and government agencies.[14] There are about 12 regional and 66 local study centres, 2 health science and 7 agricultural extension units, 75 STOU library corners, and student self-help and study groups. Indhira Gandhi Open University is planning to extend distance education services to rural areas by using voluntary and non-governmental organizations.

Student assessment, acceptance, and institutional equivalence and accreditation are also sensitive issues, especially at the tertiary levels. Institutions use widely varying grading systems, from continuous assessment to conventional examination sessions. The United Kingdom Open University runs a number of courses in which students are assessed on the basis of an unsupervised individual project.

Most institutions organise examinations at local centres. Special problems are involved in assessment; the grading and processing of tens of thousands of students' answers within a short period of time requires innovation, decentralisation, and electronic data processing. The adoption of the credit system in assessing students can improve its flexibility, and make it possible for students to take courses when and where it is most convenient for them.

It must be remembered that academic and administrative positions in DE systems require professional profiles which are not those of conventional professionals. Staff preparation and development costs should not be underestimated. The Indhira Ghandi Open University started operations offering a diploma in DE.

3. Costs versus effectiveness[15]

Costs of distance education systems will of course vary with the kind of technology used and the volume and extent of services provided, but it can be safely said that administrative costs will be higher than those of conventional institutions. In a general way, also, one can say that the fixed costs of DE systems are generally high, and variable costs low. It may well cost more to start DE programmes, given the capital outlay required, than conventional ones, and it must also be remembered that setting up DE is a long process; perhaps more than two years will pass between the design phase and the delivery of the first course, and it may be some years before the courses will reach their optimum variable cost. Costs per student are lower than conventional costs per student, costs per graduate slightly higher (see *Tables 8.3 and 8.4*).

Within schools, DE projects generally mean yet further costs: 10 per cent more of the cost per student in the Côte d'Ivoire. Radio is much less expensive than television and, with carefully designed curricula, highly cost-effective. The per-student year cost of interactive radio mathematics instruction is estimated at US$0.44 in Thailand; English instruction in Kenya at US$0.40 -- about the cost of a textbook at the primary level. Recourse to DE methods to compensate for the lack of lower secondary teachers -- technology for labour substitution -- can prove immensely cost-effective over a limited period of time, but as seen in the Radio Primaria and Tele Secundaria in Mexico, and the Instructional Television Programme in

Table 8.3 Cost and success rates: distance teaching at secondary level in some developing countries

Country, institution and date of studies	Type of project	Annual enrolment at time of study	Annual cost per student in US$[1]	Capital included in caculations?	Measure of success		Comparison between costs of distance teaching and costs of orthodox education
					Measure used	Rate	
Brazil: IRDEB 1977[2]	Secondary	8 000	107	Yes, at 7.5%	Examination passes	37%	D/t is probably more expensive
Brazil: Minerva 1977[2]	Secondary (Radio, print and some face-to-face support for out-of-school equivalency examination)	177 000	40	Yes, at 7.5%	n/a	n/a	D/t is probably cheaper
Canary Islands: ECCA (Radio School) 1978[3]	Upper primary/ lower secondary	23 000	102	Yes, discount rate not stated	Number promoted to next class after 6 months study	72.75%	D/t is cheaper
Kenya: Correspondence Course Unit 1977[2]	Teacher training	340- 2 900	517	Yes, at 7.5%	Teachers promoted as result of course	90%	D/t is more expensive
Malawi: Malawi Correspondence College 1976[2]	Secondary	3 800	254	Yes, at 7.5%	Exam. passes: as proportion of enrolments as proportion of exam. entrants	13% 21%	Cost per successful student dearer than for day schools but cheaper than for boarding schools
Mexico: Telesecundaria 1972[4]	Secondary (Use of television to extend range of schools using under-qualified teachers)	29 000	374	Yes, at 7.5%	Standardized tests administered to Telesecundaria and conventional school students	Comparable scores	Cost per student lower ($374 instead of $502) but no information about cost per completion
Republic of Korea: Air Correspondence High School 1974-77[2]	Secondary	20 000	108	Yes, at 7.5%	Examination passes	46%	D/t is cheaper
Zambia: National Correspondence College	Secondary in supervised study groups	12 000	64 to 185	Yes, at 7.5%	Examination pass rate	n/a	If success rate above 5-14% of original enrolment, then D/T is cheaper

[1] Costs converted to U.S. $ as at June 1984, using World Bank and U.S.A. deflators. [2] Costs summarized in Perraton (1982) where sources are given. [3] Espina Cepeda (1980). [4] Jamison, Klees and Wells (1978), pp. 217-235. [5] Perraton (1983); high and low estimates of costs reflect the varying costs of face-to-face supervision.

Source: H. Perraton (ed.), *Distance education: an economic and educational assessment of its potential for Africa*, Wasington, D.C., The World Bank, 1986, (Report No. EDT43).

Table 8.4 Cost and success rates: distance teaching at tertiary level

Country, institution and date of studies[1]	Type of project	Annual enrolment at time of study	Annual cost per student in US$[2]	Capital included in caculations?	Measure of success		Comparison between costs of distance teaching and costs of orthodox education
					Measure used	Rate	
Canada: Athabasca University 1979/80[4]	University	4 400[3]	1 238	Yes	n/a	n/a	Costs are within the range of comparable Alberta conventional universities and lower than that of small conventional university
Costa Rica: Universidad Estatal a Distancia 1980	University	8 150[5]	1 038	Yes	n/a	n/a	Cost per student lower than at conventional universities. Cost per credit comparable with that of larger conventional university
Israel: Everyman University 1978	University	8 000	1 266[6]	Yes	Graduates as proportion of enrolment	Forecast 37.5%	Cost per graduate estimated at $9 582 compared with $18 800-$20 500 at conventional univ.
Japan: University of the Air[7]	University	7 000	1 922[6]	Yes	--	--	Cost per graduate will equal cost at private day universities, if 50% graduation rate achieved.
United Kingdom: Open University 1971/79	University	25 000	1 872	Yes	Graduates as proportion of final registration	54%	D/t cheaper per graduate produced than orthodox university
United Kingdom: Open University 1981/82[8]	University	20 000	n/a	Yes	As above	57%	Cost per graduate through OU 62% of cost per arts graduate at orthodox univ., i.e., $13 219 (OU) and i.e., $13 219 (OU) and $21 472 (CU)
United Kingdom: Doncaster Institute of Higher Educ. 1977/78	Professional qualification	75	1 193	No	Final examination passes as proportion of entrants to 3-year course	52%	D/t cheaper. Cost per graduate are: $12 545 conventional $7 566 d/t
United Kingdom: South West London College	Professional qualification	150	833	No	Final examination passes as proportion of entrants to 2-year course	35%	D/t cheaper than evening classes but dearer than day release classes. Costs per graduate are: $4 241 day release; $4 764 d/t; and $6 268 evening classes
Venezuela: Universidad Nacional Abierta 1980	University	13 400[5]	1 571	Yes	n/a	n/a	n/a

[1] Except where shown, this table is based on Table 5 in Perraton (1982) where full references for data are given. [2] Costs converted to U.S. $ as at June 1984, using the U.S. Consumer Price Index, as a deflator. [3] Course enrolments. [4] Using the figures for 1979/1980. [5] Full-time equivalents. [6] Budgeted, not actual expenditure. [7] Muta (1984). [8] Horlock (1984).

Source: H. Perraton (ed.), *Distance education: an economic and educational assessment of its potential for Africa*, Wasington, D.C., The World Bank, 1986, (Report No. EDT43).

the Côte d'Ivoire, teachers will eventually claim and receive higher wages. Nonetheless, DE can be an interesting alternative where specialists are lacking in specific disciplines such as secondary level interactive radio instruction. The provision of in-school DE programmes for the guidance or upgrading of teachers is also a possibility to be considered.

Out-of-school DE projects, with the exception of Madureza Bahia in Brazil and the Malawi Correspondence College (see *Inset 12*), are generally less expensive than conventional training; and in-service teacher training programmes less expensive than residential courses. Even when it is more expensive, DE is sometimes the only possibility, however, given space and time constraints. The costs of the Kenya Teacher In-service Training Project were high mainly because of the small number of participants. But teacher training isnormally one of the most effective of DE's applications (see *Inset 13*).

At the tertiary level there is a good deal of agreement that both per-student and per-graduate costs are lower than in conventional universities. The United Kingdom Open University claims that in 1983-84 the unit cost per undergraduate varied between £1,400 for liberal arts and £2,340 for sciences, which compares with the UGC norm of £3,510. At the Sukhothai Thammathirat Open University, the per-student unit cost is said to be US$100 to 300, and the per-graduate cost around US$270, representing 11.46 per cent of the highest and 54.91 per cent of the lowest per-graduate cost in conventional universities. Students' fees constitute as much as 47.3 per cent of the total resources of some DE universities (Universitas Terbuka, for example) as compared with 30.2 per cent at the Sukhothai Thammathirat Open University and 68 per cent at the Korean Air and Correspondence University. Conversely, the China Central Radio and Television University is entirely government-supported.

To achieve an optimum quality:cost ratio, it is necessary to have enrolments large enough to permit economies of scale, which means a wide variety of courses. Student support keeps the drop-out rate reasonable. Especially during the initial phases of operations, drop-out rates have been high, sometimes as much as 70 per cent. It must be admitted, however, that high drop-out rates can be encouraged purposely as a means of selection. Since forecast information is crucial to planning the reproduction of materials, the problem of

Inset 12
An alternative route to secondary schooling
in Malawi

In 1965, the government of Malawi created the Malawi Correspondence College (MCC) as an alternative to the formal system, which could enroll only 9 per cent of primary school graduates. The MCC evolved gradually over 20 years as the government recognized that it offered a relatively inexpensive way to respond to the growing demand for secondary education. The recurrent cost per student in a MCC study centre is less than one-fifth of the recurrent cost of a student in a government secondary school, and the cost per graduate is slightly less than the cost per secondary school graduate.

The system is based on radio, correspondence, and the use of not fully qualified teachers who work with students in special study centres and in regular secondary schools at night. The only entrance requirements are a primary school leaving certificate and payment of a fee for correspondence materials. More than 80 per cent of MCC students enrol at the junior secondary level and the rest at the senior secondary level. Although the MCC centres were originally designed to serve working youths on a part-time basis, over 70 per cent of all students are now studying in classrooms for over 5 hours a day. By 1985 the MCC was enrolling more than 10,000 new students a year and providing to its approximately 19,000 active students 15 hours of radio programmes a week, correspondence materials, and a service that reviews and marks students' correspondence lessons.

MCC centres are generally located in simple buildings, often constructed by the community next to a primary school, and are frequently accompanied by simple housing facilities for students and teachers. In some cases centres make use of primary school buildings in the late afternoons and evenings. The teachers, who may have only a primary teaching certificate, are selected by local supervisors on the basis of their skills and interests. They are paid by local education authorities and are responsible for the general supervision of the classes. The MCC also provides classes in regular secondary schools after hours. These classes are often taught by regular secondary school teachers, who receive supplementary payments through the MCC.

Overall pass rates for MCC candidates on the National Junior Certificate Examination have been between 10 and 22 per cent over the past few years. These pass rates are low compared with those of regular secondary schools, but they are satisfactory in the light of the MCC's much lower admissions standards.

The programme became more attractive to students when the government made places at regular senior secondary schools available to all MCC students who passed the examination for the full junior certificate in one sitting and at the university to all who earned a full Malawi certificate of education in one sitting. This policy has been changed somewhat, and MCC graduates now have to compete on an equal footing with graduates of the regular secondary schools.

Source: World Bank, *Education in sub-Saharan Africa: policies for adjustment, revitalization, and expansion*, Washington, D.C., World Bank, 1988.

Inset 13
Pakistan: The Allama Iqbal Open University Programme

The Allama Iqbal Open University programmes are mostly for working teachers. They have been designed and created with the following broad objectives in view:
(1) To provide opportunities for teachers to upgrade their educational qualifications in spite of their lack of financial resources and time for study leave.
(2) To maximise the use of sources other than the classroom for education and development.
(3) To enable teachers in service to make the best use of time and effort by combining work and study for continuing education.

The pioneering and most popular course for working teachers so far has been the primary teacher orientation course (PTOC). It is the quickest and most economic. In five presentations since 1976, the PTOC reached 50,000 primary school teachers.

The course is media-based, consisting of a self-instructional package of 18 study units supported by an equal number of radio programmes, two television slots and tuition by experienced teachers. The course is an attempt to familiarise the teachers with new elements of primary school curriculum, increase their knowledge in subject content and methodology, where necessary, and provide them with an opportunity in terms of improving their qualifications by counting the course as one of the six intermediate courses. The instructional package consists of study units on school subjects, population education, training of literacy workers and use of school literacy.

The PTOC has made the following contributions :
• used media-mix for the training and re-education of teachers on a scale previously considered impossible to achieve;
• kept the unit cost close to Rs. 200.00 (= US$20), i.e. about one-sixth of the cost of a conventional six-week in-service training course;
• created study units in association with outside experts in the field, which added greatly to the value of the correspondence package;
• gave the first clear notification of the changes in curriculum to the teachers involved;
• provided teachers with a permanent set of reference material for their professional use.

Source: V. Prakasha; A. Guruge; A.K.B. Tay, *Improving the quality of basic learning opportunities: challenge and response*, Paris, Unesco, 1986, (Unesco/Unicef Digest, No. 19).

planning for quantities of materials to be produced, warehoused and delivered, with obvious repercussions in costs, is then critical.

Data concerning costs in dual-mode institutions are insufficient to draw valid conclusions, but this would appear to be a promising solution, and may well be easier to implement than to found new institutions. The costs data of continuing education for a high-level qualification and on-the-job training in companies are even more rare. Better knowledge of the respective costs of various technological solutions would of course facilitate selection among them. But in the area of post-graduate and high-level continuing training, the cost factor is not a decisive criterion, and, in any case, there is no conventional alternative.

4. Merging patterns

Despite numerous advances in the methods of instruction and communications, which have considerably widened the applicability of DE with mature learners, it is still regarded as a second-best choice, although for people who work it may be the only way to have access to more education. Distance education has developed in all sectors of education and training, but not where it is in competition with conventional formal alternatives. However, in the light of increasing demand for post-graduate courses it may be an eminently appropriate solution, given its flexibility and adaptability to lifelong learning and the requirements of continuing education.

Difficulties in comparing their success stem from the origins of DE clienteles. The typical targets are highly motivated, literate and numerate adolescents and adults with working experience who do not have access or cannot afford to attend regular courses in regular institutions. Primary and secondary school leavers often want to resume studies and acquire qualifications, and DE programmes *have been made available to them* so that they might pursue their studies. The expansion of DE at the post-secondary level can be seen either as an answer to new development needs and increased social pressure, or as a strategy for protecting the universities from a tidal wave of undergraduate students of different (lower) social and economic backgrounds. True equivalency of diplomas and recognition by the labour market is an unsolved problem in most countries, even where legislation proclaims equality. With few exceptions, preference is given to graduates from conventional institutions.

Moreover, opinion still has it that hand-made products are better than industrial ones. The academically able are admitted to regular education at the secondary and tertiary levels, while DE is offered to those that are left over. In a way, therefore, it contributes to the perpetuation of traditions of élitism. Regional and local DE systems which are not already based in an educational institution struggle to become the nuclei of new conventional institutions, adding new facilities such as laboratories and meeting rooms to old buildings.

It can take a good deal of time and persuasion to change a mindset, and it is clear that in general this is in favour of social learning. It may be possible to merge the two approaches, to alternate between DE and physical presence with the same students. DE is obviously a good tool; without help from the teacher, a student learns to dig by digging, whether he is among the ablest or the least able; but it must be remembered that understanding instructions alone is a good deal less efficient than having someone explain them to you, and that effort in isolation will be discouraging if it goes on too long.

Combinations of correspondence courses with classroom sessions enable small schools to offer broader curricula, and students to resolve the problem of conflicting class hours. This is particularly relevant for mothers who need a great deal of flexibility in the organisation of their learning time. The introduction of DE materials and techniques could aid in the development of independent study habits in regular secondary schools and universities, and, in conjunction with redeployment of staff and facilities, might help to reduce costs and increase the numbers of students accommodated. There should be no major technical or educational difficulty in substituting DE in the form of printed matter in combination with audio- or video-cassettes or computer software for a third to half of teacher:student contact hours; there are already ample proofs of the effectiveness of such techniques. Programmes of the Polish Radio and Television University for Teachers, for example, constitute an integral part of the regular Polish pre-service teacher training curriculum.[16] Provided that institutional resistance can be surmounted, the integration of DE with conventional education should be regarded as an appropriate solution, from the economic as well as the educational point of view, to problems of increasing the education supply at secondary and tertiary levels in both developed and developing countries.

5. Summary: priorities for selecting educational technologies

Under pressure for both quantitative and qualitative improvements, the use of modern technologies to improve and expand education delivery systems is no longer a marginal phenomenon. Distance education does not assume that rigid requirements in place and time are essential to the learning process, as long as communication links can be established between the teacher and the learner. Hence, DE is particularly suitable to serve the needs of learners scattered in remote areas, of mothers and of other potential enrolees who need flexibility in the organisation of their learning time.

In adopting or expanding DE programmes, particular attention should be paid to the organisation and management of student services, including channels of interaction and feedback, opportunities for practical work and assessment.

In choosing among alternative delivery services, cost-effectiveness analyses are required. Costs of DE systems vary with the kind of technology used and the extent of services provided, but, in general, administrative costs are higher than those of conventional institutions. Moreover, the setting up of a DE programme is a long process; and it may require some years before the courses reach their optimum unit costs. To achieve an optimum quality:cost ratio, it is necessary to have enrolments large enough to permit economies of scale, which means a wide variety of courses.

---

1. V.V. Ilyin, 'The USSR Financial and Economic Institute for Distance Education', In: *Distance education,* Vol. 4, No. 2, 1983.

2. D.J. Keegan, 'On defining Distance Education', In: *Distance Education,* Vol. 1, No. 1, 1980.

3. W. Perry, *The state of distance learning worldwide,* Oslo, The International Centre for Distance Learning of the UN University, 1984.

4. A. Kaye, 'Distance Education: the state of the art', In: *Prospects,* Vol. 18, No. 1, 1988.

5. J.S. Daniel, *Distance Education and national development in developing Distance Education,* Oslo, International Centre for Distance Learning of the

UN University, 1988.

6. Unesco, *Developments in Distance Education: an analysis of five Asian case studies,* Paris, Unesco, 1989.

7. There is now a second open university in Bangkok.

8. Asian Development Bank, *Distance Education Vol. II,* Manila, 1987.

9. G.R. Reddy, *Open universities: the ivory towers thrown open,.* New Delhi, Sterling Publishers, 1988.

10. Unesco, *Higher level distance education,* Paris, Unesco, 1988.

11. R. Smith, 'Growth and scope of distance learning'. In: *Distance Education Vol. I,* Asian Development Bank, 1987.

12. Unesco, 1989, op cit.

13. D. Hawkridge; J. Robison, *Organising educational broadcasting,* Paris, Unesco, 1982.

14. Unesco, 1989, op cit.

15. Among others, see: *The economics of new educational media, Vols. 1, 2 & 3,* Paris, Unesco, 1977, 1980, 1982; H. Perraton, *The costs of distance education,* Cambridge (UK), International Extension College, 1982; H. Perraton (ed.), *Distance education: an assessment of its potential for Africa,* Washington, D.C., World Bank, 1986, (Report No. EDT43); G.R. Reddy, 1988, op cit; Srisa-an Wichit, 'Financing and cost-effectiveness of distance education', In: *Distance Education,* Asian Development Bank, op cit.

16. Eugenia Potulicka, 'Poland: the Radio and Television University for Teachers', In: *Prospects,* Vol. 18, No. 2, 1988.

Chapter 9

Buildings, equipment, materials: priorities for physical planning and utilisation ·

1. Buildings and activity areas: a guide to planners

The question of facilities is rarely among the priorities of a developing country. Yet while allocation for education in these countries decreased from 5.4 per cent of GNP in 1975 to 3.5 per cent in 1986, capital investment averaged 16.5 per cent of the total education budgets during the 1970s (in Africa it was 15 per cent, in Latin America 13.2 per cent, and in Asia, 25 per cent). Between 1980 and 1985 it slipped to 10.8 per cent (9.3 per cent in Africa, 7.5 per cent in Latin America, 15.7 per cent in Asia), and has continued to diminish in favour of current expenditure, which rose from 84 per cent in 1980 to just under 90 per cent of the education budgets of 1986.

These figures reflect the overall financial contexts of developing countries and the fact remains that there is not enough space for every child, and statistics indicate that in many countries only one child out of two goes to school. Educational policies are virtually unanimous in their goal of achieving universal primary education by the end of the century. Buildings must therefore be constructed. Even the secondary schools, for which capital investment is generally reserved, suffer from lack of funding -- despite the assistance of donor agencies. Financing is required for:

- Expansion of existing schools to meet enrolment increase (this applies at primary level as well) in particular for increased access of girls to education;
- Rehabilitation of facilities, of which, according to some sources, 60 per cent are in unsatisfactory condition;
- Replacement of obsolescent furniture and equipment (this applies also to higher institutions).

In 1990, demand is outstripping supply in many countries, with consequences that are only too well known: classrooms are overcrowded and uncomfortable; teaching conditions are poor; failure together with the poor morale which is due to dreary environments swells the numbers of drop-outs.

Construction costs are rising. The cost of building a new primary school, for example, has more than doubled during the past 15 years.

Depressing as the situation is, it should more than ever encourage national authorities to explore policies of quality construction. Major considerations in selection are:

- Economy (this need not be at the expense of quality, which may in the long run entail less expense; it need not involve a reduction in space; and it must not endanger security or ignore construction standards);
- Simplicity of materials (in the selection of building materials, it is essential to choose those which will remain attractive the longest, and to avoid superfluous finishes and expensive fittings);
- Simplicity of design and appropriateness to activities;
- Conformity to standards of comfort (temperature, hygrometry, ventilation, lighting, sound insulation, etc.);
- Phase organisation (so that construction is conducted in stages);
- Local production of materials (which must be planned for appropriateness to the task);
- Employment of local manpower;
- Sturdiness (to minimise maintenance needs).

Once constructed, the learning site must function and be kept in optimum condition:

- Through full use of the learning environment;
- By limiting cover to essential areas and promoting outdoor instruction in those countries where simple shaded frames are sufficient;

- Through implementation partnerships with ministries (i.e., education/public works, communications, construction, etc.), local authorities, or communities.

a. Building services

Responsibility for the construction of educational facilities usually rests with a school buildings department or agency within the ministry of education, or a similar department in the ministry of public works headed by an architect or an engineer. In either case, a small team of professionals -- architects, engineers, designers, and draughtsmen -- base their designs on quantitative data provided by the educational planning services in the ministry of education in terms of classroom, laboratory, workshop, and administrative office requirements of a given enrolment. Unfortunately, the pedagogical quality of projects designed by either type of service does not always come up to expectations.

Designers are often more concerned with the aesthetics of a building than with providing functional and comfortable teaching space; there may not even be an educational facilities planner, who should be an educator, and if there is, he or she may not have been involved in the design phase of the project. Communication between educational planning and physical planning are essential, and should be systematic and open. Unesco regional seminars have drawn attention to this problem and have generally concluded that the ministry of education should take the initiative of establishing in its services a team of educators, sociologists, and educational facilities planners, who, together with architects and engineers, should formulate educational building policy which is then submitted to the decision-making authorities.

In order to have the most reliable possible overview of the nature of problems, data concerning the condition of existing buildings directly under the supervision of the ministry of education should be assembled. Inventories of those schools, on the basis of which the physical resources in the educational plant can be processed, are urgently required.

The difficulty in gathering sufficiently precise information to guarantee reliability must not be underestimated, particularly in countries where no such data have ever been available. Some governments have already institutionalised the process by establishing a national team in charge of the inventory of all public buildings and development projects (educational, administrative, and cultural), as well as roads and bridges, etc. The team is organised as an ongoing and continuous process, with systematic updating of information at regular intervals.

The first phase of the exercise is the formulation of a questionnaire to be sent to the school authorities, which must include questions and parameters not always within the range of knowledge of a headmaster or principal. Among these are the degree of decay of the facilities, structural defects, etc., which will have to be assessed by professionals from the community or region, or by emissaries of the ministry. The head of the institution should be the primary source consulted, however. The information to be obtained includes the following:

(i)	General data	Legal status, ownership, year of opening;
(ii)	Educational data	Enrolment by sex, level, shift teaching, and administrative staff, other staff (community activities), non-formal education, etc.;
(iii)	Physical data	Site: location, area, topography, access and services, planted areas, etc.; Buildings : general teaching area, specialised teaching areas, seminar and multi- purpose rooms, administrative and communal areas, boarding and staff housing;
(iv)	Furniture and equipment (by facility)	Types of chairs, tables, etc.; condition;
(v)	Financial data	Current expenditure by category; maintenance costs.

The collected questionnaires should be examined by decision-makers, and assessed according to quality and degree of detail of the answers. A good, precise questionnaire will of course be more likely to elicit good, precise answers. The information should then be compiled in an inventory, to be used as a basis on which to set policy for future building design.

In addition, demographic data should be provided by local authorities and specialized institutions to assess the needs for extension of school facilities in response to demand for education. An important tool for carrying out the analysis of the data is the school map.[1] School mapping exercises have already been carried out in a number of countries. They consist of locating, on a map of the country, all educational institutions at all levels, the capacity of each institution, the present enrolment by level and by sex, and the numbers of school-aged children in villages, towns and cities, making it possible to locate and evaluate the extent of the unserved populations.

These data, compared with enrolment trends, particularly of pupils coming from primary into secondary, and the inventory data, can enable authorities to define alternatives such as:

- The demolition and replacement of obsolete buildings;
- The renovation of less critically derelict or unsuitable buildings;
- Enlargement of a facility;
- Construction of new establishments.

The ministry must also decide on the most suitable size[2] of an establishment and conduct cost-benefit analyses.

The subsequent phase is the preparation of a schedule of the accommodations -- both new and renovated -- needed by each institution, on the following basis: (i) the evolution of the school map, forecasting increase or decrease in school-age populations by zones, and a forecast of the catchment areas of these zones; (ii) educational facilities to be provided (or limited) in these zones; (iii) number and size of institutions where shift systems are to be initiated; it will also have to be determined which institutions can be gradually expanded so as to do away with the shift system.

One of the options that can have an important bearing on the number, distribution and size of institutions is the extension of co-education at the secondary level. This option generally makes an establishment more economical to manage, but nevertheless requires certain special facilities such as separate sanitary and locker room accommodation, boarding, etc.

b. Preparation and planning

Construction and/or renovation programmes having been selected, detailed cost estimates are prepared, followed by plans for financing -- which include government contributions and funding from donor countries or international agencies. The choice of a site may have unexpected financial consequences if preliminary studies have not been adequate. Of particular interest to educational planners are the legal status and ownership, the extent of the catchment area, and the accessibility of a site. Site components to be considered by architects and/or engineers include:

(i)	Shape and dimensions	Shape may impede the extension of an otherwise suitable site;
(ii)	Topography	A steep slope, for example, may not only be a nuisance, but may incur unexpected costs for controlling drainoff and the erosion of foundations; costs for hauling earth could be exorbitant;
(iii)	Drainage	If a site is susceptible to flooding, infilling and foundation work may be extremely expensive;
(iv)	Soil characteristics	To find a bearing stratum under light soils it is sometimes necessary to provide deeper foundations, which can raise construction costs to impossible levels;
(v)	Access and services	If new access roads have to be built and electrical lines extended, or if the water table is very low, cost studies must be undertaken to determine whether or not the site should be purchased.

Authorities in charge of land acquisition must make sure that the enquiry has been carried out and evaluated, and all the above aspects taken into consideration before purchasing a site. In general, it is preferable to consider alternatives presented by the relevant bodies and to select the most cost-effective among them. In urban areas, where land is difficult to come by and expensive, a site may have to be programmed for intensive use to amortise the purchase price and development costs.

Shared-accommodation projects in urban areas include the construction of a science-and-arts centre which is shared by several schools, its specialised rooms (for example chemistry laboratories, language laboratories, arts-and-crafts work-shops, etc.) used by each school in turn. The advantages are (i) full use of the site (all accommodations are in use 90 per cent of the week); (ii) lower building costs (fewer specialised rooms are built); (iii) lower running costs (the centre is run by one of the full-time teachers); (iv) less responsibility accruing to the principals of the feeder schools; (v) minimum maintenance costs.

On occasion, the attention of national authorities has been drawn to changing conceptions of instruction areas and their implications for building design. The nature of the activities has evolved, and thus the so-called 'Public Works Department' classroom/blackboard teaching -- quite common in the developing world -- is challenged. A 'PWD' school consists of a series of rooms along a long corridor, each with the teacher's desk on a platform on one side facing rows of cumbersome two-seated benches. The benches are hard to move, inadaptable to growing students, and can be packed with as many as six children. There is no storage space, not even room to move.

When there are not sufficient facilities, experience shows that, in many countries, learning is possible out of doors in shaded areas, as well as in classrooms, and the design of educational facilities can support a good deal of rethinking. School-children play mathematical games out of doors. Numerous primary schools include 'discovery expeditions' and gardening activities in their schedules.

Attempts have been made in recent years to lower construction costs and at the same time keep quality at a certain standard. Partitions between classrooms have been removed or replaced with sliding, folding, or storage walls -- with mixed results. The walls are fragile, and acoustic insulation is lacking. The conclusion is fairly general that better walls, more generous space, and more flexible use of the space in each area are preferable, to allow for movement of furniture, storage, and sanitary and electric facilities. Exterior space, sheltered or roofed over, can be set up for teaching and relieve overcrowding in interior classrooms.

These trends go against the great temptation to lower costs by reducing space. Modern-day increases in enrolment and in number of pupils per class, innovation in basic materials and equipment require the abandonment of policies which are short-term cheap and long-term expensive. Unless needs are foreseen and capacities provided for, an instruction area once built is expensive to modify.

In developing countries, the State takes over a certain proportion of the school-building programmes. Where it does not intervene in the financing and construction of primary school buildings, the role is assumed by local or regional authorities. But the government should at least encourage better design of facilities at this level, and this is one of the objectives of the above-mentioned educational facilities centre established within the ministry of education. Its research and development programme should cover all educational levels:

(i) Space planning   All activities -- indoor and outdoor -- are scheduled and translated into teaching space;

(ii) Design guidelines and specifications

- Space standards   Area per pupil/place for collective teaching classrooms, small groups (seminars), or self-directed learning;
- Comfort   Protection from excessive sunshine, glare, noise; provision of adequate natural ventilation;
- Safety   Protection from fire, flooding, other natural disasters;

(iii) Building specifications   Determined on the basis of availability of building materials, spans, building regulations;

(iv) Furniture and equipment   By type of activity, size, anthropometric requirements, technical characteristics;

(v) Cost ceilings   Analysis of financial implications of various construction elements.

Design phases should produce prototypes which, once evaluated by all concerned -- both educators and designers -- can be developed and reproduced. The plans will be copied and sent to the regional services concerned.

The implementation stage of a programme presupposes (i) co-ordination between the designer (in this case the educational building centre) and the builders -- the contractors supervised by the local public works department, who should be briefed on all aspects, educational and technical, of the project, and (ii) co-ordination between the designer and the users -- headmasters, principals, and teachers, who should fully understand the conceptions of the designer and be briefed on how to use the teaching tool that is being built for them. There was a case of a 4,000-school programme that did not co-ordinate properly in these two ways; the building plans were misinterpreted by the builders, and the badly-built schools were ill-used by the teachers. An expensive lesson.

c. Construction

The architect's manner of presentation can be by illustrated manual, lectures, ministerial circulars, or whatever, as long as the explanations are clearly expressed. The quality:cost ratio will vary with the construction industry of a country and its raw material resources. If it is necessary to import cement, then wood frame or masonry load-bearing walls are preferable. If a selection must be made among several building systems, the following parameters might be considered:

- lower cost for the same performance;
- resistance to weather conditions: the longer-lasting, the better;
- minimal maintenance requirements.

University buildings, and those of other institutions of higher learning, such as technical and agricultural colleges, polytechnical institutes, etc., are sometimes intended to serve as national showcases, and are needlessly and extravagantly dressed up to look sophisticated. Built with the help of foreign funds and technical assistance, these poisoned gifts are often an excessive burden on government current expenditure. These buildings should be built with the same care as primary and secondary facilities. The most important characteristic of good design is simplicity. Spaces should be flexible, as needs vary from year to year. Maintenance should be minimal, which is to say that plaster and cement renderings should be avoided, water and electricity systems easily accessed, pipes systems strong and durable.

Traditional and local building practices may be perfectly suitable, especially in regions which are difficult of access. Most cultures have developed highly suitable building types, long-lasting structures among them, and structures that can be built according to local practice may well be carried out better and more easily maintained thereafter by workers who are familiar with the techniques. A simple guidebook, containing numerous illustrations on the construction of school buildings, could be published, as has been done in some countries,[3] by the ministry of education and distributed to local authorities.

While the question of skilled labour does not always pose a problem in urban areas, it can be critical in less populated rural zones, particularly as concerns plumbing, electricity, roofing, and other trades in which the country has few contractors with state-of-the-art technical know-how.

d. Furniture and equipment

In addition to being comfortable and sturdy, school tables, chairs, and stools particularly should be easy to move and handle, and to adapt to variations in space organisation. It should take but a few minutes to arrange an area for a different activity: to change a scene from formal lecture room to practice exercises in small groups or individual work. Furniture which can be stacked is easier to move and store, as are flat-top tables with a maximum of two workplaces, that one can combine to form larger working surfaces. The proliferation of teaching materials -- textbooks, guides, charts, maps, mathematics team games -- and the necessity for exhibiting pupils' work make it difficult to function without pinboards, and closets and shelves which are sheltered from termites, humidity, and dust. Standards should include mnimum cupboard space of 1.5m and 10 linear metres of shelf space per class of 40. The more sophisticated materials, audio-visual, microcomputers, etc., must absolutely be protected against humidity, dust, and theft. Usually they are piled up in the principal's office, where they are inaccessible, and rapidly unusable. It is also advisable to plan for a central storage room, with metal casing, and to put someone in charge of it, preferably a staff member. Separate storage facilities with different responsible individuals are a particularly good idea for schools with two or more shifts.

Specialised rooms and labs, often, in practice, either overequipped or completely lacking in equipment, should contain at least one demonstration bench, with water and electricity, and two independent sinks with taps for the students, and a network of electrical plugs. A preparation and storage room next to the lab is indispensable, and laboratories are good places for exhibit cupboards with glass doors.

Project costs can be lowered by optimising the use of spaces, thereby reducing their number. School authorities tend to allocate one classroom per class group, and it remains empty when the class is using other facilities such as labs or outdoor areas. If lecture room, seminar room, arts-and-crafts workshop and library assignments are activity-based rather than class-based, their use, and that of the classrooms as well, can be organised for full-time occupation. One can compute a use-factor, that is, the number of periods during which a space can be used as a factor of the total number of periods per week, usually 80 to 85 per cent for general subjects, 75 per cent for specialised rooms, and 60 per cent for workshops.

An organisational advantage: all of the equipment pertaining to a subject can be grouped in the subject room. But individual storage space such as lockers may be in small rooms or segments of corridors; they need not necessarily be in special rooms. Yet more use can be wrung from a space by offering courses for adults or conducting other community development activities outside school hours and during holidays. Problems raised by such activities are primarily practical -- such as the storage of (stackable or folding) adult-size furniture, and the assignment of responsibility for the use and maintenance of equipment. A solution may be another central storage facility.

e. Staff accommodation

The problem of lodging should not be minimised; it is one of the great difficulties facing national authorities in attracting and keeping teachers, particularly in rural areas. Many countries allocate staff housing within school premises, at least for headmasters, principals, and deputy principals, but not automatically for teachers. Educational authorities have different feelings about this from one country to another, but experience has generally shown that given a choice between a housing allowance and a rent-free house (charges are paid), the allocation is preferred.

There are countries in which a savings system makes the teacher the owner of a house by the time of retirement, provided that he or she has filled several posts, possibly in out-of-the-way areas.

f. Maintenance

Among the most acute problems of developing countries is the run-down condition of most State-owned buildings -- educational, cultural, administrative, etc. -- which are not cared for, and in the long run represent huge financial drains. According to some evidence, it seems that about 60 per cent of many developing countries' public buildings of over 20 years standing are so deteriorated that they can no longer be rehabilitated, and it is dangerous to allow access to them.

There is usually no provision in ministry budgets for maintenance of public buildings, furniture, or equipment. This is a deep-seated problem which requires a complete rethinking of government budget allocation. Ad hoc maintenance systems that involve teams sent out by ministries of public works only in response to natural disasters should be developed into routine systems involving also representatives of regional governments and inspectors from the ministry of education, and local communities, in co-operation with the head of the institution in question.

An annual allotment of 1.5 to 2 per cent of the construction cost of a building, and 5 per cent of the cost of furniture and equipment, should be placed in a maintenance fund to be made available five years after the opening of an establishment. Besides the structure itself, plumbing, electricity, and roofing require maintenance -- often because of vandalism, and sometimes because pupils do not know how to correctly use the sanitary facilities provided. Ministries of education should organise regular annual or semi-annual inspections of all the institutions under their authority, by regional inspection teams of masonry, plumbing, electricity and roofing specialists. Between visits, it should be the duty of the director of the school to supervise buildings and equipment systematically. Preventive inspection can signal anomalies before equipment ceases to function: leaks, clogging, electrical trouble, etc. For the larger schools it may be necessary to hire a handyman to repair things temporarily until the next inspection. If by chance there is a technical school in the vicinity, the services of its instructors, together with a team of trainees, might be enlisted to undertake repairs in their areas of specialisation.

2. Materials and equipment: quality and cost-effectiveness

a. Overall trends

Teaching is no simple thing, even when there is no lack of equipment and material. However, even without textbooks, visual aids, and other materials that appeal graphically to the understanding of a pupil, it can be challenging indeed. For many countries these items can cost between 2 and 5 per cent of the education expenditure, that is between 0.2 and 0.36 per cent of GNP. Large-scale projects which require the use of up-to-date information and communication technologies, must generally be financed through separate budgets.

The materials required for attaining the basic objectives of a developing country might be classified as follows: (i) basic materials such as textbooks, paper, and materials; (ii) intermediate materials such as science teaching equipment; (iii) modern audi-visual aids and microcomputers. A country at the basic stage will not, of course, go into audio-visual investment at the outset. But where the use of video and computer equipment is widespread in the environment, schools will feel pressure to develop technologically as well. Whatever the categories of materials and equipment, general considerations must be reviewed before specific purchasing is envisaged.

Educational materials and equipment include all physical items used directly or indirectly for purposes of education and training, to support, facilitate, or encourage transmission or acquisition of knowledge, competence, skills, and know-how. Three main categories must be considered, beginning with the most general:

- paper supplies, pencils, note and exercise books, chalk, etc.
- furniture: tables, benches, blackboards, etc.
- instructional materials and equipment: (i) textbooks, guides, charts, maps; (ii) audio-visual and electronic teaching aids (hardware, software); (iii) science and technology equipment -- some catalogues advertise more than a thousand specialised items -- and equipment for physical education and sports.

The market is larger than the part financed by the public agencies of a country; families, private schools, and the associations are also consumers of these products, and the educational demand for items such as paper and glass products should be considered in relation to the overall markets. In most industrialised countries, these products are provided locally; central authorities usually do not need to supply anything except perhaps computers to schools. Market mechanisms normally determine the availability, suitability, distribution and maintenance of educational equipment, and selection is normally in the hands of principals, teachers, or students. But in developing countries it cannot be assumed that local industry and market forces can cope with the needs of education. The flow of materials must be controlled in countries where sudden quantitative expansion and qualitative improvement have combined to push demand over the capacities of the markets to provide. Lack of maintenance, which is also due to scarcity of resources, lack of appropriate structures, lack of planning and co-ordination between structures, and the prestige of imported goods, all contribute to keeping schools poorly supplied.

In general, the materials in use are not suited to the needs or the environments of the pupils. Imported goods are designed for their countries of origin, and impede efforts to increase the relevance of instruction. As school enrolment increases, so will demand, creating problems where resources are slim, foreign currency expensive, and debt crushing. National policies for obtaining and providing suitable materials at acceptable costs, and the thoughtful planning of production, procurement and distribution, maintenance, and user training can help to forestall difficulties. But these policies are in no way limited to the education sector, and must concern departments of culture, communications, health and development, etc., as well as those of industry, commerce, and the economy. The problems must preferably be approached globally, if education is to avoid ivory tower isolation, and stay in its proper perspective as part and parcel of the life of the country.

Amidst the great variety of institutional services and directorates it becomes very difficult to devise coherent national strategies for the integration of planning and budget services, curriculum development institutes, science equipment offices, educational technology centres, etc. To anticipate their needs, many developing countries have started to produce such items as paper, chalk, textbooks, science equipment, and school furniture on industrial or semi-industrial scales, which offers the advantages of:

- Lower unit costs;
- Increased relevance;
- Reduction in imports;
- Creation of employment.

Alternatives ranging from exclusive State control to exclusive private control of design, production, and distribution have been adopted by countries, and government response to private initiatives has ranged from indifference to tight regulation of production and prices. Some countries have managed to involve both sectors in true collaboration; but experience has shown that over-extension of the educational sector, i.e. actual involvement in the manufacturing process and the running of factories, is not advisable. It is better to make a clear distinction between the role of the education sector and that of the economic, whether public or private. The education sector, as a main user and consumer of the products, must make its needs known, propose specifications, control the quality of the products offered, supervise their distribution and monitor their use. But it usually has neither the managerial capacity nor the staff to deal with the production process.

Research in cost reduction and control should be combined with research in effective learning, so that the bottom line does not become the determinant factor in selection or production. Cost-effectiveness is the criterion to be kept in the forefront of this process.

Three sources of inexpensive instructional materials have been seen to be effective: the environment, the teachers and students, and the providers of commercial packaging. A good deal of material for the lower grades can come from the environment: natural products such as stones, leaves, seashells and sticks for counting. And at higher levels, biology can be taught using animals and plants from the environment rather than prepared specimens from laboratories. Industrial packaging can be recycled -- boxes, bottles and bottlecaps, and other containers -- if households will part with them (in rural areas they may not).

Opportunity costs of products made by students and teachers may be high even if the direct costs are not. Even when a teacher has the necessary tools for making equipment, time is short, and one cannot expect technical and vocational schools to produce vast quantities of teaching equipment, either. They can make prototypes for evaluation and test purposes, and sometimes small series of items which are urgently needed, but these institutions are involved in teaching, and must not be sidetracked too far into production. Some countries have found it convenient to reduce costs by assembling parts produced in factories in the schools -- circuit boards, for example. And these activities can constitute highly interesting learning exercises. The processes of designing and creating are stimulating and relevant, not to mention conducive to practical skills; and the teacher who is trained to produce teaching aids may also be stimulated to design prototypes.

Unesco, through its regional offices and networks for educational innovation, and other agencies, such as the Commonwealth Secretariat, have encouraged teacher-and community-manufacture of low-cost devices and apparatus for science teaching. While they cannot be the sole providers of teaching aids, their contribution can be useful, and the experience of contributing satisfying, and the objects created will be eminently relevant and practical.

Commercial packaging, specially designed by educationists to be recycled or simply to serve as educational tools during use, includes notebook covers bearing such decoration as the multiplication tables, historical figures, health and nutritional information. In the Côte d'Ivoire, matchboxes bear one letter each, and have been recycled as learning devices for literacy courses. In Portugal, after the revolution of 1974, the great majority of the 15,000 primary schools then operating were without teaching materials, and the educational authorities arranged with the private sector to produce reusable packaging. Firms were asked to adapt or design packaging of widely consumed products, which then bore the stamp of the ministry *'Useful in schools'*. The mass media were drawn in to mobilise populations and sensitise teachers, and special prizes were awarded to the most effective efforts. A one-year campaign gave birth to a dozen projects, some of which involved the co-operation of competing companies, and many companies were turned away. So many packages were circulated (20 million) that long afterwards they were still found in shops. Studies showed that the materials did actually help in teaching various subjects, and the campaign contributed to awakening the interest of parents and the communities in the problems of the schools.

b. Textbooks

Textbooks are the instructional device par excellence, and central to teaching.[4] In the least developed countries, they often constitute 85 per cent of recurrent expenditure on materials. Classrooms deprived of textbooks promote little in the way of reading skills, and are obliged to content themselves with rote learning, recitation, copying from blackboards and taking lecture notes.[5] The presence of textbooks in schools is so taken for granted that teacher training institutes pay little attention to them as compared to computers, for example, or audio-visual tools. Research on their use is all but non-existent. In many countries they are the visible syllabus (they are often arranged in weekly progression), and they model the teaching-learning process. They can be designed predominantly for the teacher's or the learner's use, and can be used in the classroom collectively or outside for self-directed learning; most frequently they serve for both (see *Inset 14*). A teacher's guide usually accompanies the book, and these guides have been known to be more voluminous than the text. They may be combined with a workbook, but this imposes a new book for each pupil each year.

Textbooks reflect learning psychologies which range from the wholly teacher-centred and authoritarian, 'spoonfeeding' the student, to the learner-centred which promote creative thinking; they should be relevant not only to the socio-cultural environment of the community and the prevailing philosophy of education, but in line with the level of expertise of the teachers and the expectations and competencies of the learners and their families. At the basic levels, textbooks are particularly sensitive to the educational environment and climate.

Every book industry in the world publishes these books, and in developing countries they take the best part of the market. In making policy decisions one must be wary of measures that might stagnate the national book industry, as local publishers are quite dependent upon access to the textbook market.

Worldwide, scholarly publishing tends to be dominated by the multinational houses, especially at the secondary and higher levels, and in vocational and technical subjects (see *Inset 15*). Policy should be based on general, holistic feasibility studies and not narrowed to the education sector.

Inset 14
Textbooks and achievement

The influence of textbooks appears to be stronger within rural schools and among students from lower income families. In rural Brazil, for instance, students with parents who had received no schooling were almost three times as likely to pass primary school if they had used two or more books (67 per cent graduating), compared to students in this same group who had no textbooks in school (only 24 per cent graduating). Among students with parents who had completed primary school, 73 per cent of all pupils with at least two books passed primary school, versus 61 per cent of those with no books (total sample equalled 1,006 primary school students). Similarly, a study of 6,056 Malaysian youth found that the availability of books in school was more strongly related to achievement among lower income children from Chinese and Indian ethnic groups.

Clearer evidence on the magnitude of the effects of textbooks comes from more recent studies which have employed experimental research designs -- thereby holding constant student background and other school factors. For instance, a controlled evaluation in the Philippines provided textbooks to 2,295 first- and second-grade pupils within 52 schools. A control group of similar schools was also selected. Books were then introduced at ratios of two pupils per book and one pupil per book in alternate classrooms. Achievement gains resulting from the intervention were substantial. In first grade science, performance was .51 of a standard deviation higher within the experimental classrooms, .30 higher in mathematics, and .32 higher in Togalog. The .51 change (in units of the standard deviation) indicates that the mean score achieved by 50 per cent of all students was obtained by 69 per cent of those students in the treatment group. This improvement is twice the impact of what would be gained by lowering class size from forty to ten students

The influence of the textbook programme on achievement was greater for children with parents who had received less schooling. The correlation between the child's social class and science achievement was modest for all students. Yet this association was not at all evident for pupils receiving textbooks. Nor did the child's social class influence gains in achievement scores. Interestingly from an efficiency viewpoint, the concentration of textbooks (2:1 versus 1:1 pupil to book ratio) made no difference on levels of pupil achievement. The magnitude of effect on Togalog and mathematics was more modest. This may be the result of greater difficulty in using these latter texts relative to the science volume, as reported by the teachers.

Source: B. Fuller, *Raising school quality in developing countries: what investments boost learning*, Washington, D.C., World Bank, 1985, (Education and training series, discussion paper No. EDT7).

Inset 15
Transnational publishing houses in Arab States

The results of field studies undertaken in Egypt, Lebanon and Jordan, as well as information collected from various sources on other Arab States, have shown that the market for imported foreign books is mainly run by British, French and American transnational companies. The French companies are predominant in the Maghreb countries and the Lebanon; however, they have very little or no business activity in English-speaking countries such as the Gulf States, Jordan, Sudan, and very reduced activities in countries such as Egypt where the French book market only accounts for 3 per cent of the imported book market.

Over recent years, Soviet scientific books edited in English and Arabic have started to appear on the Arab market, particularly in Egypt, Syria, the Yemen Democratic Republic, countries which, over the past three decades, have sent students to the Soviet Union for university studies. On their return they recommend the use of Soviet books in technology and pure science.

Large publishing houses in the Federal Republic of Germany and Japan have also started to make their appearance in the Arab market, in a few relatively restricted fields, and for English language editions. However, these attempts on the part of Soviet, German and Japanese companies have had relatively little effect, since their exports only represent 1 per cent of the turnover in imported editions.

Books supplied by transnational companies in the Arab region cover the following four main fields:
- school textbooks (for general and pre-university education);
- scientific manuals (for university education and research);
- general literature (for main public, children's books, paperback and glossy editions);
- dictionaries and encyclopaedias.

Transnational publishing companies are the main suppliers of educational goods and services for the Arab region. Their turnover represents 70 per cent of the market as a whole for educational articles, followed by 22 per cent for scientific and professional equipment, 5 per cent for computers, 2 per cent for audio-visual documents, and 1 per cent for educational games.

British companies hold most of the market for English school textbooks in all of the twelve countries that were previously British colonies. In the Lebanon and Saudi Arabia, American and British companies share the English school textbook market. Altogether, three to four American and British publishing houses and four French publishers are the main suppliers of textbooks in the Arab States region.

Source: J. Akl; E. Khoury, *Sociétés transnationales et systèmes éducatifs: études de cas en Egypte, au Liban et en Jordanie*, Paris, Unesco/Arab Fund for Economic and Social Development (AFESD)/Arab League for Educational, Cultural and Scientific Organization (ALECSO), 1985.

Constraints affecting all categories of costs -- design (including testing and confirmation by learner use), production, distribution, and use -- must be considered at all levels: the authorities and specialists, the policy-makers and planners, the school administrators, the curriculum specialists and authors, the publishers, and the printers. The interaction of political, economic, administrative, educational, and technical participants will finally determine the quality of the teaching-learning conditions. The promotion of textbooks as a major element in educational development has long-term implications. Their production requires considerable and sustainable resources, both personal and fiscal, and it takes several years from author's pen to student's desk. Their distribution is sensitive, because equity would have them provided free to those who cannot afford them.

In most industrialised countries, they are provided free in any case, but under the pressures of economic recession, developing countries have been obliged to ask families to contribute; in China, North Africa and the Philippines, for example, textbooks are sold at subsidised prices. Some countries produce semester-sized books to reduce size, and thus their price. Even poor families are usually willing to pay if a textbook costs less than 1 per cent of the per capita GNP, but the most acceptable range is 0.1 to 0.5 per cent.[6] Sometimes books are sold or rented in wealthier areas and provided free to the poor populations. Financial participation of the family not only encourages pupils to take care of their books, but stimulates the industry because each book is used by only one child. If the textbooks are the property of the school and must be returned at the end of the year, children in rural areas have nothing to read during annual vacation. In some countries, authorities are now trying to sensitise communities by making the distribution of schoolbooks and materials the occasion for a village ceremony.

Design and testing are often neglected, and yet they are critically important. The development of a manuscript requires time, and high-level expertise; specifications must be established concerning the length of the book, its size, whether it shall be used collectively or individually, and the type and quantity of illustrations. When these have been worked out between educators and publishers, and cost estimates established, a good manuscript will require the input of a team working under a subject-matter specialist. Tryouts, field testing and learner verification will increase the quality and efficiency of the draft, and prove highly cost effective if undertaken before the book goes to press. But it takes two to three years. Common practice is to assign to a teacher or a university department the task of writing the manuscript, and then having it approved by a commission. At university level, where books are less teaching machines than portable information sources, the problem is in selecting and/or adapting the best publication, and coping with the copyright costs. Domestic production of textbooks is clearly the responsibility of the education sector, and even if it is decided to import them, there must be control over their contents and designs.

The composition, printing and binding facilities necessary to book publishing may not exist in a country, although the advent of computers has lowered the costs of composition, speeded it up, made great flexibility in format and presentation possible, and facilitated the inclusion of graphs and illustrations. But these technologies require expertise, not only in handling but in maintenance of sophisticated equipment. Printing facilities, both government and private, are the most visible part of the publishing process, and many textbook development projects, intra- or extra-nationally funded are mainly -- sometimes wrongly -- focused on the procurement of printing equipment. To be managed economically, production machinery must be in use all the time -- three shifts a day, six days a week, year in and year out with no breakdowns and no pauses due to running out of raw materials. It may be cheaper to have textbooks printed outside the country. Transnational publishers often print in countries where wages are low. It may also happen that heavy duties are imposed on paper, but not on completed books -- or vice versa -- or that the views of the ministry of education are in conflict with those of industry. The size of the market determines the possibilities for economies of scale, and makes textbook production in a small, multilingual country, such as those of the Caribbean or Oceania, exorbitant (see *Inset 16*).

Textbooks are bulky goods, sensitive to climate and requiring dry warehousing. Shipping is problematic; long-term storage of large print-runs means losses. And the most serious problem in starting local manufacturing units from scratch is finding sustainable fiscal and human resources. Some countries are finding it difficult under present economic conditions even to replace and repair equipment, and to import the raw materials needed to keep their production processes going.

Inset 16
Textbook publishing in small countries

Despite an enormous increase in the number of countries which produce textbooks of their own, there are still a fair number -- small countries and island communities -- where populations are often too small to make the production of textbooks viable. In some areas, examination councils have been formed which resulted in standardisation of curricula and textbooks, opening up possibilities for regional publishing negotiations with inter-regional publishers for bulk supply at bulk prices. Three West African countries, Senegal, Côte d'Ivoire and Togo, have created a regional publishing house, 'Nouvelles Editions Africaines', through which they share textbook publishing and printing costs. It is also possible to negotiate with a publisher to produce a special edition of a textbook locally. With various amendments to suit local conditions, desktop publishing and offset printing are making it easier to fill needs for small print runs.

Source: Unpublished Unesco report.

Moreover, in countries with neither a proper publishing industry nor commercial booksellers, local production does not solve the problem of provision of schools. Enrolment data are inaccurate; needs cannot be precisely forecast or provided for. Road networks are inadequate, and books arrive late in remote areas when they arrive at all. It has been reported that it takes at least six months to get books from a distribution centre to mountain communities in Nepal, and that about 50 per cent of the cost of the book (as opposed to 2 per cent for the plains regions) is incurred in transporting them: on horses, bicycles, light aircraft, lorries, or someone's head.[7]

Production and distribution must be prompt if educational requirements are to be respected; and that means more warehousing space. It is a costly venture for a ministry of education to go into the establishment and maintenance of a fleet of transportation vehicles, but sometimes there is no alternative, not even the possibility of borrowing military equipment and operators.

Distribution difficulties are so acute in many countries that it is probably a good idea to plan on a book life of three to five years, on the use of each title by several cohorts, on the avoidance of centrally produced worksheets, handouts or other small materials, and on staying put as far as curricula are concerned.

The aspect most frequently neglected in costing textbooks, and this in developed countries as well, is the cost involved in seeing that the teachers know how to use the book and have the teacher's manual. This is a cost that falls to education, whoever is in charge of producing and distributing. Regular training sessions and distance education would enhance teachers' use of textbooks enormously, and supervisers as well should be asked to help.

Integrated planning, co-ordination and interaction between concerned parties in the framework of a precise division of tasks is the key to progress in this area. Altbach[8] says, "The keys to effective textbook development are not massive fiscal expenditures or crash programmes, but rather careful co-ordination, attention to the articulation between the education system and the publishing industry, linking curricular development and the expansion of enrolments to textbook requirements, and the involvement of the necessary expertise in the development of relevant and high-quality textbooks. The textbook situation in any country depends on the state of the publishing industry (including printing capacity, the availability of paper, and the distribution network), the presence of competent authors (and the research and testing facilities to ensure relevant textbooks), and the educational system."

The issue of textbooks is graphically illustrative of the need for effective management. The solution will be country specific, (or regional for some textbooks) and can range from simple subcontracting based on tenders (for foreign-language textbooks) to the creation of agencies to develop, produce, and/or provide and distribute textbooks to the nation.

c. Equipment for teaching science and technology

The current revolution in science and technology affects the most fundamental objectives of education. Among its main roles now are preparation for living in a scientific and technological world, the acquaintance of the students with its concepts, and their initiation into the uses and applications of technology in daily life. Science and technology must be introduced at an early stage, and constitutes one of the critical elements in the renewal of primary education.

Chalk and talk will never suffice. If science is to be taught, special facilities, the level of sophistication of which will vary with the level of the pupils and the use which they intend to make of it, are required. A science laboratory is not needed in the lower grades; the experience of many countries, including the industrialised, has demonstrated that neither formal laboratories nor expensive equipment is necessary to provide satisfactory science education. With more relevant curricula, science and technology can be related to everyday life by making full use of the tools and utensils available in the community and the resources of the environment. Learning outcomes can be higher, at lower cost, than with traditional 'science-for-science's sake' approaches.

Infrastructures and advanced equipment are necessary at the upper secondary and tertiary levels, of course, where contemporary approaches to science teaching integrate practical work with theory.

Curriculum development is prerequisite to, and predates, textbook development and the purchase of equipment. Where the curriculum and equipment are determined by separate departments, lack of co-ordination will cause problems. After curriculum reform, and the production of a textbook, equipment is normally developed. But it may happen, and be discovered too late, that the text requires items which are far beyond production or import capacities, and the text has to be revised. It may be impossible to do that. If the textbook and equipment had been developed simultaneously, it would undoubtedly have worked better.

The study of science has at least two purposes: to understand scientific principles, and to use scientific knowledge to arrive at certain objectives. It is impossible to develop this kind of mental perspicacity if science training consists only in the simple recall of information. A minimum of equipment is required, and teachers must be sufficiently trained to be confident of using the equipment without fear of liability for damage or loss. Also, equipment must not be purchased for educational institutions, particularly at the secondary and tertiary levels, until provisions have been made for its maintenance (see *Inset 17*). Spare parts must be available, and as teachers are not maintenance technicians, the latter must be available within a time short enough that the school does not become demoralised by breakdowns. It may be perfectly reasonable to invest in sophisticated equipment, but not if it cannot be used.

Curriculum reform should go hand in hand, when possible, with the development of equipment especially designed to facilitate the understanding of scientific concepts.

Inset 17
A secondary school science project in Zimbabwe

Zim-Sci came into operation in 1981 as an emergency programme due to sudden expansion in secondary school enrolments after independence. It constituted a response to a lack of science teaching facilities and a shortage of qualified teachers. The project covers the first four years of secondary science education, emphasizing a practical approach. The experiments provided in study guides together with the basic kit equipment are so designed that pupils can perform experiments themselves. The nature of the materials in the study guides is such that it promotes and sustains a classroom environment in which questioning, problem-solving and critical examination of information are integral elements. The Zim-Sci materials underwent reviews and revision in the light of feedback from teachers and the evaluation studies carried out by internal and external experts. The establishment of a 'marketing system' within the ministry of education was an important step towards ensuring the supply of equipment. In stimulating interest in Zim-Sci materials and equipment within Zimbabwe and in neighbouring countries, the marketing system plays a paramount role in promoting sub-regional co-operation among countries in Africa, especially those facing similar educational problems.

Source: Unesco, *Education and training policies in sub-Saharan Africa: problems, guidelines and prospects,* Paris, Unesco, 1987.

In conventional practice, schools are provided with demonstration apparatus representing modified versions of equipment for research or industrial use. The items needed are numerous and diverse, and originate from many industrial sectors -- wood, metal, plastic, glass, chemicals, etc. A typical primary school list includes more than 100 different items; science laboratories often catalogue more than 500, some of which -- test tubes, beakers, etc. -- are sold in quantity, but it is still very difficult for a developing country to manufacture all these components, especially those required by science laboratories.

Not only are items of equipment dissimilar, the performance of practical experiments requires that they be obtained in large quantities. Student-centred science teaching means that each group of six to eight students will require a set of some 50 items ranging from instruments for measuring to test tubes, that is a minimum of

250 items for each school, provided the curriculum does not demand a fixed sequence, in which all students would be involved in the same activities at the same time. If students work individually, of course, the quantities must be multiplied by six or eight, and on a national scale the numbers will run easily into the millions. A yearly replacement rate of 10 per cent is reasonable where youngsters are handling equipment, and this adds up to a heavy burden for the country. Many have recognized the need for curriculum reform; but there is still a critical lack of specialists in the field of equipment design and manufacture -- a field not closely related to teaching -- which impedes the development of science education.

Design should be based on specifications and curriculum rather than procurement-oriented. Physical and curricular functions as well as environmental and ergonomic constraints must be defined. Careful judgement is required; automatic selection of the most expensive item because it must be the best, or the least expensive item because money is short, is the surest way to wastage, and to ending up ill-equipped. Not all items need be specially designed, but care must be taken to balance costs against efficiency, ease of use, and facility of maintenance. In the lower grades, it is advantageous to use items from the community with which the children are familiar, such as measuring cups, scales, weights, yardsticks, or knotted strings in use at local markets. Science is related to daily life, and should not be confined to laboratories. It is precisely irrelevance which explains the failure of transfer of practices and materials initiated in developed countries. Prototypes of whatever origin should be field tested before they are mass produced or mass procured.

Standard lists of equipment for planning and setting priorities, drawn up simultaneously with the curricula and textbook plans, are advisable in cases where all needs cannot possibly be satisfied. Then one can proceed to careful screening of the materials, to determine which can be produced in the country, and which must be imported. *Table 9.1* illustrates the production and acquisition options that are often presented to educational authorities. Design, production, and procurement efforts for all levels must be co-ordinated in order to take advantage of whatever economies of scale are possible, and to allow full use of staff, equipment, and facilities.

Table 9.1. Options open to educational authorities for production and acquisition of science teaching equipment

Production at National level	Production at district & provincial levels	Production by teachers, parents & pupils	Acquired from abroad
State production centres	State workshops[1]	Teacher training centres at national, provincial & district levels	Purchases ex catalogue
Large private enterprise	Co-operatives[1]		Local designs produced wholly or partially abroad
	Small private[1] enterprise	Co-operative workshops	Unicef/Unesco assistance
	Artisans[2]	Village craftspersons	Aid through other agencies
		Classroom, school workshop and home	Aid through bi-lateral programmes
Large quantities	Small batches	Individual items	Small quantities
Small precision items	Bulkier equipment	Pedagogical value attached to making	Designs & processes not available locally
High technology	Level/sophistication within skills of local manpower	Short lifespan of item	
Plastics		Simple hand tools	

Source: Unesco-Unicef, *Improving the quality of basic learning opportunities: Challenge and response,* Co-operative programme Digest 19, 1986

[1] Production, sites, sources
[2] Indications, appropriate targets.

Where the national industrial base is not yet strong, costs of total manufacturing can rapidly exceed those in more developed countries, especially if all components must be produced in the same plant. Planners must also provide for local assembly of imported components. Government and private sectors can and do promote local initiatives such as centralised manufacturing and distribution and *ad hoc* institutions. In the Philippines, a Science Education Centre is attached to the university; it prepares textbook scripts and, in collaboration with the college of engineering, designs equipment. The unit actually produces a few sophisticated items, in large quantities; but most equipment is produced by private manufacturers using designs approved by the Centre. In Madagascar, the Centre National de Production de Matériels Didactiques, established in 1976, has several woodworking, metalworking, auto-mechanics, electrical and general workshops, which manufacture a wide range of equipment from local raw materials. It has training facilities to initiate teachers in the use of the materials and in minor repairs and maintenance. Similar units have been set up in Burma, China, Ethiopia, Kenya, Democratic Korea, the Republic of Korea, Nigeria (where there are several units), Thailand, Turkey, and Venezuela, and other countries are in the process of developing them. State factories or small-scale industries have been developed to provide such equipment in India, Pakistan, Vietnam, and some countries -- India and Turkey for example -- are already exporting.

These techniques of production, along with plastic processing, glass-blowing, and biological and chemical production, are of great interest to labour-intensive countries such as these, and Unesco and other agencies are helping to promote their self-sufficiency in these areas. Central science equipment clearing houses must be provided for storing, sorting, and distributing local as well as imported goods. These units should also handle the repacking of chemicals in small quantities -- a highly labour-intensive activity. The science education centres of some countries also fill the role of a central store; in others, there are separate units (see *Inset 18*).

Inset 18
Science equipment in Nigeria

Equipment for teaching integrated science was imported at first in Nigeria, then gradually replaced by locally produced equipment. To reach this goal, the government set up a Science Equipment Development and Manufacturing Centre, which now mass produces and distributes equipment to all schools in the country. Emphasis was also placed on repair and maintenance of equipment. With help from Unesco, Regional Science Equipment Centres have been set up throughout the country, and serve all of its secondary institutions.

Source: Unesco, *Education and training policies in sub-Saharan Africa: problems, guidelines and prospects*, Paris, Unesco, 1987.

For reasons of economy, the financing of higher level science and technology laboratories should be computed as part of the building construction costs. In Latin America, a Unesco/SECAB joint effort has subsidised the design, construction and assembly of low-cost compact laboratories with locally produced elements for science teaching, in the place of more expensive, imported, conventional laboratories. Shipping fragile scientific equipment is more problematic than shipping textbooks, and must be carefully planned. Warehousing and transportation must be provided, and of course implicit in these requirements is close and comprehensive administrative supervision and control. Teachers must be instructed in the use of the equipment, whether during their period of service or beforehand, and this means a new, practical dimension in academically oriented teacher training. As a first step, facilities for training and retraining should be set up and a local network of science (teaching) resource centres developed, to offer guidance, lend special materials and equipment, and monitor their use.

Some countries have opted for setting up city-wide computer centres at which students from all the schools receive instruction, and which receive other community activities and adult education classes. Some give support to science teachers' associations, science clubs, equipment producers' associations and fairs.

Some of these items should be considered as investments, and schools should be required to maintain inventories. Administrators and teachers worry about student damage to equipment and theft of microscopes, computers and other expensive items, and keep them locked away so securely that they are used only exceptionally, notably during inspections and official visits. To ensure replacement of broken or stolen equipment, and protect administrators and teachers from liability, insurance should probably be considered, and continuous maintenance of this equipment is vital.

d. Audio-visual communication and computers

Here we are referring to the use of material such as slides, tapes, transparencies, films, video-cassettes and microcomputers in schools, as a means of solving teaching and learning problems in regular classrooms and streamlining education. These tools do not significantly alter the traditional teacher-student relationships. Even computers have aroused little evidence of altered teaching patterns that might lead to significant savings in ordinary school outlays.

There is a common belief that the media can improve learning quality, but it is difficult to demonstrate, and also to estimate, how much learning one gets for how much investment. The introduction of audio-visual equipment usually reflects changes in curriculum objectives (language instruction is a good example), so that the 'additional' learning is actually *different* learning. Moreover, as can be seen from *Table 9.2,* costs vary with the use to which the material

Table 9.2: Comparative costs of audio-visual equipment per student according to mode of utilisation

Equipment		Use	Rate of use	Annual cost	Annual cost expressed in % annual cost per student in traditional context (6,000)[1]	Hourly cost
Photographic	a)	introduction to picture-taking, instant processing	20 hours, in groups of 12	400	6.7	20
	b)	production of finished work; processing and printing effected at school	30 hours in groups of 12	750	12.5	25
Video	a)	recording-broadcasting	50 hours a year, classes of 25 students	50	0.8	4.5
	b)	video coverage course during the year	1 one-week training	75	1.25	5
	c)	basic production	production of one 15-minute programme a week for 25 weeks, in groups of 5	850	14.2	140
	d)	elaborate production	production of one 15-minute programme a week for 25 weeks, in groups of 5	2260	37.6	200
	e)	autoscopy - heteroscopy	90 hours per student per year	1575	26.2	17.5
Language laboratory	a)	20 booths used 1 hour every two weeks, i.e. 15 hours a year		370	6.2	6
	b)	example of a language laboratory where one-fifth of the programmes are produced by the school		561	9.3	37.4

[1] The annual cost per pupil aged 11 to 15 years was estimated at FF 6,000 in France in 1980, that is, at 750 hours a year, FF.8.00 per student-hour. FF.8.60 = US$1.00 (1984).

Source: Unesco, *Technical and economic criteria for media selection and planning in educational institutions,* Paris, Unesco, 1984, (Educational studies and documents, No. 48).

is put, whether it is used collectively or individually, and whether it is teacher or learner-oriented.

Below a critical time of exposure to a tool, learning is difficult to measure, and only catalytic effects are to be expected. If students are shown two 20-minute films or video-cassettes a week (this is often a maximum), the total yearly exposure is 20 hours, which can hardly balance 900 hours of instruction. But educational objectives related to basic technological culture, media education and computer literacy will ultimately become world-wide, and will inevitably mean expenditure for this equipment. A school can use existing cassettes or films, or it can try to produce materials relevant to its context. It can select the software which is appropriate to its needs, and invest in hardware with which it is compatible, or it can invest in hardware and develop the software. The use of each tool must be optimised to avoid unnecessary duplication of formats and apparatus. It must be noted that some equipment requires specialised classrooms; classical examples are language and photo labs, closed-circuit television studios, and computer rooms.

An already fairly frequent experience in developed countries justifies the use of audio-visual equipment in schools. They are an aid to instruction, create motivation and awareness, and speed the learning process. Teaching laboratories are particularly effective for higher-level intensive professional training and retraining, where opportunity costs of students' time are high (languages, micro-teaching, multimedia self-teaching systems, computer simulation). At lower levels they are often used to overcome learning difficulties in normal and (especially) handicapped children, to aid visualisation, or to facilitate understanding of difficult abstract notions. They are expected to contribute to diversifying teaching processes by varying learning activities and the size of learning units (individual to small group to class to amphitheatre).

But in developed as well as developing countries the most critical factor in the impact of audio-visual equipment upon learning is the teacher and his/her willingness to venture into technical areas. Research has shown that the teachers are the prime variable: their inertia or resistance is usually at the bottom of projects that fail. Another critical element is of course the availability of high-quality software. With hardware, once the financial hurdle is crossed, problems are easily ironed out; but lack of resource banks, film, and supplies, and other software-related problems, remain. A third problem is the organisational pattern of the school. audio-visual techniques should be encouraged only in schools where environments and human resources are favourable.

A special case would appear to be required as concerns computers, which are rapidly becoming the symbol of modernisation in education. It is unlikely that the computer will ever constitute the unique tool of education, but more than 80 per cent of those working in education today will still be active in twenty years, and so will the facilities they are using. The place and role of computers must be determined in context with those of other technologies: printing, audio-visual, etc. Experience leads to believe that the introduction of computers into education is not a mere inclusion of a tool, but a revolution that will have far-reaching repercussions at all levels of the system, its methods, contents, management structures, modes of teacher training, and relations between the school and other social institutions. Spontaneous development and *laissez faire* policies have led to impaired functioning and wastage, and more than any other equipment, computers require co-ordinated and systematic acquisition of hardware, selection of software, and training of personnel, in which staggering financial resources over long periods of time are debated against rapid technological change.

It must be remembered that computer technology is both a science to be taught and an aid to progress in other technologies. There are conflicting views as to the usefulness and educational value of computer science as a subject in general pre-university curricula, and studies have shown[9] that the effects of Computer-Assisted Instruction (CAI) are mixed:

- Improvements in performance attributable to the use of computers are comparable to those obtained with other innovative methods;
- Weaker students seem to profit most from computer-assisted teaching;
- Progress declines over time;
- The higher the level of education, the less the benefit; secondary level simulation exercises get the best results from a cognitive point of view;
- CAI requires extensive and expensive teacher training;
- Software is often inadequate.

Thus a number of countries have been less interested in CAI in recent years. While it is assumed that computers increase learning capacity, the best and most effective form is not yet certain. Computer-assisted instruction is still in its infancy, and the aims which support it, the variety of methods, and the differences in the socio-cultural environments and objectives of each society, along with psychological and institutional resistance have yet to be properly explored or dealt with. Social pressure has made it difficult to limit it in some countries, however, and it appears advisable to prepare for predictable change by ensuring the development of high-level expertise in the fields of computers and their applications to education, and by running a few pilot and future-oriented projects.

3. Summary: Priorities for physical planning and utilisation

The most important things for decision-makers to keep in mind in the context of educational facilities include:
- Keeping pedagogical concerns uppermost and aesthetics further down on the priority list;
- Encouraging design that is appropriate to cope with the evolution of pedagogical methods, and in which space is easily adapted to whatever activities it is needed for: lecture halls, seminar spaces, multi-purpose worksites, and specialised areas such as laboratories;
- Promoting design which optimises techniques for protecting the building and minimising maintenance;
- Establishing a revolving fund to cover maintenance of buildings, furniture, and equipment.

In setting priorities in the use of materials and equipment, due consideration should be given to research in cost reduction and control combined with research in effective learning so that the bottom line does not become the determinant factor of decision. Again, cost-effectiveness criteria should be used.

Textbooks should be relevant not only to the socio-cultural environment of the community and the prevailing philosophy of education, but in line with the level of expertise of the teachers and the expectations and competencies of learners and their facilities. Textbook production requires considerable and sustainable resources, both fiscal and personal, and time.

Curriculum development is prerequisite to, and predates, textbook development and the purchase of equipment. Lack of co-ordination and synchronisation will cause problems. Equipment design should be based on specification and curriculum rather than procurement-oriented. Physical and curricular functions as well as environmental and ecomomic constraints must be defined. Standard lists of equipment for planning and setting priorities, drawn up simultaneously with the curricular and textbook plans are advisable when all needs cannot be satisfied. The financing of expensive higher level science and technology laboratories should be computed as part of the building construction costs.

The most critical factor in the impact of audio-visual equipment upon learning is the teacher and his/her willingness and ability to venture into technical areas.

---

1. See J. Hallak, *Planning the location of schools: an instrument of educational policy,* Paris, Unesco:IIEP, 1977.

2. The generally recognized maximum for a primary school is 400 to 450 pupils, with 10 teachers (including the headmaster or headmistress); for a secondary school, 750 to 1,200, with 25 teachers plus a director.

3. Afghanistan, Chad, Mexico, and Nepal, among others.

4. A.M. Verspoor; J.L. Leno, *Textbooks as instruments for the improvement of the quality of education,* Washington, D.C., World Bank, 1986, (Report No. EDT50).

5. S.P. Heynemann; J.P. Farrell; M.A. Sepulveda-Stuardo, *Textbooks and achievement: what we know,* Washington D.C., World Bank, (Staff working paper No 298). M.E. Lockheed; S.C. Vail; B. Fuller, *How textbooks affect achievement,* Washington D.C., World Bank, (Report no EDT53)

6. F. Orivel; F. Sergent, 'Foreign aid to education in sub-Saharan Africa: how useful is it?' In: *Prospects,* Vol. 13, No. 4, 1988.

7. K.C. Yadunandan, 'Nepal: for better planning of textbook production', In: *Prospects,* Vol. 13, No. 3, 1983.

8. P.G. Altbach, 'Key issues of textbook production,' In: *Prospects,* Vol. 13, No. 3, 1983.

9. M. Carnoy; H. Daley; L. Loop, *Education and computers: vision and reality,* Paris, Unesco, 1987, (ED/87/WS/37).

Chapter 10

Beyond the school systems: priorities in managing non-formal education programmes

Non-formal education has proliferated over the past few decades, radically altering the contours of the educational field. Even the least informed observer will have noticed that the educational field is highly diverse. While the school remains the dominant institution in education, it is no longer the only path that individuals can take to pursue explicit educational and training objectives. A wide range of educational possibilities have developed outside it, and are expanding rapidly.

This chapter will attempt to give, first, a sketchy overview of the various functions, fields and organisational modes of non-formal education. The ways and means by which NFE can help in two major challenges in developing countries -- expanding literacy and skill training -- and which deserve increased encouragement and support, will then be looked at more closely. Particular attention will be paid to illiterate adults, unserved children and drop-outs, as the major target groups of non-formal literacy schemes, as well as to the possible responses of non-formal training to the needs of the informal and the traditional sectors of the economy.

1. The manifold facets of NFE

Non-formal education is highly heterogeneous: it applies to many fields, many activities, many audiences; it is financed by various agents, public and private, and offered in varied forms. It can be very loose, or so structured as to look very much like formal education. But it can get to the most educated as well as to the most depressed sectors of the population -- rural women, isolated indigenous populations, child workers, etc. -- which the formal sector sometimes cannot reach.

NFE deals with everything from literacy campaigns to computer technology. It is sometimes in a favourable position to compete with or outdistance formal education, but it can also be used to supplement the formal services.

In most cases, NFE varies with level of development. In the poorest developing countries, apart from those which have extensive literacy campaigns, NFE programmes are not sufficiently developed. In fact, in many countries of low economic levels, the potential of NFE is far from being fully utilised.

It seems somehow paradoxical that it is the more educationally advanced countries which generate the most demand for NFE.

To different degrees in different contexts, four broad areas of NFE emerge parallel to the formal school systems: paraformal education, popular education, education for personal improvement, and professional training -- so classified because they:

- respond to different needs;
- serve different clienteles;
- are organised by different agents;
- have different relationships with formal education systems.

Table 10.1 proposes a classification of different types of non-formal education and of their respective modes of organisation. The classification is based on the results of a few studies on non-formal education in various parts of the world. There may, of course, be different ways of categorising the very diverse types and forms of non-formal education, but the one adopted here is particularly relevant.

Paraformal (evening classes, distance education, etc.) refers to programmes that provide a substitute for formal schooling, i.e., offer a 'second chance' to those who cannot attend regular schooling. Popular is explicitly targeted to serve marginal groups. It is the least institutionalised component, including adult literacy, co-operative training, political mobilisation, and/or community development. Education for personal improvement (music, languages, sports, etc.) is provided by clubs, cultural institutions, and associations, and in most cases paid for by the client. Professional or vocational NFE

Table 10.1: *Organising Agencies*

Organizing agent	Public	Private				
		Firms	Churches	Trade unions	Volunteers	Profit-making organ.
Paraformal	xxx		x	x		x
Popular	x		xxx	xxx	xxx	
Personal improvement	xx	x		x	xx	xxx
Professional/vocational	xxx	xxx		xx		xxx

xxx: Important
xx: Secondary
x: Marginal

Source: IIEP, *The diversification of the educational field,* Paris, IIEP, 1989, (Mimeo).

training can be provided by firms, trade unions, private agencies, and of course, schools.

The first distinction to be made is between public and private. Governments are often important organisers of out-of-school educational activities -- not only ministries of education, but also other ministries and public services -- and local authorities are taking increasing interest in these varied and flexible forms. It is in paraformal activities that governments generally play an important role; for example, a survey[1] of Latin American literacy programmes shows that of 14 countries, the programmes of 11 were run by public administrations, 2 by private agencies and 1 by public and private institutions. A survey of Burma, Brazil, China, Cuba, Somalia, Tanzania, USSR and Vietnam[2] equally concludes that governments play predominant roles. Governments are also very present in professional training and, to a lesser extent, personal improvement schemes. They are involved to a limited extent in popular education, and even then work primarily through local governments. It is the churches, trade-unions and other non-profit organisations that are most involved in popular education activities, while enterprises and profit-making organisations primarily operate in the fields of professional and personal improvement.

There is then no such thing as a typical NFE institution. NFE organisers are very different from each other and highly specialised; but many links are being developed between them, notably a process of sub-contracting of the private sector by the public sector, and between institutions in the same sector. Thus it is sometimes difficult to make clear distinctions between their enrolments, or to evaluate costs. The following will concentrate on three areas which rely heavily on the public sector for organisation, financing, and operating: literacy programmes (targeted on adults, primarily), services for unschooled children and dropouts, and vocational training for skill development.

It is not claimed that non-formal education is a panacea, or that it can substitute entirely for formal education. There are implementation problems. But it has been seen that NFE programmes that are economically and politically integrated, adequately financed, and placed in appropriate legal frameworks or loosely co-ordinated with FE programmes can be successful, especially in reaching otherwise problematic populations.

2. Expanding literacy

a. Adult education

Adult education is perhaps the most important area of action in literacy programmes, but we use the term 'literacy' to include any measure that follows from or substitutes for formal education to advance literacy. Despite progress in school enrolments, only a few countries have literacy rates near 100 per cent. Industrialised countries suffer from what is called the functional illiteracy of significant segments of their populations. In developing countries, many adults, especially in rural areas, are illiterate, and many young people drop out too early to be literate, or at least to remain so. Thus the ubiquitous problem of supplementing formal school programmes. Literacy campaigns have been conducted in socially and economically diverse countries, and it is not easy to assess their impacts. Where there is any information on these efforts, the demarcation between formal and non-formal education is fuzzy and the results may be imputed to either.

Often deemed unsuccessful, for lack of political will, lack of resources, lack of post-literacy structures, lack of motivation on the part of the potential clients, and perhaps public perceptions which do not include sensitivity to the value of literacy, it is our premise that these programmes could -- at low cost -- raise the literacy rates of cohorts of young people and of whole populations. Smaller programmes rather than great nationwide campaigns might be more effective and easier to control[3] (see *Inset 19*).

Experience accumulated by many countries indicates the advisability of two-level approaches, in the school system, and in the community (see *Table 10.2*).

Inset 19
Kenyan literacy programme

A literacy programme was introduced in Kenya as part of a global development strategy on which the country's Fourth Development Plan (1979-1983) was based. A department of adult education was established within the ministry of culture and social services, whose role was one of stimulation, supervision and technical support for the literacy programme (training of literacy personnel through short-term seminars and correspondence courses, preparation of primers and other teaching materials; regular supervision of teaching staff; collection of statistical data about enrolment, centres and teachers; organization of national literacy tests).

The methodological approach promoted by the department was functional, aiming at establishing systematic links between literacy teaching and the everyday activities of participants. Learners were supposed to become functionally literate in a period of 9 months, which corresponds to some 300 to 400 hours of literacy class attendance.

For those who have obtained a literacy certificate, a post-literacy programme has been developed and corresponding learning materials have been prepared. In certain urban areas, a few centres prepare neo-literates and primary school drop-outs for taking the CPE (Certificate of Primary Education). In order to reach the general public, special programmes have been broadcast.

Between 1980 and 1987, 108,485 learners were formally certified.

A study shows that the main problem which the Kenyan literacy programme is facing is its limited coverage and the difficulty of sustaining its growth. Enrolments have been regularly declining and the number of literacy certificates delivered has remained at a very low level (in 1985, 5.09 per cent of the learners became certified). This decline was not a result of a reduction of supply but a rapid demobilisation of the demand. The central issue is therefore the motivation of the learner, which determines his/her decision to enrol, the regularity of attendance and the perseverance to continue. The learners' motivation can be sustained by active literacy methods adapted to adult learners and leading to quick results in order to sustain their interest (which means that the teachers have to be properly trained and motivated too). But there is also another point: the learners are more motivated (to learn and retain) when they can use literacy skills in their everyday life.

Source: G. Carron; K. Mwiria; G. Righa, *The functioning and effects of the Kenyan Literacy Programme: a view from the local level.* Paris, Unesco:IIEP, 1989, (IIEP Research Report No. 76).

---

b. Response to unserved children and early drop-outs

Factors in both educational systems and environments are among those most responsible for inhibiting the access of children to formal education, and discouraging those who do attend. An educational response must be as diversified as the target groups themselves, its conception and design planned just as activities are planned in the formal systems although the planning and implementation procedures may be partly different.[4] Difficulties peculiar to NFE might include:

- identifying the unserved populations, understanding their motivations, assessing their attitudes;
- analysing the specific educational and general conditions in their areas;
- selecting key partners with whom to set up educational projects: representatives of the formal education systems, development officials, political and economic advisers, community representatives, etc.;
- isolating the educational needs, finding and estimating resources, defining aims, means, and an evaluation system.

Targets are specific and limited, and these actions may not have much of an impact on enrolment or literacy in quantitative terms. But a drop in the ocean though they may be, they can play very important roles in the lives of the people they do reach. They can also serve as starting points for extending benefits, and as follow-up to activities of the formal systems. Being directly concerned with immediate local life, they can draw problems to the attention of central agencies and help to formulate appropriate solutions.

The project in Maharashtra State, India, described in *Inset 20,* is one of the numerous examples of effective NFE (among those one could also cite the tutorial schools and colleges in the Indian sub-continent) which illustrate the validity of an NFE activity as an extension of the formal school system.

c. The two-level approach to literacy

Irrespective of their specific target groups literacy programmes have to be rooted in both the school system and the community (see *Table 10.2*).

Table 10.2: *The two-level approach to literacy*

I. ON THE SYSTEM LEVEL

Political will and support	- setting framework by law - including literacy in national development plans - allocating funds judicially to insure regular financing.
Administrative organization base on principle of duality	- an autonomous central literacy office to define orientations, programmes and exercise a regulatory function, offering incentives to promote local initiative (national literacy prizes and awards) - local municipalities to execute the programmes, with responsibility for adopting them to local conditions.

Collaboration between literacy departments and other ministries, public and private organizations
  to coordinate actions and
  maximise results
	- coordination cells at the various levels
	- regular information systems (meetings, papers)

to find and use more resources	- agreements with public and private enterprises and voluntary organisations. - when feasible, the use of civil or military services to recruit trainers;
Staff training and mobilisation	- short initial and regular in-service training for those engaged in literacy programmes at each level - systematic literacy training (especially adult methods) in regular teacher training. - emoluments when feasible;
Support of school supervisors	- school visits, meetings of adult educators in a given area, organised by supervisors.
Teaching aids	- basic didactic material (books for students and teachers, posters, literacy teachers' books) - modern media such as radio, television, rural press, DE literacy programmes.
Evaluation and research	- creating a Research Department, preferably attached to a university, to evaluate the programme continuously, rectify if necessary, and measure effects - research on information systems, data collection, indicators for evaluation, methods and pedagogy, follow-up necessities (post-literacy, printed materials for neoliterates ...).

II.   ON THE COMMUNITY LEVEL

Adapting teaching (methods and contents) to the local population's needs	- using adult pedagogy - teaching in local languages according to expectations of learners - organizing community work - involving development officers
	- setting up community centres to organise and manage activities;
Co-ordination between formal primary and literacy programmes and teachers to stimulate feedback between school and communities, children and adults	- at trainers' level: meetings, elaboration of common community development evaluations and use of facilities; - at learners' level: mobilising young adult learners to participate in common activities, such as cottage production of teaching materials, monitoring.

(i) At the system level

Political will and support is an essential condition for success. Literacy activities must be integrated in national development plans and receive adequate allocations in human and financial resources. Legal and fiscal benefits could be offered as incentives to organising entities, lotteries might be organised, and awards made to learners who complete well-defined courses of study.

At the same time, it is the prerogative of the State to enlist the efforts of other institutions, such as NGOs and mass organisations. Where the government is not decisive, these organisations will probably be ineffectual as well.[5]

Administrative organisation should be based on a 'principle of duality'. Central levels develop standards of quality and norms, provide training to adult educators and financial support. Local levels initiate, execute and adapt programmes to local conditions.

If literacy departments collaborate closely with other public or private organisations, concerted action can optimise the resources available. Priorities and programmes can be examined and implemented via meetings of the representatives of the various ministries, universities and trade unions, state governors, and mayors.

Inset 20
NFE in Maharashtra State, India

To provide primary education to illiterate girls aged 9 to 14 in a rural area in Maharashtra State, 89 non-formal evening classes were opened with an enrolment of 1,431 children, 1,040 of whom were girls. In these areas it is usually the boys who go to school, the girls being kept at home to do household, agricultural, or construction work.

Attendance at the evening classes was voluntary; the children could remain in the system in spite of irregular attendance, although this was normally very good, except during the heavy rains, at festival time, or when agriculture demanded particularly long, hard work. The classes consisted of reciting songs, poems and stories, and playing language and number games. Homework consisted of attention to personal cleanliness and good health habits, collecting specimens from nature and waste materials for learning aids, and practising traditional crafts.

Most of the parents agreed to send the girls to the classes because they felt they provided opportunities for relaxing and enjoying social contacts; also, the classes were within short distances of home, and if parents needed a girl at home she could be sent for in a hurry. Some of the parents, particularly mothers, who had been to primary school and dropped out, wanted to give their daughters a chance which they had missed. And finally, it was observed that literacy of girls has come to be looked on as a means of improving their marriage prospects.

In offering classes in these remote areas, project organisers have appointed only local teachers, none of whom, as it happens, had previous professional training. Their qualifications range from secondary school certificates to completion of primary school. Communication among the villagers, teachers, and pupils is excellent, as they all know one another. Teachers are trained in pilot centres, five days of every month, in a centrally located village. Locally oriented teaching materials are prepared with their help.

The pupils -- about 20 per class -- help to organise the classes and clean the classrooms. There are no bells signalling the beginning or end of the activities. Pupils arrive as soon as they can, and leave as late as they can. Most of the pupils complete an equivalent of standard grade 4 within a period of two years, and learn a good deal about health, sanitation, group living, self-teaching, and decision-making in the process. During the first year of the programme, only a very few drop-outs occurred.

Source: Unesco/Asian Programme for Educational Innovation for Development (APEID), 'Education for rural development: a portfolio of studies', In: *Education for disadvantaged women*, Bangkok, APEID, 1982, Vol. 2, pp.10-12.

Regular information on programme implementation, progress and problems can be disseminated and private funding mobilised. A fairly reliable source of adult educators is the civil or military service.

Staff training and mobilisation are crucial to the success of a literacy programme. Skilled teachers may be recruited from the formal system, adult educators and rural developers from the communities; these people are generally paid for their services, but volunteers can also be attracted. Specific training for the task should be provided to all: in-service literacy training (adult pedagogy) can be provided systematically in teacher training curricula; initial literacy training should be provided to all those engaged in the programmes, and a network of pedagogical and organisational support services, replete with radio and television where possible, might be mounted and made available to them. The issue of emoluments must not be neglected, but they do not guarantee enthusiasm below a certain level; and it must be said that without the establishment of an atmosphere of importance, neither paid employees nor unpaid volunteers will be enthusiastic for very long. Once the organisation begins paying its staff, it will not be able to revert to volunteer labour, and having both paid and unpaid people doing the same work often causes problems.

Support from school supervisors is very welcome in these programmes. They should be compensated enough to be able to visit the literacy classes regularly, and to organise meetings with the teachers. They can also play administrative roles, liaison with the central level, for example, and make pedagogical suggestions to the teachers. Teaching aids, provided free to teachers and at low cost to learners, can be very effective both in ensuring a homogeneity in the classes and in motivating learners.

Evaluation and research are essential. It may be necessary to create a research department to evaluate programmes continuously and detect and rectify problems as quickly as possible. A good information system, such as MIS, might furnish indicators to assess internal efficiency, methods and pedagogy, follow-up activities, etc.

(ii) At the community level

Studies show that the motivation of the learner to attain literacy is a good deal more important to the success of a programme than curriculum content.[6] Still, teaching methods and contents must be adapted to the real life of a community. Opinions diverge, but it is generally felt either that literacy and numeracy should be paramount, and other subjects of interest to the learners included, or that curricula should focus on production techniques or politico-ideological questions. In deciding the aims of NFE and FE as well, each country must set its aims, keeping in mind the fact that an overheavy burden both in range of topics and technical complexity will trample the confidence of already overworked learners.

Teaching methods can vary considerably, but adult learners must be treated with respect and patience, and there must be no hint of patronising attitudes. The teachers' attitudes, and their relations with a community, are as important as knowing what they are talking about.[7] Local languages can and should be used, if the learners are thereby facilitated in their learning; and a good many other ideas occur to those who take the time to ponder on educational quality, attendance, and educational outcome. Simple projects can be undertaken by communities; rural development officers can be involved in the programmes; community centres can be set up to help with management and implementation.

Co-ordination between formal primary and non-formal literacy programmes can stimulate feedback between school and community, and between children and adults, in ways that are very constructive.

- *For trainers:* meetings of teachers and (adult) educators to exchange information and if possible plan community development activities.
- *For institutions:* organisation of libraries and co-operatives, mobilising common activities for children and adults.
- *For children and adults:* school and community linkages to produce cottage educational materials from local resources; peer monitoring; etc.
- *For drop-outs:* a chance to benefit from either or both systems according to their own time constraints.

This package of fairly ambitious measures is not the only way towards the eradication of illiteracy. It may be regarded as a means of focusing on fundamental aspects to be considered when contemplating the requirements of a given population.

3. Skill training

Nowadays, countries can choose from a considerable array of training delivery systems.[8] In general, formal programmes can best provide training in a representative sample of skills which concern one broad occupational field or several related fields. They are however limited in their capability to provide training in very specific skill areas, largely because of the difficulty of rapidly adapting equipment, curricula, etc.. to the varying and fast changing skill needs of specific employers. Furthermore, formal vocational training generally aims at responding to skill needs in the modern employment sector, whereas the vast majority of the working population in most developing countries is engaged in the traditional sectors of agriculture and handicrafts and the informal sector.

Non-formal programmes offer a wide variety of training alternatives in cost, length and type of training which can help overcome the existing skill gaps.

Much has been written and said about the crucial role that firms, especially large firms, 'inter-firm' and 'university-industry' networks, can play in highly specialised as well as in *ad hoc* skill-specific and job-specific training aimed at meeting new or changing skill requirements (due largely to technological change and the exposure to increased world-wide competition). This section will, therefore, limit itself to dealing with essential aspects of and experiences in non-formal training for the traditional and informal employment sectors; for many years in the future, these sectors can be expected to remain the main occupational sectors in a large number of developing countries.

The informal economic sector is characterised by the 'smallness' of the work unit, often consisting of only one or two individuals, with ten full-time workers constituting the upper limit of informal enterprises. It is really made up of many 'sub-sectors' -- small entrepreneurs and establishments; independent and casual workers engaged in craft work; workshop production and commercial and service jobs -- which have different training needs. Training must rather be 'tailor-made' and respond to the immediate needs of individual establishments. It has to be low cost, as the trainees in the informal sector and their families generally cover the cost of training by paying 'learning fees' to masters who take on apprentices. Finally, factors such as long working hours and reluctance of employers in the informal sector to become involved, have to be taken into account. On-the-job training or flexible training in small groups at the local level (mobile training teams), which make use of the existing infrastructure of machinery and equipment in small enterprises, constitute adequate responses to the particular constraints of the informal sector.

Low-cost training alternatives should be looked for, but not at any rate. If the investment in a programme is too limited to ensure a minimum level of instructional quality and student achievement, the cost-effectiveness of the programme will be actually very low. Besides, minimum levels of investment, adequate maintenance and management capabilities constitute major prerequisites of cost-effectiveness: all too often, the inability to maintain and repair tools, machinery and equipment at a level necessary to ensure optimal amortisation of investment may contribute to unreasonable and extremely high capital costs. In many cases the lack and inadequacy of instructional materials seriously hamper the effectiveness of non-formal training. Above all, the administrative capacity necessary to ensure the viability and sustainability of the programme has frequently proved to be insufficient.

In developing more or less centralised agencies that provide key support services (evaluation; advice; development and delivery of instructional materials, etc..), public authorities could help overcome these difficulties. Governments could also envisage encouraging successful formulae of non-formal training by special incentives (certification; subsidies, etc.).

Youths and adults who have had to leave the formal system before attaining any professional qualification constitute a large group in the informal sector; they deserve particular attention. One of the major problems faced in organising activities aimed at this group is the low level of literacy and numeracy characterising the beneficiaries. According to the special needs and difficulties of the target groups, programmes may have to include elements such as basic subsistence support (food, health care, shelter, etc.) and social services (counselling) besides the training component.

Numerous programmes for street children (see *Inset 21*) are presently run by various international and national, governmental and non-governmental organisations; they attempt to provide training which takes the specific needs of this target group into account.

Inset 21
Amal: a family reunification and vocational
training programme for street children in Sudan

The children are offered full accommodation for an initial period
of two to three weeks, during which time they receive some literacy
classes in the mornings and sport-recreation programmes in the
afternoons. During this period, project staff carry out investigations
into the backgrounds of the children, who are then provided with the
means, such as transport, to rejoin their families.

Where family reunification is not feasible (as in the case of most
children from Southern Sudan), the children are transferred to 'Beit El
Amal' (House of Hope). This is a longer-term residential facility
providing not only accommodation, but also regular education and
vocational training.

The approach that is followed involves, first, interviews by social
workers with the street boys in Khartoum. This is followed by visits
of counterpart social workers in the rural areas to the boys' homes
and local technical training facilities prior to reunification. The
project relies on developing intensive relationships between the social
worker, the boy, the family and training institutes. This is a
time-consuming activity but reportedly relatively cost effective given
the good results thus far achieved. It is also reported that as a result of
this approach about 300 boys have been successfully reunified and
150 of these have been employed or engaged as apprentices in local
workshops where they earn a modest, but regular, salary. The
programme is estimated to cost about US$156 per reunified child.

Source: 'The emerging response to child labour', In: *Conditions of Work
Digest,* (ILO), Vol. 7, No. 1.

In a large number of developing countries, training for rural
development provided through both formal and non formal delivery
systems will also remain a primordial concern in the coming years.

Over the last decades, a good many programmes have been
implemented for farmers, with the idea that the more educated a rural
population is, the more productive it will be. This may or may not be
so, but productivity is found to improve with increased literacy and
numeracy -- fractions particularly, which are necessary to calculate
dosages in applying products to the fields. Where experimentation is
part of the timetable, and there is a positive general economic and

social attitude towards innovation in the community, the programmes have been found to be more closely correlated to production (see *Inset 22*). Furthermore, rural-based training schemes seem to be particularly efficient when they are combined with a package of initiatives aimed to address production and market-related concerns.

Inset 22
The Botswana Brigades

The Botswana Brigades are a rural-based training scheme. The small autonomous training and production units are controlled by a local board of trustees. Training is given to 16- to 18-year-old primary school leavers and mainly focuses on local occupations. One day is spent on academic upgrading and trade theory, and four days are assigned to practical work. The service and production activities of the units provide a way to offset training costs, and often include community development activities. The objective is to generate income, support community development and provide practical training.

Production activities contain a natural link between the training and the buyers of the product (surrogate employers). As products are designed, produced and marketed, the necessary technical skills for each step are identified and can be built into the instruction. This mechanism allows for adjustment on an ongoing basis. Moreover, instruction is directly tied to its application. In fact, because there is more control over the design of the training and wider arrays of practical activities to offer trainees, production centres can achieve a more satisfactory combination of theoretical and practical instruction than conventional on-the-job training.

Source: UNDP, *Education and training in the 1990s: developing countries' needs and strategies,* New York, Education Development Center, 1989, (Policy Discussion Paper).

Training aimed at addressing rural development objectives has to cope with a population with little free time, restricted resources, often low levels of basic education, and difficulties in forming groups large enough to organise cost-effective training. Further exploration and development of new instructional technologies which can be centrally prepared and standardised, and at the same time less dependent on inflexible delivery systems, is urgently needed.

Training systems, be they formal or non-formal, take time to mature. Experience suggests that non-formal training programmes face the same difficulties in building up and maintaining quality as formal programmes. New non-formal training should, therefore, be started on a small scale that can be effectively administered and managed until greater experience is gained and until linkages with employers and other social institutions, notably at the local level, are well established; cautious incremental expansion of training schemes is also required in order to ensure sustained investment in these schemes over a relatively long period of time. In any case, concentration of investment in the most effective training schemes and in those elements required for maintaining instructional quality (adequately trained and paid instructors, instructional resources, evaluation systems, efficient programme administration) are major conditions of the quality and success of non-formal training.

4. Summary: guidelines for establishing priorities in NFE

Non-formal education and training can obviously play a major role in meeting the still widely unsatisfied basic educational needs and essential skill requirements for development. Despite the manifold forms and fields of NFE initiatives, experience points to certain common conditions on which the effectiveness of NFE generally depends to a great extent:

- sufficient administrative and management capacities;
- experimentation before the expansion of NFE schemes;
- regular cost-effectiveness control;
- careful choice, development and delivery of adequate instructional materials;
- flexible organisation adapted to the specific needs and constraints of the learners, which often goes alongside a certain decentralisation of management;
- integration of non-formal education and training services with other development activities;
- linkage between non-formal education and training and the educational and social institutions at the local level.

253

1. C.E. Beca, *Alfabetización y post alfabetización en América Latina,* Santiago de Chile, Unesco : OREALC, 1987.

2. H.S. Bhola, *Campaigning for literacy: eight national experiences of the twentieth century, with a memorandum to decision makers,* Paris, Unesco, 1984.

3. See Unesco/UNDP, *The world of literacy. Policy, research and action.* Ottawa, International Development Research Centre, 1979; and Unesco, Office of Statistics, *Compendium of statistics on illiteracy,* Paris, Unesco, 1988, (Statistical reports and studies, 30).

4. See J. Hallak, *Planning the location of schools,* Paris, Unesco:IIEP, 1977.

5. A. Lind; A. Johnston, *Adult Literacy in the Third World. a review of objectives and strategies,* Stockholm, University of Stockholm, Swedish International Development Authority, 1986, (SIDA Education Division Documents, No. 32).

6. Ibid.

7. Ibid.

8. UNDP, *Needs and strategies for education and training in developing countries in the 1990s,* New York, Education Development Center, 1989.

Chapter 11

Managing the system: priorities for management and administration

More people and more financing are involved in the administration and management of educational systems, in most countries, than in any other sector of activity, and it is extremely important that its machinery be efficient and smooth-running.[1] Data on the size, efficiency and performance of developing countries' administrative systems are neither comprehensive nor systematic, but partial evidence suggests that they reflect their jagged histories. For the most part their structures were never designed to handle the massive school systems of today, and in addition to that, their quality and efficiency usually leave a good deal to be desired. As is to be expected, educational administrators are almost always selected from among the teachers, who attain, fairly late in life, administrative positions which neither their training nor their experience has ever prepared them for.

Few developing countries have adequate administrative training facilities. As a matter of fact, in both developing and industrialised countries, communication and information systems are invariably sluggish, and data are seldom available to administrators when they need it. It follows that administrators find it difficult to monitor the educational systems, and heavy routine impedes innovation and initiative. Administrative procedures are invariably cumbersome and dilatory: add to that the image of an ageing functionary not accustomed to taking initiative and we have the perfect formula for a dysfunctional system. Coming fresh and eager into a system like this is disappointing if not crushing. It takes more than professionalism to perform under such circumstances.

The recession of the 1970s and the subsequent restrictions on · educational budgets affected the resources of administrations to such an extent that in some countries of Central America and the sub-Sahara the outlays for operating and managing school systems were more or less symbolic: little or no resources for transport, office equipment, supplies, or maintenance. What is covered is the salaries of a small number of persons, who belong neither to the civil service nor to the teaching profession, and not enough money is allocated to implement even the most routine tasks. If any of the recommendations here regarding policy, priority, or strategy are to be carried out, if the quality and efficiency of education systems are to be boosted, if the suggestions of the preceding chapters are to be implemented, a certain minimum of resources must be found by governments and directed toward the administration of their educational structures.

1. The case for modest strategies of improvement

The most important tenet in setting about improving educational systems is to keep reform measures modest and manageable. Many countries, often with the support of international agencies, have started off too ambitiously, and the mistakes have been proportional.

It may or may not be a good idea to bypass administrative structures to get quick results. A new idea for reform sometimes moves governments to enlist younger, more motivated (perhaps better paid), elitist staff, give them a direct line to the minister's office, and ignore the entrenched bureaucracy. Sometimes it works. But it may not work forever, and how does one go from *'emergency structures'* of this kind back to the old routine? If the bureaucracy in place feels no sense of commitment or responsibility for the new policy, if it has been parachuted in over their heads, they will simply wait until things return to normal and they can go back to doing their jobs.

The recent experience of a Latin American country is illustrative. A new minister of education decided to computerise the operations of the department. A computing centre was established, with young and eager staff fresh from a prestigious foreign university. It had the status of a 'general directorate', that is, far higher than that of the division of statistics and information of the planning department, and direct working relationships with the minister and his staff.

During the first two years of its existence, no statistical yearbook was produced (software was developed, however). The data collected by the old division of statistics were demanded by the centre. They were not checked as well as they had been, and the young team had little experience of the actual goings on in the schools. The centre's first printout was quite useless. The country had a habit of changing ministers fairly suddenly, and that is what happened. The new minister was less interested in statistics, and the centre gradually declined. The old division, confirmed in its suspicions by the centre's failure, went back to producing and processing school data the way it had always done.

Massive injections of financial resources and ambitious plans for reform may get fast results. But most problems of educational administration are common to the rest of the public sector as well, and unless they are addressed globally they will tend to persist, or to resurface. Some problems have their roots in the culture and traditions of the societies, and require solutions very different from just pumping money in. Fast results may not be permanent results. Administrative machinery is composed of human beings, and human beings take time to change. Some changes may even take generations. The replacement of senior managers through early retirement schemes might keep the administrations younger, but even lowering the age of retirement requires time and funds over and above their actual costs, which may not be noticed until one has to pay them.

We should never overlook the fact that the *routine business of education is much more important than grand designs for reform.* If schools do not open their doors, if textbooks and supplies do not reach the pupils, if teachers are not paid, the best policies, plans, or reforms will serve for very little. In our view, the improvement of administrative machinery must always begin with the everyday functions of delivery. This is already a challenging and difficult undertaking, requiring time, political commitment, and the enlistment of social support.

2. Guidelines for the improvement of routine management

At least eight major routine tasks require to be managed effectively and efficiently, especially where resources are scarce:
- Setting of objectives and curriculum planning;
- Organising the school year and the agenda;
- Budgeting and finance;
- Recruitment and deployment of human resources;
- Juggling of space;
- Management of student flows;
- Supply and delivery of materials and equipment;
- Control and assessment of performance, and consideration of feedback.

Strategies for the improvement of these routine tasks cannot be established on general bases. Current administrative structures and the conditions prevailing will determine what results are expected, what measures shall be taken, and how long it will be before the effects will be felt. The important thing to remember is that reform must be gradual.

a. Diagnosis of the administration

To bring about even gradual change in an administration, it is first necessary to know how it is working now. A study of its *modus operandi* will include (i) the nature of management responsibilities; (ii) the process of day-to-day decision-making (often concentrated in the office of the permanent secretary or minister); (iii) the degree of shortfall between the present number of managers and those needed, particularly, and sometimes crucially, at middle level; (iv) the practices established for handling routine activity;[2] (v) the 'warning' indicators and feedback used to adjust the administrative system and prevent disruptions; (vi) implicit and explicit incentive systems.[3]

A major management constraint concerns the co-ordination of public and private organisational structures. Because they vary widely in size, status, and mode of operation, and because there is little communication from one to the other, the components of school systems challenge the capacities of those in charge of their management. Co-ordination for its own sake is rarely useful; what is required is to map out the major administrative responsibilities and make a flowchart of the entities involved. In this way ministry management will be less fragmented and responsibilities (and accountability) can be smoothly delegated to the various levels in the machinery. Mechanisms for the exchange of information, for consultation, and for negotiating joint undertakings can then be set up, and the clogging of all channels at the bottleneck of one office is obviated.

The structuring of a network of loci of task management, if it is done well, will contribute simultaneously to the reduction of duplication and the pooling of resources for economies of scale. Co-ordination is vital to the administration and management of an education system if it is to serve the development policy of a country. And of course, that is what educational planning is all about.

b. Training

Having assessed and confirmed the level of unmet demand, a long-term planning frame for management training must be constructed (up to 10 years), especially in countries which continue to rely heavily or exclusively on foreign sources for high-level administrative personnel. A shorter programme is probably excessively costly, requiring the removal of too many managers from active service; and the risk is high that it will not train enough management personnel to be cost-effective.

As concerns the institutions of higher learning, the most immediate problem to be addressed is usually the scarcity of middle-level administrators, whose potential for liquidating the long delays in task management -- by sharing among themselves the work which is usually concentrated in the front office of the ministry -- is impressive. The senior management of a university is usually chosen from among its most prestigious professionals, and these officials often turn out to be mediocre administrators; (middle-level) assistant secretaries can do a good deal to improve the routine administration of a university.

c. Information technology

Dissemination of information is never a substitute for management skills, but it is an important complement to them. As management control expands, the able manager can administer a wider range of responsibilities if her/his information channels are well oiled. In many countries, shortages of trained people make decision-making highly concentrated, which means long delays and increases the probability that decisions will be slapdash. The information technology now available can reduce delays and increase access to data. If local managers are indeed to be well trained, a transition period in the life of the administration will impose added burdens on present staff. Information systems can facilitate their tasks at a minimum cost, and the current generation of microprocessors requires fairly short introductory training. Low investment and maintenance costs also make them a very attractive option for some countries.

d. Sharing and exchange of facilities and services

Countries of small size must capitalise on every opportunity for economies of scale. In areas such as textbook production (making full use of printing facilities), distribution (taking advantages of possibilities for combining deliveries of various goods), teacher training centres (placed, perhaps, at the disposal of several schools), synergy with the department of public administration, for example, in managing staff files and salary payments. A few countries use the internal mailing services of their departments of defence to carry correspondence courses to and from remote rural areas that the postal department has trouble reaching.

It is suggested that some of the services of one sub-sector might be sub-contracted to others for the sake of efficiency -- for example the management of final primary examinations assigned to the centres that conduct secondary examinations; planning and research activities to specialised university departments -- or to other ministries. School health and nutrition services might more efficiently be provided by the ministry of health; school buses managed by transport departments, data analyses by information services.

e. Incentives, seniority, and advancement

It is probably better to have no incentives at all than to bother with incentives which are not perceived as worth having. But if they are substantial, they should be precisely defined in terms of time so that they are not taken for granted. A special fund is sometimes established in budgets and phased out after a specified number of years.

Financial rewards are obviously not the only motives for doing a good job. A major conditioning variable in the management environment is the attitude of the society toward its bureaucrats, which in turn is conditioned by the degree to which employment and advancement is merit-based as opposed to ascriptive. It is true that to greater or lesser degrees, 'modern' dynamism and innovation are spreading throughout the most dynamic areas of the private sector, and into specific segments of the public sector. Without going against their value systems or traditions, countries want to encourage the kind of behaviour which combines dynamic personal initiative with dedicated social responsibility, for this is the behaviour that makes bureaucratic systems work. The role of a worthy developing government is to maintain a commitment to managerial quality without sacrificing localisation rates (the speed with which foreign staff are replaced by local staff). Most senior managers in developing countries belong to the old school, and large numbers of young professionals, some of them well trained, languish in powerless posts. Unfortunately it is never very clear what the speeds of localisation and retirement should be. It is a long walk on a high tightrope. Choices must be delicately and carefully made.

f. The private sector

In a number of countries the private sector is very important in delivering education, and this pertains to all levels of the system. It can be highly heterogeneous, as far as quality is concerned, encompassing the best and the worst of a system. Where investment is directed towards this sector, it should be for the purposes of (i) helping the various entities organise and co-operate among themselves; (ii) introducing a spirit of co-operation with the public sector; and (iii) contributing to the quality of service offered. There is no simple model, but it is usually a good idea for educational administrations to improve the effectiveness of the private sector and to promote co-operation with the public.

3. Some priority areas

After a copious diagnosis of an administrative system, definition of educational objectives, identification of priorities (which will vary with the deficiencies identified and the diagnosis pronounced), and formulation of strategies, certain sector-specific principles might apply.

a. Illustrative examples by level of education

Primary level priority may go to regionalisation and localisation of teacher recruitment (recently observed in Guatemala), production and distribution of textbooks (for example in Jamaica), decentralisation of decision-making in organising the school year, localisation of responsibility for repair of buildings, delegation to school principals of management of funds raised through the charging of fees, or under the policies of some governments, assignment of authority to parents' associations and communities.

At the secondary level it may be felt that priority should go to strengthening the management role of the individual schools. Small schools can be managed by trained principals, and new terms of reference can be formulated to define their tasks -- for instance the organisation of the use of equipment and facilities. Larger schools may require the services of a school board with broad managerial responsibilities including relationships with the ministry and the local authorities. The ministry might implement special in-service management training programmes for school heads, their assistants, and department directors. Scholarships and sabbaticals might be awarded to encourage these officers to seek such training. Manuals might be provided to managers at various levels, and incentives offered to organise summer workshops to discuss issues and exchange management experiences.

Possibilities for improving technical/vocational/trade schools are diverse and numerous. Examples include increasing the autonomy of a school so that it can (i) manage its specialised facilities (shops, laboratories, etc.) and organise intramural activities and extramural contractual work; (ii) set yearly phase-outs and additions of subjects according to the local labour demand; (iii) develop cost-effective proportions: trim some streams and expand others; (iv) establish a school fund for part-time recruitment of community specialists as needs develop. These and other similar measures all involve tradeoffs. Their validity must be periodically assessed by central government departments, and priority adjustments made to fit educational objectives to their findings.

As compared to general education, vocational/technical has many partners, each seeing the issues from its own perspective. Co-ordinating councils can be set up to facilitate interactions among ministries of education and of labour, agriculture, health, etc., employers, teaching and non-teaching staff, and school administrations, and to establish policy, plan, and regulate the training sector as a whole.

The priorities of higher education vary considerably with the size of the system, its types of component (universities, colleges, institutes, etc.), its history and the degree of prestige of its institutions, and the proportion of private as compared to public institutions. In many systems management and administrative attempts at co-ordination are hampered by the very conditions which make co-ordination necessary. Ideally, even if the policy of the government is to promote competition among them, the institutions, however disparate, should all be covered by umbrella mechanisms such as university councils, grant commissions, etc. Through these the government can co-ordinate the missions of all the institutions, while each maintains its autonomy. In some countries special legal provisions -- which are not easy to arrange -- may be required; in others, wide differences in status (wealthy and prestigious private universities cohabiting with poor community colleges) may make it entirely unrealistic to attempt co-ordination. At the institutional level, training will differ with the priorities of the individual unit. A given establishment may be in need of support in developing curricula, recruiting staff, financing day-to-day operations, conducting examinations, etc.

In the non-formal sector, the highest priorities include research, evaluation and assessment. The lack of data pertaining to non-formal activities is usually what blocks attempts to develop the sector. Once some basis is established, coherent relationships among these activities, between them and the formal system, and with ministries and agencies can be plotted out. For example, literacy and adult programmes can be associated with primary education; skill development and non-formal activities with apprenticeship schemes; rural extension programmes with technical and vocational training. It may be unwise, however, to attempt co-ordination at the implementation level, unless it is limited to a small geographical area, a district or village, where physical proximity makes it easier. The NGOs can be very effective in this regard, and their initiatives are generally eminently worthy of support. NGO field workers should be trained, especially in the fields of needs assessment, course organisation, data management, reporting systems and human relations.

b. Two common policy options

Determining what are the main priority areas in a particular sector in a particular country will depend on a variety of factors, including its economic prosperity and policy, its previous demographic growth and educational development -- all factors that have been fully discussed in this book. But there are certain policy options that are being considered today by a wide variety of countries, and which pose particularly tricky administrative problems.

It may be helpful to look in some detail at two such options that many countries face or are considering: (i) increasing cost recovery through fees or other charges, together with the introduction of student loans; (ii) organising teaching in large classes.

These examples are given as illustrations of the type of educational innovation that administrators or managers may consider as a way of using existing resources more effectively or mobilising new resources.

(i) Introducing student loan schemes

A number of developing countries in Asia and Africa are considering the introduction of student loans as a way of increasing cost recovery, by requiring those who benefit from higher education to contribute to its cost through the repayment of a loan (see *Inset 23*). But how would an administrator design a student loan programme? A recent study[4] that examines the feasibility of student loans in developing countries lists ten policy choices that have to be made (see *Inset 24*).

Inset 23
Student loan agencies in Jamaica and Barbados

In Jamaica, the Students' Loan Bureau was set up in 1970, with initial capital provided by the Bank of Jamaica, partly financed by a loan from the Inter-American Development Bank (IDB) and partly by counterpart funding from the Jamaican Government. Since it was established, the Students' Loan Bureau has awarded over 12,000 loans. The Student Revolving Loan Fund (SRLF) was set up in Barbados in 1976, also financed through a loan from IDB. Both are specialised agencies, with responsibility for day-to-day administration of student loans on the basis of terms agreed with the government, which provides guarantees against default and also subsidises the interest on student loans.

(ii) Teaching in large classes

Classes of more than 60 pupils are a structural fact in many developing countries, and should not be treated as abnormal. They constitute, in fact, a means of democratising education, and help to relieve pressures of social demand. It should be remembered that they were also common in the advanced countries at the beginning of the industrial age. But in today's developing countries, large classes often operate under unfavourable physical conditions, shortages of teaching materials, underqualification of teachers, and short-term palliative measures will not suffice to correct them. Governments must devise positive policies which treat oversized classes as a fact of life, and make them effective as rapidly as possible. The ways and means of implementing them need not necessarily be very costly. The first draft of a forthcoming Unesco publication, *Innovations for large classes: a guide for teachers and administrators,* which was discussed by African educationists at a seminar in Dakar in 1986, provides some suggestions of possible innovations, mechanisms and resources that could be utilised to make large classes more effective (see *Tables 11.1 and 11.2*).

Inset 24
Designing a student loan programme

A policy-maker or administrator who favours the idea of student loans, but is still at the stage of designing a loan programme, faces a number of policy decisions. First and foremost, there are political decisions:
- What is the aim of the loan programme?
- What is the policy on fees and cost recovery?
- Is a loan programme feasible and politically acceptable?

According to Woodhall, once the political choices have been made and the overall objectives of a loan programme are established, the policy-maker must choose between various options in the design of a loan programme. These choices can be summarized in terms of ten practical decisions that have to be made:

1. What form of financial aid will be provided for students? Will all aid be provided as a loan, or will grants, scholarships or other forms of aid also be available? What will be the relationship between student loans and other forms of aid?
2. Who will administer the loan programme? Will it be the responsibility of banks, or of universities and colleges, or will a new agency such as a State-owned student loan fund be established?
3. Who will be eligible for loans? What criteria will be used to select eligible students?
4. What proportion of students will receive loans?
5. What size of loan will be provided? What will be the average and maximum annual loan, and total borrowing limit?
6. What will be the repayment terms for student loans? What will be the interest rate and the length of repayment?
7. How much burden of debt should students be allowed to accumulate? Will provisions be made to ensure that students do not face excessive debt burdens, or to reduce the burden of debt in particular circumstances?
8. How will loan repayments be collected? What measures are necessary to keep default to a minimum?
9. Will the loan programme incorporate incentives? Will favourable loan terms be granted as a reward to students who achieve high grades, or to influence student behaviour and choice?
10. How flexible will the loan programme be? Will there be special provisions for particular categories of student, e.g. married women, or those who study abroad? Can mechanisms be developed so that the loan programme can adapt to new conditions?

Source: M. Woodhall, *Lending for learning: designing a student loan programme for developing countries*, London, Commonwealth Secretariat, 1987.

Table 11.1 Possibilities for innovation at the school or class level

Action on	Innovations
Teaching methods	• Judicious and monitored introduction of active methods: Sports and physical education; Productive activities; Diversification (introduction of population education, health, nutrition, etc.); Peer tutoring.
Materials	• Listing of resources that might be tapped in the environment • Pupil and class collections • Production of educational materials by teachers and pupils
Class size	• Group assignments within a class • Parallel classes (taught by one teacher) • Release of a teacher through redistribution • Double- or multiple-shift systems
Premises	• Cleaning and maintenance • Varying arrangements of pupils in classrooms • Scheduling alternate activities on the same premises • Equipping one room as a laboratory
Time	• Introduction of flexible timetables • Reassignment of time, for remedial work, for example
Relations with educational authorities	• Record keeping • Circulation of information
Resources within a school district	• Involvement of parents and other members of the community • Listing of potential sources • Use of resource persons • Parents' associations • School boards • School co-operatives, productive study • 'Twinning' of schools with firms
Other resources	• Listing of potential sources • The school inspectorate • Support centres -- for training, materials, research services, etc. • Enlistment of networks of correspondents • Sponsoring, international community twinning, other contacts Establishment of links with neighbouring schools
Testing and examinations	• Continuous assessment • End-of-course certification
In-service training	• Appointment of a teachers' council

Table 11.2 System-wide action plan for dealing with large classes: immediate and medium-term measures which administrators and managers might consider in responding creatively to the necessity for oversized classes

	Administration and management	*Curriculum content*	*Teacher training*	*Teaching materials*	*Facilities*
Immediate	Simplify and standardise records and communication Decentralise management Limit repetition; put age limits and other qualifications on exams. Relax timetables Enlist support of school inspectors	Renew curricula and add fields such as physical education, productive work, use of mother tongue Clearly define priorities: reading, writing, science education	Self-instruction Workshops for the production of teaching aids Distance teaching Annual conferences	Systematise school production of written materials through support, guidance, use of radio, and involvement of supervisors Produce collective vocational/technical materials in training institutions	Develop norms and standardise plans Seek assistance for investment in human capital (from specialised consultants) Seek assistance to provide industrial materials
Medium-term	Develop statistics Establish a directorate for planning and programming Revise budgetary nomenclature Upgrade status of non-teaching staff Systematise information policy	Improve relevance and applicability of curricula to economic, social, religious and cultural values and to employment Phase introduction of reforms rationally	Integrate initial and in-service training Scale seminars down from national to local levels Support in-service training to implement 'major' (5-, 10-, 20-year) plans Train administrative and managerial staff	Set up printing works or publishing house within framework of national book policy Develop national education-related industries (stationery, furniture, equipment) Use radio to develop distance teaching and non-formal education	Improve school mapping Fit out a writing room in each school Develop documentation centres and facilities for practical work, and integrate into, e.g., science teaching Establish networks of resources and backup centres through specialised nation-wide or provincial institutions

4. Establishing conditions for improving administration

Three major concerns are basic to the interests of most educational administrations.

a. Staff recruitment

Staffing problems are manifest in under-utilisation and mis-utilisation of the skills of those who have them, and motivation for efficiency. The dangers in ignoring these facts of life are serious. Well-known management methods from industry and the competitive service sector -- banking, insurance, etc. -- are easily adapted to our needs. Methods should be decided for the public sector as a whole, from central, through regional, to local levels, to (i) rationalise the use of present staff, (ii) identify the surpluses and deficits in each administrative unit, (iii) establish training needs and provide in-service training, (iv) experiment with new standards for recruitment, promotion, and deployment, on the basis of skill and performance rather than political affiliation, and (v) define a system of incentives to improve efficiency.

Over a transition period of several years these measures will require supplementary resources. There will be better emoluments for better qualified people, indemnities for early retirement of untrained senior managers (if there is a pool of younger, better trained managers available), expenses for training programmes for both the new staff and those with seniority, and there will be incentives.

A well thought-out agenda will be necessary for the gradual elimination of political interference in staffing, as well as the integration of the workers' unions into the machinery for defining the new management mechanisms. At face value, these conditions may look daunting in the short run of most countries. Cost implications are particularly intimidating, and the conditions themselves go against entrenched traditions, and entrenched political opposition. Where these problems are most difficult, it is probably a good idea to go at it in phases, as a long-term strategy.

b. Information collection

Without data, it is impossible to run administrative machinery rationally. Even the efficient performance of routine tasks such as starting off the school year, conducting examinations, appointing teachers or preparing the following year's budget -- imply the availability of basic statistics for use as a springboard. Some countries cannot afford to publish such statistics as school enrolment figures more than once every four or five years; others collect regularly perhaps, but without any clear view as to their purpose, and publish them sporadically in massive volumes, partially processed, and rarely looked at. Very few countries have orderly structures for collecting, processing and publishing the data on which their administrations could run sleek systems.

Starting with the very simple and easily operated Management Information System (MIS), gradually expanding it to serve the major requirements of its administration, the Republic of Korea established a commendable system. In the beginning a good system will be expensive. Computers and the people trained to use them are rarely available in the ministry. Financial resources will also be required to train people at the grassroots level to collect data and check for reliability and regularity. But compared to the cost of running an ill-conceived educational system, these amounts are very small indeed, and within the capacities of the tightest budget. More challenging is the step from the first phase of experimentation with the MIS, into its routinisation and application to the various levels of decision-making and management. This step must be taken gradually. Even in some of the least developed countries, finance ministry budget offices, and particularly directorates of public expenditure, have introduced more or less sophisticated MIS to monitor the management of public spending. With the increasing use of computers and data bases in the public and private service sectors, it is more than likely that the generation, processing, and use of information will be more and more accepted by educational administrations.

c. Rules and regulations

If misuse of public funds and arbitrary practices are to be avoided, a country must legislate against them. But if regulations are too complex, too numerous, too difficult to understand and apply (and they often are), the country might just as well not have them; they will be ignored, or serve only to slow things down. If they are too simple, and this applies often to centralised systems, they cannot be applied to the variety of concrete, specific problems that educational administrators are regularly faced with. The dilemma is that once the rules are established, it is very hard to change them, even after they become obsolete.

The regulations established should cover the use of ministry cars, for example, telephone expenses, petrol, computers and other equipment, and monitoring structures set up to see that they are not ignored. Assuming a decided political commitment, the issue might be addressed in phases.

Phase 1 will be concerned with the need for transparency, and wide diffusion of the rules through the proper channels (for example, identification of government and public properties -- cars, equipment, etc. -- with easily visible labels).

Phase 2 may concern itself with the gradual but steady adaptation of existing rules for internal operation, for example between the central ministry and the regional offices or the director of supply and equipment and the sub-sectoral directors; or between the office of the budget of the ministry of finance and the general administrator of the ministry of education; and so on. The challenge is to reconcile the need for rigorous management and control with that of maintaining and encouraging initiatives at all echelons in the machinery.

Phase 3, the most difficult to implement, consists of renovating the rules that apply to 'actors' in educational administration: parents' associations, teachers' unions, local authorities, etc. To stimulate the participation of communities, particularly in financing in cash or in kind the operation of their school, new rules should be established to give them more say in that operation. Their input may conflict with the views of the teachers. This phase requires experimenting, exploring, playing by ear.

5. Towards a hybrid administrative machinery

Proper consideration of the three factors in improvement -- financing, decision-making, and execution -- involves a number of tradeoffs: centralisation versus decentralisation; public versus private; autonomous versus bureaucracy-administered. It may be useful to state here that systems are rarely one or the other. Even universities are not entirely autonomous, for example, and it is hard to imagine a centralised system of NFE or a completely decentralised system for defining educational priorities. Systems are defined by their position between the two extremes, and decentralisation is successful only to the extent that a good central administration is there for backstopping, support, and regulation, as the experience of some industrialised countries shows. Both centralised systems, such as the French, and decentralised systems, such as the British, have tried during recent years to move toward what might be called 'hybrid' administrative systems, in which the management of activities is decentralised -- the responsibility of individual schools and universities -- and the responsibility of the ministries and local educational authorities is more clearly defined: setting educational objectives, addressing policy issues, and regulating the overall educational system.

It is still too early to judge these experiments, and the results and applicability of similar experiments in other countries will depend on how well they are adapted to those countries. What they do suggest is that regulations must be clearly laid out and known and understood by all the 'actors' involved. The government and the schools must be familiar with and understand the allocation formula; there must be unambiguous demarcation of which activities shall be under the responsibility of the school, and which shall remain with the government; the priorities which have been set by the government must be known to all; and the initiatives and freedom of action of principals in the management of their schools must be plainly defined. Some developing countries have tried to go beyond the rhetoric of 'participatory planning and administration', and have experimented with specific new rules and regulations in areas such as buildings and nutrition, splitting responsibility among the central administrations, local authorities and communities, and parents' associations. The results have been promising, for example as in the case of the Plan Tripartido for primary school construction in Guatemala. Hybrid NFE administration has also been particularly effective.

It is important to distinguish between *decentralisation*, which is the delegation of authority from the centre to the regions or institutions, and *deconcentration*, which is simple assignment of execution under the aegis of the centre (see *Inset 25*). There is no empirical evidence to support the preferability of one system over another in all countries, but it is probably true that:

•   In very poor countries with very weak administrative machinery, highly centralised systems may be preferable until some progress is made. Where money and skills are scarce it is more necessary to use methods which permit economies of scale and the attainment of global targets such as unity and equity. This is not intended to mean, of course, that legal arrangements cannot be made to allow local initiatives within limits, and parallel expansion and improvement of management systems in the private sector.

Inset 25
Different examples of decentralisation

Provincial school boards were recently granted much greater voices in the allocation of funds in the *Republic of Korea;* matching funds were set up, for example, and the boards were consulted during the personnel hiring processes. They were not, however, consulted during the curriculum-development processes.

Thailand adopted a number of innovations to improve the quality of its schools, among which was transfer of decision-making responsibility for curricula and staff recruitment and training to school clusters, improvement of the quality of supplies, and accountability for student performance. Twelve regional offices were strengthened and equipped for the new responsibilities.

Primary decentralisation in *Botswana* is extensive, covering employment of teachers, remuneration of principals, and management of buildings. Each district development committee has technical and political charge of planning; the ministry defines curricula.

Since the Arusha Declaration of 1967, *Tanzanian* regional development administrations and district development councils have been in charge of monitoring the primary schools. Curricula and teacher management remain under the control of the central administration, as does the entire administration of the secondary system. But the new set-up allows better integration of primary development with due consideration of regional and local concerns.

Papua New Guinea is a country with a long tradition of decentralised administration. The Provincial Education Boards were established in 1952. But since 1978, each of these boards has had the responsibility for planning its own system, which includes community grade schools, provincial secondary schools, and NFE. There have been difficulties, but there is general satisfaction with the arrangement.

- In the more advanced countries, formulae which divide responsibilities between the central government (which keeps the responsibility for defining and adopting objectives, managing the overall system, controlling quality and establishing norms and standards), the schools (responsible for routine management) and the users -- the students, their parents, the firms and other employers -- would be conducive to transparency in the application of the rules, and to efficiency of administration. They may be however, too difficult for implementation in the short run, as the British experience shows.

- In other countries (neither excessively poor nor advanced), in-between systems which fit in with their political commitment, socio-cultural conditions, and resources, can be developed.

Unexpected costs are a nasty surprise. From comparable experiences in other countries, data can be drawn to see that such costs are foreseen. We are not sure where on the scale centralisation-versus-decentralisation the longest-term cost-effectiveness will be found. A certain degree of experimentation will be necessary. But decentralisation is always costly in the short term, as the recent decentralisation effort in France has shown. Redeployment and recruitment involve expense, but ministries of finance are finding that it is worth it in terms of long-term reduction in demands on the central budget (and transfer of financial obligation to the provinces or regions, of course), which is from their point of view a primary concern.

All things considered, then, hybrid systems which gradually divide responsibilities between the central systems, the local administrations, and the users appear the most attractive on grounds of both cost and efficiency, if they:
- establish diversified information systems adapted to the needs of all 'actors';
- clearly specify and diffuse the rules and regulations, and the criteria for incentives;
- develop administrative and managerial capacities through recruitment and training; and
- redirect resources adequate to finance the above.

Most of the developing countries start out with fairly centralised administrations, and moving toward hybridisation will be slow and difficult. No planner is eager to incur the displacements, or to enter into the long negotiations necessary to adapt regulations and redefine duties, ranks, and power bases. Where elementary and secondary teachers' unions exist, they are forces to be considered, and in any case the support and enthusiasm of these essential elements in the business of education must be enlisted if the sector is to run well. On the tertiary level there have always been institutions which enjoyed wide and solid autonomy, and they have brooked very little interference in their routine management. Today, however, many of them suffer more or less serious problems of inefficiency. New sensitivity to economic cycles has made them particularly vulnerable: uncontrolled expansion in fat years is followed by drastic adjustments in facilities, staff, and management of student flows in lean years. Thus some kind of hybridisation introduced gradually is seen as a valid possibility at all levels in the sector.

6. Summary: priorities for management and administration

The most important conclusions to be kept in mind for setting priorities to improve management and administration are the following:

(i) Resources must be found by governments and directed towards the strengthening and improvement of education and administration services, if any of the suggestions developed throughout the book are to receive serious consideration for implementation

(ii) The most urgent action to be taken in many countries is the improvement of routine management. To achieve this, the improvement of the administrative machinery must begin with the everyday functions of delivery. It is suggested that a thorough diagnosis of the administration be carried out, training programmes for personnel be implemented, a system for establishing and assimilating information be established, improved efficiency in the use of facilities and services be sought through economies of scale, incentives be introduced to improve management of personnel, and co-operation and co-ordination with the private sector be organised.

(iii) There are priority areas for action in each component and segment of an educational system. These should be established in the light of a variety of factors, in particular the policy options that are being considered by the government. For example, teaching large classes -- a fact of life in many developing countries -- requires proper administration and managerial support. Again, the introduction of student loans to increase cost recovery in higher education requires a fairly detailed administrative design for proper implementation.

(iv) Three major concerns are to be taken into consideration in programmes for improving administration: addressing staffing problems, routinising the management information system, and regulating the functioning of the administrative entities.

(v) There are at present conflicting arguments in favour of centralisation and decentralisation in administration. A system which would combine decentralisation in implementation and centralisation in policy and quality control seems to be an advantage in many industrialised countries. On the other hand, in very poor countries with weak administration a centralised system would perhaps be preferable in the short run.

---

1. A. Bordia, 'Decentralisation in educational administration: the third world perspective', In: C. Malpica; S. Rassekh (eds.), *Educational administration and multi-level plan implementation: experiences from developing countries,* Paris, Unesco:IIEP, 1983. See also C. Beeby, *Planning and the educational administrator,* Paris, Unesco:IIEP, 1967 (Fundamentals of educational planning, No. 4).

2. In some countries the recruitment of a primary school teacher -- screening, selection, interviewing, checking with the various units of the ministries of education and finance, sometimes votes of Congress, even the approval of the Executive -- can take two to three years. The prohibitive costs of such processes, justified by the need for transparency, must surely be reducible without danger of misuse of public funds.

3. The performance of a school supervisor is often judged on the basis of the statistics which they periodically submit. This practice should be replaced with one in which emphasis is placed on the number of schools visited, and the quality of the support delivered.

4. Maureen Woodhall, *Lending for learning: designing a student loan programme for developing countries,* London, Commonwealth Secretariat, 1987.

Part IV

Memo to donors

Chapter 12

Priorities for international assistance

Twenty years ago the Pearson Report on international development[1] spoke of the "pivotal role of education in development policy" and the need for fundamental change both in the educational policies of the developing countries and the nature and magnitude of international aid. This last chapter is devoted to a discussion of what problems still exist despite considerable achievements since publication of the Pearson Report in 1969, and what remains to be done in the coming years to improve and strengthen international co-operation in HRD.

1. International educational assistance: a reminder of past and present trends

International assistance to education amounted to US$4.25 billion in 1986, according to Unesco sources.[2] Compared to the some US$600 million that external sources provided in 1969, this is an impressive achievement. However, recent trends in assistance to educational financing show that after a considerable increase early in the 1970s, international educational assistance levelled off until the beginning of the 1980s -- bilateral aid until 1980, multilateral until 1983.[3] The OECD Development Assistance Committee has reported a net decrease in educational assistance among the major bilateral funding sources since 1980, despite the fact that overall development assistance from these same countries over the same period increased by 45 per cent. The difference must therefore have come from multilateral sources, particularly the development banks.

Fluctuations in the dollar rates since 1980 have reinforced the general downward trend. The value of the dollar doubled between 1981 and 1984, and has declined against other currencies since then. The purchasing power of aid granted consequently rose between 1981 and 1985, more or less in step with the rising value of the dollar, but has declined since 1985, thus aggravating the situation of stagnation in the aid-receiving countries.

Overall, the share of education in total development assistance has remained modest: 5 per cent of multilateral financing, and 11 per cent of bilateral figures. As *Table 12.1* shows, there are no discernible trends in the relative priority of education in the eyes of the multilateral agencies between 1980 and 1986.

Table 12.1: Percentage share of education in total development assistance of multilateral banks and funds, 1980-86

Agency	1980	1981	1982	1983	1984	1985	1986	Average 1980-86
African Development Bank	4.7	2.4	6.4	8.8	7.2	10.1	7.5	6.7
Arab Multilateral	1.5	0.8	1.8	3.6	1.5	5.4	2.1	2.4
Asian Development Bank	4.5	5.2	3.8	6.7	5.4	3.5	4.2	4.8
Caribbean Development Bank	2.1	4.4	5.1	6.3	3.1	2.0	4.6	3.9
EDF/EIB	4.6	3.2	6.0	8.7	7.1	4.3	2.6	5.2
Inter-American Development Bank	2.9	2.6	9.5	6.2	0.7	3.0	5.9	4.4
World Bank	3.8	6.0	4.0	3.8	4.5	6.5	5.1	4.8
Total	3.8	4.9	4.8	4.7	4.0	5.8	5.0	4.7

Source: Unesco, *Trends in external financing of education: annual report for 1986*, Paris, Unesco, 1986.

External aid received per capita and per pupil varies widely from country to country. But, generally speaking, compared to the some US$100 billion spent on education by the governments of developing countries, external development assistance in the period covered by Table 12.1 is not very significant (i.e. around 4.2 per cent). At one extreme, in the sub-Sahara, Nigeria received US$0.10 per capita, Botswana nearly US$20. As a rule, the most populous countries of the region receive less per capita than small countries, regardless of income.[4]

An analysis by type of aid shows that grants and soft loans have declined in proportion to loans. The World Bank's IDA credits are very favourable (maturation 35-40 years, servicing less than 16 per cent), but they must be reimbursed by the receiving countries. Furthermore, less than 50 per cent of World Bank lending for education between 1981 and 1985 benefited from these IDA credits, which go to the poorest countries only; other countries receive IBRD loans at variable interest rates that are fairly close to those of the international financial market.

Bilateral assistance for education is also partly loans and credits, at more or less preferential rates of interest. Grants to educational projects are usually earmarked, restricting the receiving country's choice of equipment, experts, etc. to those selected in advance by the donor country. The share of education in the loans from those multilateral aid agencies, which transfer resources without fees, is decreasing: education's share in UNDP disbursements went from 6.9 to 3.4 per cent between 1975 and 1984; in those of Unicef it went from 20.8 to 12.3 per cent.[5]

Assistance from non-governmental organisations, now representing an estimated 5 per cent of the total aid to education in developing countries, is however reported to be on the rise. An analysis of the distribution of financial aid by level of education reveals the following patterns:

- Less than 5 per cent of all financial assistance to education went to the primary level during the 1980s (about US$180 million per year) in spite of the fact that the international donor community considers it imperative that primary education should receive priority in educational financing.
- Secondary education and training took a larger share of the 'foreign aid cake': 15-17 per cent of the total external aid received by sub-Saharan Africa since 1980 for education has been directed towards the secondary level.[6]
- By far the largest part of this goes to vocational and technical education. Between 1980 and 1986, general secondary education in the sub-Sahara received US$10 per student annually; for vocational/technical it was US$200 per student.
- Higher education is the privileged sector from the point of view of assistance. Without indirect subsidies, the sub-Sahara receives US$400 yearly for each student; with subsidies (for registration fees, etc.) it hits US$1,000 per student[7] -- compared to about US$1 per pupil at primary level.

At all levels, the scope[8] as well as the cost-effectiveness and use of external support to such crucial educational inputs as buildings, equipment, textbooks, etc., require rethinking.

These problematic trends in external aid to education may be related to a shift in development assistance, especially bilateral, towards sectors in which assistance is considered to be more urgently needed. They are in contradiction with the now generalised acknowledgement of the individual and social returns on education, especially basic education, in developing countries. More generally, as has been argued in this book, it is human development that is at stake.

Of course, decreasing external investment in education may also be due to persisting criticism from a number of quarters as regards the value of educational assistance. There are still those whose doubts about whether it does any good at all discourage future commitments on the part of the international community. Two decades ago, Coombs[9] stated that very little could be said to answer the question, but at the same time called upon readers to at least distinguish those criticisms which were justified from those which were not. External assistance, while it has engendered or reinforced certain of the developing countries' problems, has unquestionably brought relief of others, and it is not necessarily because a system of education is inefficient that the aid offered to it was inefficient. As Phillips put it,[10] "The more inefficient a system is, the more it requires the right kind of aid."

Providing the right kind of aid is easier said than done. Bilateral and multilateral agencies have put a good deal of effort into finding approaches which would satisfy the requirements of both donors and recipients, and as we shall see below, a good deal more will be brought to bear before those approaches are sure.

2. Major operational issues of international co-operation in education

Converging assessments conducted by multilateral agencies, among them the OECD's Development Assistance Committee, isolate four areas in which inadequacies of preparation and implementation tend to reduce the overall cost-effectiveness of external aid: human resources, financing, co-operation structures, and time.

a. Human resources

According to a recent UNDP survey,[11] the lack of understanding of local contexts on the part of experts still constitutes a major problem for national experts and educational decision-makers in developing countries.

Furthermore, technical assistance incurs expense for the receiving countries, even when the salaries of the donor or assisting agencies are covered by those agencies. Housing, air-conditioned offices, and other facilities provided by the host countries can in some cases be as costly to them as the salaries of equivalent nationals would have been.[12] Also, delays in filling posts can mean costly waste, costly lack of co-ordination, costly time lost, for both the assisting agency and the country.

Of course, adequately trained local labour is not always available when it is needed. The country may simply not have the professionals that a project requires, but in some cases it is the 'self-contained' nature of the project which is at the root of the problem. These projects still do not take sufficiently into consideration the necessity for leaving expertise behind on completion of a project. A notable example of the contrary is the UNDP requirement that all (or most) projects involve full-time national counterparts of the foreign appointees.

b. Financing

Where planning is inadequate or non-existent, management of projects and programmes supported by external aid is difficult, and results are compromised. Specific problems have included the following:

• Liquidity problems on the part of funding agencies, due to irregularity in the flow of contributions from Member States.

• Difficulties on the part of the receiving country in meeting the recurrent costs of new educational facilities or services initiated by externally funded projects. Waste of resources and frustration have been suffered by both the supporting organisations and the countries assisted -- a high price to pay for neglect. Preliminary planning must include an assessment of the long-term affordability of an endowment and its general compatibility with the resources, structures, and priorities of the receiving country.

c. Structures

Most of the frustrations and failures experienced in co-operating for the development of education are rooted in the very structures of co-operation, which is conducted in terms of *projects*. It is unrealistic to expect that a new institution or a strategy for sustained quality improvement can be developed and consolidated within the four- to five-year period generally assigned, or within the scope -- an isolated segment of an educational system -- generally targeted. Imbalances are virtually invited by this sort of selectivity, and certainly no integration is provided for, even within the sector, not to speak of interaction with the others. Moreover, local contexts are extremely varied, and cannot be adequately taken into consideration within the confines of a project structure. The effects of a development project can hardly be lasting if it is not rooted in local traditions and expectations, yet it has not been the consistent policy of international assistance to seek close conformity with national development policies, and local communities and educational managers have generally not been sufficiently involved in preparing, monitoring, and evaluating externally assisted projects.

Local institutions for the co-ordination of external aid from the various sources are virtually non-existent, which means that the help received from abroad is not assimilated in an orderly, organised manner, and a good deal of it is wasted. It can even happen that a government is unable to spend the moneys received before the expiration date of a project.

The receiving educational system is fragmented by specific foreign aid, and the assisting agencies themselves work in isolation. Where it exists at all, co-ordination is narrowly limited, and inevitably there is duplication of effort, resulting in waste of human and material resources. Efforts have been made by some agencies, notably the UNDP, Unesco, and the World Bank, to improve co-ordination. But a good deal remains to be done.

d. Time

Preliminary assessment of a proposed permanent improvement in an educational system takes more than the three or four weeks normally allotted by international organisations to on-site feasibility studies, and even these are considered to be too costly in the light of the overall resources to be endowed to the project. During operations, teams of experts are assigned to projects to make progress assessments, but they rarely remain at the site long enough to actually see any progress. Time over-runs in project implementation are also a dismally familiar occurrence in international co-operation ventures. On average, the normal four years projected by the World Bank was estimated in 1980 to run usually to seven,[13] and these figures probably still hold true today. Turnover among foreign experts, and the long delays required to fill vacant posts, badly timed training of local personnel, logistic problems -- introduction of new equipment, opposition to innovations in curricula, etc. -- and many other unforeseen difficulties make these project extensions imperative.

Obviously timing and synchronisation of the mobilisation and use of resources at the various stages of implementation are vital if waste, inefficiency, and even failure to attain the objective are to be avoided.

3. Overcoming present inadequacies of aid in education: ten commandments

Both the aid-receiving countries as well as the international donor community are becoming increasingly aware of the manifold problems of external assistance to education. But the task of making substantial improvements will be harsh. The following 'ten commandments' propose, against the background of lessons from past and present experiences, some major general and operational guidelines for future international co-operation in education:

1. Make education and HRD a top priority sector for international aid.

Increased investment in human resource development, particularly in education, is justified on all grounds: human, political, technical, economic and ecological. Hence, the appeal to donors to significantly boost the magnitude of their support to this field of development requires no lengthy explanation here.

Some might feel that insufficient absorptive capacities in a number of developing countries set limits to further increase in external aid to HRD. Actually, the absorptive capacity -- performance in disbursement and execution of programmes -- of a country varies with a number of factors, but does not seem to vary in a simple way with size or income level. On-site feasibility testing, market research, and appraisal of the programmes to be implemented are good ways to assess this essential quality in the recipient country, and should be a routine part of preparation phases. More often than not, the country's needs are so immense that they would justify a good many more extensions, in both dollars and years, than the funding agency could possibly commit. The poorest countries are of course those most likely to be targeted by these agencies in the first place; their educational and training systems are in such bad shape that, without massive support, they cannot hope to produce trained or educated people. Here, 'built-in' strategies of programme implementation are recommended. Countries should benefit from support packages, including small-scale programmes with loose management, traditional investment projects, rehabilitation and strengthening of the school system, support for the operations budget, and perhaps support to the global improvement of the sector. The packages could be evolved through a pooling of efforts of different agencies, including those of NGOs which might possibly take on some of the small-scale projects.

In the case of countries that suffer from structural budgetary deficits and high indebtedness, special arrangements -- in particular more imaginative modes of funding -- are required. At the risk of going against orthodox concepts, according to which external resources should finance investment but not recurrent expenditure, it has to be pointed out that the future of education in the countries concerned will be hampered in an irreversible way unless the necessary funds to ensure the 'basics' of educational development are made available, i.e., training and decent salaries for teachers, teaching and learning materials, maintenance and repair of equipment and buildings, etc. With a view to improving a country's own financial capacity, original formulae of external funding of education should be given particular consideration, for example *swapping debt against education*.[14] Swaps which provide external support and at the same time include debt reduction techniques in situations of chronic structural deficit are presently being tried out on an experimental basis in the area of environmental development and could perhaps be introduced experimentally in education.

2. Adopt a global concept of HRD

As discussed in Chapter 3, concentrating on one area of human development at the expense of others results in imbalances. Even where clear HRD priorities can be determined, they generally change over time and with different levels of development. At any rate, action responding to priority problems in certain educational sub-sectors and levels makes sense only if parallel convergent initiatives at the other levels and in other sub-sectors are taken. A recent UNDP survey[15] clearly indicates the prominence of a global concept of human development in the minds of educational policy-makers and NGOs. Among the factors perceived as promoting human development, primary education and access to education for girls and women (repercussions of female education on health and family planning) are seen as primordial. Major concerns are also: economic development and the generation of employment, the low quality of general secondary education, the irrelevance of vocational education to prevailing practical demand, and the inadequacy of the content and management of post-secondary education and research in the face of specific socio-economic environments.

No doubt, from the point of view of individual countries that still have low enrolment ratios (i.e. less than 80 per cent of the age-group), sectoral allocations would put the focus on basic education and adult education. In this respect, a major international undertaking, involving four multilateral agencies (Unesco, Unicef, the UNDP and the World Bank) and a number of bilateral agencies, is the *World Conference on Education for All,* which will take place in Thailand in March 1990. Hopefully, one of the outcomes will be a significant increase in international encouragement to basic education; and when governments themselves confirm their commitments by redirecting their energies and resources towards the generalisation of primary education and adult literacy, using both formal and non-formal delivery systems including new educational technologies, they should receive a gratifying boost from the international community. A Unesco World Conference to reduce illiteracy, also planned for 1990, should help create the synergy which will be necessary to spur worldwide efforts towards this massive achievement.

Increased support must go to non-formal education, in conjunction with support to the equivalent levels in the formal systems. Without NFE, a country cannot hope to serve the socio-economic groups which are beyond the reach of its formal system. Data on the effectiveness of NFE are not profuse; yet donor agencies could contribute to the advancement of equity by helping governments to reach out to marginal youth, working children, and illiterate adults, by supporting NFE organisms that expand the efficiency of formal systems by catering for drop-outs and offering training (in the form of apprenticeships, for example) and skill development for employment in the informal/traditional sectors.

Regardless of the scope of the literacy problems that a country might have to struggle with, one of the most repeated and pressing requests on its education system is to synchronize its endeavours more closely at all levels with what are often perceived to be fast changing employment structures and work requirements.

At the sub-sectoral level, projects which aim at improving the quality and relevance of specific segments of the education and training system, can be decided only on the basis of a given individual country. The choices might take into consideration the following factors:

- the possibility of sharing the risks in innovative approaches with the international community;
- an objective point of view when scrutinising projects that involve major capital investment and can lead to substantial unforeseen recurrent costs;
- the need for caution in launching pilot projects and multiplier programmes for which funding for development and follow-up is not assured;
- the opportunity for reinforcing and improving existing programmes, institutions, or projects set up in earlier aid cycles, with due attention to inevitable maintenance costs.

3. Establish support to HRD within the framework of national development policies and firm mutual commitments

External aid to human resource development can increase its meaningfulness to a considerable extent by ensuring its compatibility with the receiving country's development context and its national policy priorities; only at the country level will it be possible to set up a coherent framework for HRD within which donors can provide more than 'aid in trickles'. Implementing this idea of international co-operation for a more comprehensive approach to human resource development means accepting a certain number of practical implications:

Genuine commitment to fixed objectives must be forthcoming from the receiving countries' authorities, and assistance offered from abroad must respect these objectives. If the developing countries themselves are not firmly dedicated to the achievement of certain clearly-defined educational policy objectives, improvement cannot come from abroad. Bilateral and multilateral agencies will not be much interested in the ever greater efforts that will be required of them unless they can be sure that their contributions are going to make any real differences. If their interventions are to respect the receivers' wishes, the receivers must *have* wishes; and they must be certain, on the basis of painstaking assessment and reflection, that these wishes reflect as much as possible the genuine needs of their countries.

The implications for development agencies are in the direction of promoting enhanced diagnostic capabilities in the developing world that are sensitive to each country's particular HRD demand/supply concerns and socio-cultural contexts. In particular, it will be necessary to wean national governments from dependence on external diagnostic standards and methods, towards constructing their own HRD radar systems as they see them. Support and technical assistance will of course in many cases be needed for explicit inter-agency co-operation, system design and technical training, in this more co-ordinated HRD piloting approach.

Co-ordination in the public sector interface between education and employment in the past has been mixed at best, and where it exists it has often been limited to the vocational-technical sub-sector, where an uneasy correspondence has been derived with the purpose

287

of linking educational curricula to various occupational skills' taxonomies. Seldom however has the sort of gravitational shift towards mutuality of purpose in integrated HRD been successfully addressed, and traditional separations and inter-agency rivalries have in some cases exacerbated conceptual and bureaucratic divisions.

One area in which there may be room for promising and pragmatic initiatives is the information field. A major weakness in the developing country approach to solving intractable HRD problems (such as graduate unemployment) is the shortage of analytical, *diagnostic* capabilities in-country. An awkward double dependency is thus set up in educational policy making, for example, where (i) exploratory analytical research and diagnostics are performed by outside experts, usually funded externally, and policy recommendations are made for government consideration, then (ii) implementation projects are designed and executed, ostensibly to solve the problem, following external recommendations, often funded by the same external agencies involved in the original diagnostics. The incestuousness of this arrangement seems inescapable and inevitable until countries develop the capabilities for performing their own diagnosis in HRD.

The advantage of developing country designs in this area is that labour market information systems are often less developed and bureaucratised than those in the industrialised countries, where the relevant public data series have often been incrementally derived over long time-periods, usually for reasons other than strategic policy (e.g., tax computation for industrial establishments). Recent innovations in household survey designs in Malaysia by the ILO, for example, and in key informant surveys in other countries, offer useful models for extension to wider strategic use in HRD planning. The implications for governments are for closer education/labour ministerial co-ordination in the design, conduct and interpretation of these statistical approaches to HRD problem diagnosis. In Burundi, the government has recently been exploring this concept as part of a proposed inter-sectoral approach to educational planning, with initial emphasis on modern sector employment and skills structures.[16]

Donors must respect the fixed medium-term objectives of HRD and, at the same time, remain open to feedback from the aid-receiving country and flexible enough to adapt their support policies. Some of the funding agencies are already militating for a 'sector' rather than a 'project' approach which could more readily handle the financing of broad reforms and policy changes. This would appear to be wise, although there is an in-built danger with a sector approach of interference of donors in national competence in deciding on the scope and magnitude of policy changes. There is no simple solution to the dilemma. Probably by balancing the pros and cons of sector and project approaches, funding agencies and recipient countries will come to a 'hybrid' system of co-operation built upon both approaches.

4. Widen the time horizon of international co-operation in education

Donors must stretch contributions over longer periods of time and not expect visible results overnight. Most of the changes desired take decades to be appraised, for attitudes to be altered, traditions assessed dispassionately, and for concepts to be adapted on the basis of the evidence encountered.

In general, government officials from donor countries are not able to commit themselves for the long periods that are necessary to conduct educational action in a coherent and sustainable fashion. Terms of office are limited in time, and budgets provide commitment on a yearly basis. However, a more adequate duration of co-operation programmes could probably be guaranteed if donor governments were to sensitise public opinion in their own countries through campaigns and leadership. In this way it might be possible to extend public support beyond the term of a given government's mandate. Multilateral co-operation is, in principle, in a better position to cope with commitments to medium- and long-term HRD improvement. Indeed, first attempts in this direction are presently being made: for example, the UNDP's Jakarta Plan of Action on Human Resources Development, which was set up in 1988 after consultative meetings of governmental, non-governmental, and international representatives, is taking the important step of lengthening time-frames to 13 years.

5. Focus on long-term extension and improvement of the receiving country's institutional capacities

Quantitatively, external aid alone will never be able to develop or maintain a country's educational system. Through institution-building it can exert catalytic effects, however. Institutional development can, at the same time, help reduce the still very heavy import dependency not only of external capital quality inputs (equipment, buildings) but also of technical assistance in the education sector. For developing countries, catching up with the rest of the world in the production, distribution and maintenance of material inputs to education, as well as in the generation, sharing and effective use of knowledge (especially in science and technology), means first of all the training and retraining of decision-makers, planners and implementers in various segments and at various levels of the educational system.

Unesco, UNDP, and ILO have been committed to the development of human resources for educational planning and management for several decades. The Unesco Regional Offices, and in particular IIEP, have invested considerable efforts in the training of educational planners and administrators at the central level, and increasingly at regional/provincial levels. Altogether, over a period of 25 years, IIEP has provided long-term training for 800 senior officials and short-term training for a further 2,000 officials from 140 countries. But the demand for training still far exceeds the supply. In response to these needs, some training institutions -- like IIEP -- have been expanding the impact of their training programmes by providing 'training of trainers' or 'cascade courses' as well as 'on-the-job training' for planners and administrators. The courses, symposiums, workshops, and seminars that are offered vary in type, duration, and content according to their specific aims and target groups. For example, the World Bank's Educational Development Institute offers short training seminars for top-level policy-makers and HRD officials from developing countries.

There is also a need for a more systematic and holistic approach to the upgrading of institutions and structures in a general way. The best-trained planner can be impeded by the lack of proper support. The training of a single specialist in a teacher/training institution or a curriculum development centre will not change the ways of thinking and operating of a whole institution.

Training is useful primarily to expand awareness and skills; but if there is no action targeting the staff in charge of operations and the daily conduct of routine tasks, there is little use in increasing the awareness of the top-level actors.

Accurate planning and management procedures for educational materials, for instance textbook distribution, presuppose the availability of instruments for collecting and processing data, and of regular lower-level staff to perform these duties. Training must thus be integrated in a strategic and systemic vision of HRD development, combining institutional support with various types of training and upgrading of staff at least at three levels: besides the key decision-makers (mainly senior officials and central government), school directors, supervisors, administrators and technicians, responsible for implementation and execution, must be targeted, along with the intermediate-level curriculum developers, managers of distance education, and the assessment specialists, who have responsibility for design and operations.

Institution-building has been increasingly emphasised by international, governmental, and non-governmental organisations over the past few years, as well as by higher education institutions. 'Co-operation packages' are being offered which, along with information and personal exchanges, include training in university teaching and management of staff, and the services of consultants in institutional and personnel development.[17]

6. Ensure the financial sustainability of HRD programmes.

While a developing country's financial commitment to HRD is essential, sustainability of government policy, strategies for generating adequate resources, and cost control and saving, will, of necessity, involve increased and increasing foreign assistance for a number of years. New procedures will have to be explored to generate resources, particularly to share the risks involved in launching industrial and commercial projects. Partnerships could be formed between firms in developed and developing countries, or between firms within a target region, for the production of textbooks, reference books, dictionaries, atlases; science equipment; paper, notebooks, chalk, rulers; and basic school furniture. Foreign funding can be helpful for the creation of factories and small businesses to fill national and sub-regional needs, which can be more extensive even than those of the educational system itself. Entities involved in financing small businesses and industries might also be drawn into these activities, which certainly go beyond the interests of education and training alone.

One of the ways in which aid agencies might reduce the financial drain on developing countries is by developing local and regional institutions. If students can study in high-quality local higher institutions rather than in foreign universities, great savings in foreign exchange can be made. In 1979 the foreign exchange necessary for higher education of developing countries' students abroad amounted to US$2.9 billion - 17 per cent of the interest repayment on their combined foreign debt.[18]

Savings can also result from improvement in the internal efficiency of educational systems, through quality control; changes in modes of evaluation, testing, etc.; enhanced educational management and guidance; and training schemes for administrators. Multilateral agencies have used these roads to cost-effectiveness, and bilateral agencies are increasingly using them as well.

The capacities of developing countries to control costs and optimise HRD resource allocations can be extended by assisting with the setting up and implementation of programme-linked budgeting and investment procedures, more comprehensive, unified public budgets, and more adequate financial information systems. International support has made it possible to set up such procedures in a number of individual nations, and they have already proved to be fairly effective in holding costs down.

7. Support strategic areas of educational sector management

Such strategic areas and 'instruments' for which developing countries might consider enlisting the support of agencies are:

- incentives (perhaps supported by local communities) for educational personnel: here, international co-operation can (i) facilitate the exchange of experiences; (ii) promote motivation experiments for teachers and other educational personnel; (iii) support financial and non-financial incentives to improve the effectiveness of rural schools; (iv) finance training and other such opportunities.
- teacher support and guidance: international co-operation can help to encourage the production of methodological guides and reference materials to be supplied to teachers; supervision and counselling can be reinforced through 'networking' at the local

level; resource centres can be created; distance guidance can be provided via radio, professional journals, etc.

- improvement of assessment and examination structures: educational and vocational guidance services can be developed, with the financial support of international co-operating agencies, by clearly defining achievement and performance levels, by standardising examinations and setting up examination boards and certification norms for recognition of non-formal training, and by creating guidance and counselling services at the secondary level, etc.
- development, design and distribution of teaching materials: international co-operation can provide financial support for textbooks, science equipment, and at the tertiary level, libraries and laboratories.
- rehabilitation and full use of buildings and other facilities -- laboratories, workshops, libraries, etc. -- and provision for maintenance, repairs, upgrading (water and electrical systems), and storage facilities.
- development of secondary- and tertiary-level distance education, and financial support for non-formal training: design and development of materials, student support services, provision of free (or low-cost) access to existing distance education materials and promotion of regional co-operation in this area. Distance education and self-learning methods and materials could be tried out in formal and non-formal settings.

8. Improve the administrative machinery of the countries concerned

If co-operation projects are to have lasting effects, donors and aid-requiring countries must be careful to ensure that:
- priority is given to the development and strengthening of the existing educational administration machinery in a country,
- a component for improving the machinery of educational administration is included in education projects,
- the strategy is designed in such a way as to entrust implementation to that administrative machinery.

When it is not possible to keep responsibility for a project in the hands of the existing personnel for one reason or another (extreme poverty of the administration and incapacity to handle an innovative experiment are the most common reasons, but it may also happen that a programme has to be rushed so as to complete it before the end of a legislative term or an election), perhaps part or most of the responsibility can be transferred to temporary teams, preferably on a clearly defined, short-term basis, with stated provisions for re-transfer of responsibility from the *ad hoc* unit to the stable force. The re-transfer should take place gradually while the work is being done, so that when the unit is phased out, the experience gained has been absorbed by the stable team.

Both donor and recipient programme managers will find this difficult to adhere to. But failure to do so is tantamount to merely leaving footprints in the sand. Termination of the project will be closely followed by oblivion; and neither the administrative functionaries nor the system they administer will benefit by its having existed. The lasting output will be a degree of irritation on the part of people who have got used to streamlined operations in their educational system, and that is about all.

9. Support 'South-South' and multi-level co-operation

In the past decade or two, South-South co-operative projects have been developed which aim at the exchange of information through regional co-operation among developing countries. The 1978 Buenos Aires Plan of Action gave rise to the TCDC (Technical Co-operation among Developing Countries), and, as concerns education, Unesco has given particular attention to TCDC as a channel for the development of regional literacy programmes and improvement in the quality of primary education, regional co-operative networks for educational innovation, and various inter-university networks. Collaborating in joint activities defined in common fosters self-reliance and co-operative action among partners. These forms of co-operation provide stimulation to innovators by allowing them recognition beyond their home environments, and help to develop inter-personal contacts among those facing similar problems in different environments. In a way, these contacts take the place of hiring foreign experts to renovate or innovate programmes.

Other inter-governmental regional programmes promoted by Unesco -- the Major Project in the Field of Education in Latin America and the Caribbean, the Regional Programme for Eradication of Illiteracy in Africa, the Regional Programme for Universalisation and Renewal of Primary Education and the Eradication of Illiteracy in Asia and the Pacific, and the Regional Programme for Universalisation and Renewal of Primary Education and the Eradication of Illiteracy in the Arab States, for example -- are based on the TCDC principle. They all seek to combat illiteracy by expanding the coverage of primary education and increasing support to adult education. They may differ in specific objectives, modes of operation, and organisation, but in high-level regional meetings, they discuss priorities and national implementation plans, and provide a very sound basis for international co-operation.

Networks for educational innovation on a regional level were initiated in Asia in the mid-1970s (see *Inset 26*), and have been since extended to Africa, the Arab States, the Caribbean, and Southern Europe as a strategy for the furtherance of educational exchange through international co-operation between participating institutions. In the regions they cover, they have become central to strategies for the delivery of education. Their effectiveness might be explained by the following factors:[19]

- decentralisation of decision-making regarding allocation of programme funds, with strong inputs from the network participants;
- development of national infrastructures as the main driving force for educational innovation;
- an ethos of self-help on the part of the participating countries, and an expectation that network activities will be followed up, or pursued parallel with national projects financed by the countries themselves;
- promotion of contacts between persons with operational responsibilities at the intermediate levels, i.e., people who are not central government, but concretely involved in broadly defined innovative activities;
- continuous critical assessment of the results of educational innovation in the light of national development requirements.

Inter-expert and inter-institutional networks require support. They can help to overcome one of the major obstacles to professionalism and expertise on the part of nationals, which is lack of access to specialised information, research results, and reports on the innovations and experiences of other countries in their fields. One such network is the Research Review and Advisory Group, with sub-regional networks in various parts of the world, which was created in the mid-1970s and mandated to synthesise research on educational issues in developing countries. It provides information services to researchers and policy-makers in both hemispheres.[20]

In the framework of inter-university networks, which have developed with the help of both bilateral and multilateral agencies, North-South and South-South co-operation in research and the management of higher education has been encouraged. These mechanisms, involving several partners, supplement numerous twinning relationships between universities from developed and developing countries.

Despite their efficiency, these networks are not given the priority that funding sources assign to national programmes or twinning systems. The implicit assumption is that TCDC can or should be supported entirely by the developing countries themselves. The countries and institutions devote considerable resources in kind and considerable human energy to these set-ups, but the budgets of the poorest countries cannot possibly stretch across the operation of a central unit, co-operating units, and the processing and dispatching of information on a regular basis. They cannot afford international meetings. Some of them need help to provide the bare essentials of office furnishing and travel allowances, without which they cannot participate in the network activities at all.

To effectively assist developing countries it may often be necessary to set up joint financing mechanisms and to conduct activities of various kinds and at various levels: inter-country and regional courses, as well as specialist seminars, workshops, study tours, mobile-team missions in a country (or even within an institution), training activities. An ongoing training programme for administrative staff at various levels in Ghana is a case in point. It is funded by the government of Ghana, with financial support from the World Bank, the UNDP, and Unesco, and receives intellectual support from the IIEP and other specialised institutions. Activities within countries are usually financed on a country-by-country basis, inter-country co-operation and regional activities being more difficult to set up. But it is the intermingling of national, regional, and international activities which is most effective, and also most in line with the innovative spirit of partnership, as opposed to the donor-recipient relationship which is much less successful.

In planning co-operation activities in education, it must not be forgotten that without follow-up -- which, at least at the higher levels, should include access to professional expertise and opportunities for personal exchange -- training serves for little. Specialised NGOs can be very useful in providing such expertise, in supporting the establishment of professional associations in the countries, and encouraging foreign associations to extend their operations to developing countries.

10. Promote co-ordination and organisational integration in international co-operation

Many externally financed programmes would have infinitely more consequential impact if support were integrated, crossed institutional barriers, and operated not only at the national level but also at the regional level. Furthermore, emergency situations are often unforeseen at the planning stages, even when 'contingencies' are part of the planning. The lack of a technician, who could have made a critical repair in a day or two, has more than once caused the demise of a project. But without established procedures, those in charge in the field may not even know what kind of specialist or technician they need when a breakdown occurs.

An emergency support service should be provided through inter-agency agreements, and be on call for urgent technical needs. This sort of service could work as an insurance system, subscribed to by projects, or reimbursed for calls by the projects at cost. Eventually, the regional service could become an inter-agency unit, maintained at common expense. Such arrangements have worked well on inter-school and inter-university bases. Besides keeping the equipment in shape, this sort of team might provide the latest information on new developments in equipment and materials. Common project services could also be organised at the national or provincial levels for procurement and maintenance of equipment, information gathering and processing, and production of printed, audio-visual, and other teaching materials.

Today, various agencies (often with the support of the UNDP) run projects in schools and non-formal settings to improve the quality of life: WHO and WFP focus on nutrition and health education; Unicef on maternal health and childcare, UNFPA on family planning and other population concerns, UNEP on environmental education, UNFDAC on problems of drug abuse, WHO on 'AIDS' prevention. These programmes are offered directly or through executing agencies such as Unesco, the ILO, the FAO, and non-governmental organisations. They all use the same types of equipment and technical staff for the production of printed materials, and their modes of intervention are similar -- participatory education, group discussion, promotion campaigns -- but adapted to specific actions. Common use of basic logistic structures would mean economies of scale, fuller deployment of scarce facilities and expertise, and improved implementation. Co-ordination could be in the hands of the countries themselves, and the catalytic role to be played by UNDP should not be overlooked. In this way, needs would be fulfilled efficiently, without waste or duplication, and facilities made available to education where they are needed, regardless of the sponsoring agency or the local edifice.

4. Summary: priorities for international co-operation

Overall, the share of education in total development assistance has remained modest: 5% of multilateral financing and 11% of bilateral figures; after a considerable increase in the 1970s and a levelling off at the beginning of the 1980s, it has actually declined during this decade.

The overall effectiveness of international co-operation in education tends to be reduced by inadequacies in four major areas -- human resources; finance; structures; and time. Chapter 12 gives a brief overview of major problems in these areas and develops 'ten commandments' for the consideration of donors and co-operation agencies:

1. Make education and HRD a top priority sector for international aid

Significant increases in aid to education are justified on all grounds. The receiving countries' absorptive capacities need prior assessment and possible insufficiencies should be tackled through 'built-in' strategies of programme implementation. Imaginative modes of funding, such as swaps for example, are required in the case of heavily indebted countries.

2. Adopt a global concept of HRD

In order not to provoke serious imbalances within national education systems, external aid to HRD projects should give due consideration to possible changes of HRD priorities over time and make sure that initiatives conducted in the various sub-sectors and at the different levels of education and in other HRD-related sectors are convergent.

3. Establish support to HRD within the framework of national development policies and firm mutual commitments

Only at the country level will it be possible to set up a coherent framework for HRD within which different donors can provide more than 'aid in trickles'.

However, national policy priorities and objectives have to be clearly defined and firmly respected by both the countries concerned and the assistance-providing agencies.

4. Widen the time horizon of international co-operation in education

Most of the educational progress desired requires many years of sustained and coherent efforts to become a reality. Bilateral and multilateral co-operation have to be reconsidered with a view to possible shifts towards medium- and long-term HRD improvement.

5. Focus on long-term extension and improvement of the receiving country's institutional capacities

Genuine aid to sustained educational development in the receiving countries needs to be focused on national institution-building. A holistic approach to the upgrading of HRD institutions and structures has to be adopted; among the various steps which can help reduce dependence on capital inputs and technical assistance from abroad, training activities with 'multiplier effects' (training of trainers, seminars for national decision-makers, etc.) deserve particular attention.

6. Ensure the financial sustainability of HRD policies

The various possible strategies for enhancing the financial sustainability of national HRD policies have to be further explored and encouraged: generation of resources by international or bilateral partnerships between educational goods- and services-producing firms in developed and developing countries; foreign exchange savings by developing national or regional educational institutions (especially universities and research centres); cost savings resulting from improvement of internal efficiency; and enhanced control and allocation of resources.

7. Support strategic areas of educational sector management

Such strategic areas and 'instruments' for which developing countries might consider enlisting the support of agencies are: motivating incentives for educational personnel (financial and non-financial); educational support and guidance services; modes and structures of assessment and examination; rehabilitation and use of buildings and equipment; development and distribution of teaching materials; distance education.

8. Improve the administrative machinery of the countries concerned

In order to avoid that they be merely followed by oblivion, externally-supported HRD projects should systematically include components for improving the national administration and be designed in such a way as to entrust implementation to that administrative machinery.

9. Support 'South-South' and multilevel co-operation

International co-operation in education should envisage the provision of increasing support to networks and platforms of regular exchange among developing countries, (such as Unesco's Regional Educational Innovation Networks) as well as those interconnecting educational institutions and experts of various types and status in developing and industrialised countries; such forms of co-operation have indeed proved their effectiveness for HRD capacity-building in a great number of cases over the last two decades.

10. Promote co-ordination and organisational integration in international co-operation

Externally-financed HRD programmes would have infinitely more consequential impact, facilities and expertise would be more fully used and emergency services more easily provided, if support was integrated, crossed institutional barriers and operated not only at the national but also at supra-national -- especially the regional -- levels. Co-ordination could be in the hands of the receiving countries themselves; but the catalytic role which could be played at the international level, by UNDP in particular, should not be overlooked.

---

1. L.B. Pearson, *Partners in development,* New York, Praeger, 1969.

2. Unesco, *Trends in external financing of education. Annual report for 1986,* Paris, Unesco, 1987.

3. Ibid.

4. F. Orivel; F. Sergent, 'Foreign aid to education in sub-Saharan Africa: how useful is it? In: *Prospects.* Vol. 18, No. 4, 1988.

5. William Experton, *Le financement de l'éducation en période d'austérité budgétaire,* Paris, Unesco Division of Educational Policy and Planning, 1988, Mimeo.

6. Ibid.

7. Orivel & Sergent, 1988, op cit.

8. A. Magnen, *Educational projects: preparation, finance and management,* Paris, Unesco:IIEP, 1990, (Fundamentals of educational planning, No. 39).

9. Philip H. Coombs, *The world educational crisis: a systems analysis,* New York, Oxford University Press, 1968.

10. H.M. Phillips, *Planning educational assistance for the Second Development Decade,* Paris, Unesco:IIEP, 1973, (Fundamentals of educational planning, No. 18).

11. UNDP, *Education and training in the 1990s: developing countries' needs and strategies,* New York, Education Development Center, 1989, (A policy discussion paper).

12. Orivel & Sergent, 1988, op cit.

13. World Bank, *Education: a sector policy paper,* Washington, D.C., World Bank, 1980.

14. 'Approaches to debt reduction', In: *Finance and Development,* September 1989.

15. UNDP, 1989, op. cit.

16. J.E.S. Lawrence, *Integrating HRD on the ground*, Paris, 1989, Unpublished mimeo.

17. G. Van der Mohlen, *Evaluation of international co-operation: a synthesis report for the Commission of the European Communities*, 1988, Mimeo.

18. S.P. Heyneman, *Investing in education: a quarter century of World Bank experience*, Washington, D.C., World Bank, Economic Development Institute, 1985, (Seminar Paper No. 30).

19. Unesco, *Impact evaluation of the Regional Networks for Educational Innovation for Development*, Document 129 EX/INF.7, submitted to the Executive Board of Unesco during its 12th session, 1988.

20. See for example *Norrag News*, November 1986.

IMPRIMERIE GAUTHIER-VILLARS

Imprimé en France